as two children. he is a Crown Counsel in the Chambers, a role in which he has had to prosecute numerous drug traffickers. He has had six novels published, including *A Web of Dragons* and *The Phoenix Pact*, both of which are available from Headline.

Also by Michael Hartmann

A Web of Dragons
The Phoenix Pact

Tigers of Deceit

Michael Hartmann

HEADLINE

First published in 1990
by HEADLINE BOOK PUBLISHING PLC

First published in paperback in 1990
by HEADLINE BOOK PUBLISHING PLC

10 9 8 7 6 5 4 3 2

ISBN 0 7472 34434

Typeset in 10/12½ pt Times
by Colset Private Limited, Singapore

Printed and bound in Great Britain by
Collins, Glasgow

HEADLINE BOOK PUBLISHING PLC
Headline House,
79 Great Titchfield Street
London W1P 7FN

For my mother
for ensuring that I had the opportunities
I never deserved and for teaching me
that there is another world out there.

HONG KONG

High Summer, The Year of The Dragon

It was the graveyard watch, 4 a.m., and dark as death when the junk heaved-to off Sha Chan Island. Monsoon rains beat down. Within twenty feet nothing could be seen, just black, swirling rain-washed oblivion. It was a perfect night for the trade in *pak fan*, white powder as the Cantonese called it, the stuff of dreams.

Up in his wheelhouse the master of the junk, an old Chinese of Hakka descent, wizened and arthritic, chain-smoked, grinding out each butt under the heel of his rubber sandal. The minutes began to pass. Five . . . ten . . . fifteen. Where were they? He paced the wheelhouse, muttering obscenities to himself, peering out into the night.

Something must have gone wrong. They had never been this late before. Why hadn't he received their radio signal? They always signalled as they approached. He sucked deeper on his cigarette. What if the other vessel had been seized, what then? The junk groaned in the swell. How much longer dare he wait?

'There, to starboard! I can see lights through the rain!' It was his son, the eldest, shouting. 'It's coming fast, straight at us!'

The master flew into a panic. it had to be the navy in their highspeed interceptors. 'Head west! Head west!' he screamed at his son.

But a moment later he heard the shrill bleep of the junk's radio – two short jabs, three long. It was the signal, exactly as agreed. Sweat broke out on his brown-blotched forehead. He gave a loud sigh, shaking his head, muttering to himself. Then, as the other vessel, a fibreglass speedboat, drew alongside, rage took over.

The old fisherman scurried out of the wheelhouse into the rain to vent his pent-up agitation. 'Where have you been?' he yelled at the two-man crew. 'Idiots, you couldn't navigate your way across a bridge!'

The two men in the speedboat shouted back in gutter Cantonese: 'Fuck your mother, old man!'

'Fuck your mothers, too!'

'Hey, *lo gwei* – old ghost – just give us the stuff. We're running late.'

'Whose fault is that? Monkeys!' Leaving his second son to supervise the transfer, the master returned to the shelter of his wheelhouse. 'Never again,' he mumbled to himself, 'never, never, by all the gods, I swear.' But he had sworn that same oath a dozen times before. It was his way of releasing tension, that's all, as empty of intent as his junk was of fish.

The master dealt in a different kind of catch these

days: dope, smack, Thai Horse, China White, it went by a thousand different names, but it all came from the same source: the sap of the opium poppy. Brought down on mules from the distant mountains of the Golden Triangle, from Burma and Laos, it was smuggled on to Thai trawlers. Out in the wild reaches of the South China Sea, the boats took transfer of the stuff. That was what he fished now, heroin. And if he didn't die in jail, he would end his days a rich man.

Down in the speedboat, as it tossed in the waves, the two-man crew struggled to secure the four sealed drums that were lowered to them. Then, with the drums lashed down, their fingers bleeding, they headed north-east, back into Hong Kong waters.

Their worst fear – the same as the old Hakka fisherman's – was the sudden appearance of navy interceptors. Even on a storm-swept night like this they knew they could be picked up on radar. That's why their speedboat, as sleek as a javelin, was equipped with a 300 h.p. outboard engine. But they saw no other vessels except for a few tramp steamers, and within thirty minutes they had entered a small cove sheltered by the high hills of Lung Kwu Tan.

This was rural Hong Kong, the western periphery of the New Territories. Set back from the sea among the banyan trees stood a cluster of stone cottages where fisherfolk had lived since before the *gweilos*, the foreign ghosts, had first come to colonise. Small, scruffy sampans bobbed at anchor and somewhere far off a dog barked as the speedboat drifted alongside the stone jetty. One of the crew scrambled up the steps. He paused, sheltering his face from the rain, then he made his way along the jetty until he reached an old Taoist shrine, a shrine to Kwan Tei, the god of policemen – and thieves, too. He whistled once, nervously, unsure what was best. Then he called in a half-whisper using the Triad term of respect: 'Hey, *dai lo* – elder brother – are you there?'

A figure emerged from the darkness. 'You're late,' said Cheng Tak-shing.

'We couldn't locate the junk, not on a filthy night like this.'

'Get the stuff ashore. Hurry. How many drums?'

'Four, as you said.'

'Good. Hurry. The van is back there in the trees.'

Oblivious of the rain that soaked his red cotton shirt and black denims, Cheng watched his two followers struggling with the drums. But he made no offer to help. They were Sun Yee On, like him, except he was an office bearer in the secret society, a 426, while they were only rank and file, street muscle, coolies. They followed him. That was the way of the Triads.

At thirty-three years of age, Cheng Tak-shing was short and squat with the over-developed shoulders of a weightlifter. He was balding, half his scalp bare, and possessed a frying pan face that was round, flat and small-featured – except for his eyes. It was those green-black, frog-like eyes that had earned him his nickname, Dai Ngan, a name everybody knew him by but few called him to his face. The English translation of it on his criminal record sheet read simply: alias 'Popeye'.

Cheng had trafficked in white powder since puberty. He was Chiu Chow and the Chiu Chow were notorious drug traffickers. In Hong Kong courts, so the legend went, a Chinese jury would convict a man of trafficking the minute they heard his Chiu Chow accent. Cheng had been to jail three times, twice for drugs, once for false imprisonment. And eighteen months earlier he had been charged with murder, too.

He had killed the man, a rival Triad, by hacking off his head with a melon knife. But in Hong Kong, with its *gweilo* law, witnesses had to stand up in court to prove the charge. And that's what had saved him. In Hong Kong, even in matters of murder, business was a sacred thing. There had been no family members involved, no question of revenge, just a little face to be saved by the dead man's Triad associates. Cheng's Sun Yee On colleagues had initiated settlement talks with the Crown witnesses, all 14K. Meals had been eaten, money paid, and at the trial the witnesses had done everything necessary to ensure the jury could not convict. So Cheng had walked free, his reputation enhanced a hundredfold. Everybody knew of Dai Ngan now. Everybody knew he would kill without a qualm.

Cheng waited impatiently until the fourth drum had been loaded into the back of the van. Then, driving the vehicle, he took the road towards Tuen Mun, turning off before the town along a dirt track. It was a steep, difficult climb and the first grey vapours of morning shrouded the trees when he pulled up in front of the deserted farmhouse, an old stone dwelling.

There was a man sheltering in the farmhouse doorway. He carried an umbrella and wore a wet, rumpled suit. Timorously, he came forward. 'I'm Ng,' he said in high-pitched Cantonese.

'You're early.' Cheng was visibly displeased. 'I told you what time you should be here.'

Ng stuttered in reply, 'I thought it would take longer to get here. I'm sorry . . .'

Cheng climbed out of the van. Ng didn't impress him: round-shouldered, pasty-skinned, frayed shirt collar, fake Rolex on his wrist, the gold rubbing off. But they said Ng was a good drug chemist, trained years back in Shanghai, traditionally the home of the best chemists. 'All right,' Cheng said. 'Your equipment is inside. Follow me.'

But Ng's attention had been diverted. He was gawking at the four drums being unloaded from the van. 'How much is in them?' he squeaked.

Cheng smiled. 'Two hundred and thirty units.' He enjoyed the startled reaction on Ng's face.

A 'unit' – approximately seven hundred grams – was the common measurement used by Asian drug dealers. But Ng, a chemist, used more standard indices. 'That's more than a hundred and sixty kilos,' he mumbled out loud as he made the conversion. Then, louder, he protested, 'But you never told me it would be this much. I had no idea—'

'Don't look so scared.' Cheng spat in the red mud at Ng's feet. 'Only a hundred units are for processing for the local market. We got it cheap. It's old heroin base that's been stored up in Laos.'

'What about the rest?'

'That's Number 4, nothing to do with you. It's for export to the States.'

Ng burped with an attack of nerves. 'It's been more

than a year since I processed heroin base.'

'I've got all the chemicals.'

'But you're talking about seventy kilos . . .' Ng hesitated, still worried by the amount. 'By the time I've bulked it out, you're going to have nearly a thousand pounds of stuff. It's going to take me a week or longer, a whole week, coming back every day. Where are you going to store it all?'

Cheng unbolted the farmhouse door. 'You're paid to be a chemist not a storeman.' He glanced at his watch, grimacing. 'Your equipment is up in the cockloft. Get up there now and check it. And stay there until I tell you. Like I said, you came too soon. So hide your face. There's a couple of important men coming, the seller from Laos and one of the local investors. You start your work once they've gone and not before. Don't let them know you're here otherwise we're both in trouble. And keep your eyes to yourself. You understand?'

Ng's nervous blink indicated that he understood only too well. He entered the farmhouse, sniffing the sharp smell of acid, and hurriedly climbed the ladder into the attic where the cluttered paraphernalia of his profession had been stored.

It was Ng's job to convert the old heroin base into the weak mix, about thirteen per cent pure, which Hong Kong addicts consumed. First, he would have to break down the compressed blocks, a dirty off-white in colour, by dissolving them in hydrochloric acid. Then caffeine, hundreds of pounds of it, would have to be added to the liquid to bulk it out. Minuscule quantities of strychnine would provide taste, and the mixture would then be cooked over gas stoves like vats of soap. When the acid evaporated, the resulting paste, as malleable as potter's clay, would be minced into granules and the granules baked dry in microwave ovens. The end result was what the Hong Kong police called Number 3, ready for sale on the streets.

Squatting in the cockloft, Ng was a frightened, unhappy man. Dealing with this much heroin base would be long, dangerous work. Once he started, he knew the stench of acid would be detectable half a mile away. And if he was caught . . . oh God, if he was caught, it didn't bear contemplation. The tariff for this much stuff was so high he would never get out of jail alive. If only he had known, he would never have agreed to the job. But it was too late now. If he tried to back out, Dai Ngan would kill him.

Dry-mouthed, he began to take inventory of his equipment: four zinc tubs, four microwaves, plastic bowls, spatulas . . . Suddenly, in the distance, he heard the distinctive crunch of tyres on wet gravel.

Ng knew he was forbidden to look out, he knew he should stick to his own business. He also knew all about Dai Ngan's reputation for violence. He hesitated for a moment, fingers trembling, but the temptation was too great, the attic window barely a step away . . .

The approaching vehicle was a Mercedes 500 SEC, metallic gold in colour, a common enough car in cash-rich Hong Kong. But it was the number plate that riveted the chemist's attention. In the murky gunmetal grey of dawn he couldn't make out the first two letters but the sequence of four numbers that followed were clear:

8888, the luckiest combination of numbers in the Chinese lexicon. A sequence like that, guaranteeing good fortune, must have been auctioned off by the Government for a hundred thousand dollars or more.

Ng saw two men climb out of the Mercedes, but both carried umbrellas which shielded their faces. They shook hands with Dai Ngan who had stepped out to greet them, spoke briefly to him and then the three hurried inside.

Lying flat with his face to the floor, Ng tried to peer down between the boards. The four drums were being cut open. He could hear the hiss of the oxyacetylene torch and glimpsed the bright, phosphorescent sparks.

Then the first of the two visitors spoke. Ng could not see the man but his voice was distinctive, gravelly and soft, the voice of a fond uncle. He spoke fluent Cantonese but it wasn't his mother tongue. He had to be the supplier, the one from Laos.

'As I promised, Ah Leung. See for yourself. The heroin base may be old but it is still in perfect condition. My own Tiger Claw brand. You won't get better, not at the price.'

The second visitor, the Hong Kong investor, answered, 'You never let me down, Tinko.'

'I value your patronage, Ah Leung.'

'And I value the service you provide.'

'The Number 4 – also my own Tiger Claw brand – is guaranteed ninety-six per cent pure. You can test it.'

'I don't think that will be necessary. We are men of trust, Tinko. It all appears to be in excellent condition. That's all that concerned me, that the merchandise hadn't been spoiled in any way.'

'Good, then our work here is done. I am always – how can I put it? – a little nervous so close to so much merchandise in a foreign place. I will feel much happier drinking tea back at the hotel.'

The one called Ah Leung laughed softly, mockingly. 'Don't be so concerned, Tinko. You are perfectly safe here.'

'Ah, but age has taught me to be cautious, my friend.'

'When do you return to Laos?'

'I fly out this afternoon for Singapore and then on to Vientiane.'

'It sounds as if Hong Kong is not to your liking.'

'No doubt it has many good things . . .'

'Well then?'

'It also has many good policemen.'

There was a moment's hesitation before Ng heard Dai Ngan interject for the first time. 'I assure you, I would know about the police before they got within a mile of here.'

'I have a formula that has served me well over the years,' answered the Laotian in his soft sing-song. 'For every policeman in a place like this there will be three informers. And informers don't need to get within a mile, Mr Cheng, they are already eating at your table.'

Dai Ngan was clearly stung. 'Are you saying we are not trustworthy? Is that what you are suggesting?'

'I mean no offence,' the Laotian replied. 'It is simply the nature of our business.'

Carl Drexel, forty-eight years old, a native San Franciscan, was working late that night. Nursing a mug of decaffeinated coffee, the agent in charge of the activities of the DEA – the US Drug Enforcement Administration – was attempting to draft a memo to Washington concerning travel allowances for his agents. Drexel was good on paper but mindless red tape like this induced brain death and he was on his fourth attempt when the telephone rang. He expected it to be his wife. This was the third night in a row that he had been late home. But it was Danny Abbott on the line, a local cop with the rank of chief inspector in the Narcotics Bureau. Drexel put down his pen, welcoming the interruption. 'Hi, Danny, how are things going?'

'We've got him, Carl. Jesus, I can still hardly believe it. But we've got him!' Danny Abbott couldn't contain the triumph in his voice. 'At long last we're going to nail the bastard!'

'Hold your horses. Who are we talking about here?'

'Leung Chi-ming, that's who.'

'Christ alive!' Drexel sat bolt upright. He took off his reading glasses, gold-rimmed bifocals, and dropped them on the desk. 'Are you sure?'

'One of my informers has just got through to me. He's been employed as a chemist for a shipment that came in three nights ago, a huge bloody amount – one hundred and sixty kilos, he says.'

Carl Drexel gave a low whistle of appreciation. 'But how does your informer tie in Leung Chi-ming?'

'Just as we always suspected, Leung is one of the financiers.'

'But your man is only a chemist, one of the workers. How would he know?'

Danny Abbott laughed. 'Because Leung has cocked it up, that's how. I always knew it, Carl. All we had to do was wait, that's all. I always knew that one day Leung would poke his shitty little rich man's head out of his hole.'

Drexel could feel his own excitement building. It was incredible news. 'But has your informer seen him, I mean right there with the stuff? Can he make a firm I.D.?'

'Not seen him, no, not exactly.'

A note of cynicism crept into Drexel's voice. 'So what exactly did he see?'

'Leung was there to inspect the merchandise, that's what my man says. He was there with the seller, a man he called Tinko – probably Tinko Chaiwisan.'

'Chaiwisan?' Drexel was surprised. 'So Uncle Chicken came out of Laos for the deal, did he? He's a wily old bastard, half Chinese, half Laotian. Where's Chaiwisan now?'

'Flown out.'

'So we've lost him.'

'But Leung Chi-ming is still here, still in his mandarin's palace up on the Peak.'

'But if your informer didn't see Leung, how is he able to pinpoint him?'

'First, he's got the registration number of the car, a Merc – Leung's own car. Second, he heard him referred to as "Ah Leung" a dozen times or more.'

Drexel paused, waiting. 'Is that it?'

'Christ, what more do you expect, a signed confession?'

Carl Drexel liked Danny Abbott. Danny was a good operator. But he was young, too excitable. Every ticket he bought was going to win the State lottery. A little more caution was needed. 'If it really was Leung Chiming out there, good luck to you,' he said. 'But from what you tell me, Danny, this is purely a local scene. There's no way DEA can get involved.'

'You haven't heard it all yet, Carl.'

'Okay, fill me in.'

'My man says that over half the stuff – eighty kilos of Number 4 – is headed for the States.'

Now Drexel was interested, very interested indeed.

'Just wholesale, Carl, out on the streets of New York, do you know what we're talking about? A hundred million US. That's got to be big bucks in anybody's book.'

But Drexel was more interested in the human targets, the suppliers like Chaiwisan, the financiers, brokers, the mules who couriered the stuff, and especially the buyers in the States. 'What about this guy of yours,' he asked, 'is he prepared to stay in and feed us information?'

'He's scared shitless. But yeah, sure, if we can give him the right kind of guarantees.'

Drexel chuckled. 'New identity, new passport, a little noodle place on Sunset Boulevard.'

Danny chuckled, too. 'You don't put your life on the line for truth and justice, not any more.'

'Just the American way of life?'

Danny laughed. 'Especially if you're Hong Kong Chinese with 1997 looming up.'

Drexel was sold. 'Okay,' he said. 'So we need to talk. Where do we meet?'

'Remember that little place in Tsim Sha Tsui, the Sichuan restaurant?'

'The New China. Yeah, I know the place.' Carl Drexel drained his coffee mug. 'Tell me, Danny, have you reported this to your boss man yet?'

There was the slightest pause before Danny Abbott answered defensively, 'When I'm good and ready.'

Drexel shrugged. 'It's your play, Danny, but is there any percentage in bucking the system?'

'Bugger the system!' Danny Abbott's long-stored antagonism spilled over. 'You and I have suffered too much grief over Leung Chi-ming as it is, Carl. This time, when I make my initial report, I want those myopic assholes paying attention. Don't worry, I know what I'm doing. The New China in half an hour, okay?'

'I'll be there.' Leaving his unfinished memorandum on the desk, Drexel grabbed his jacket and headed out of the US Consulate down Garden Road. It was a sweltering night with humidity up in the high nineties and within a dozen paces the sweat was sluicing down the creases of his heavy, lugubrious face. He knew that by the time he reached the MTR – Hong Kong's subway – he would look like he had stepped out of a sauna fully clothed, the one dripping *gweilo* amid five thousand trim and very dry Chinese. It was one of the few things he felt self-conscious about here in Asia, his Western bulk and his Western propensity for copious sweating. Tonight, though, his thoughts were too firmly fixed on Leung Chi-ming to care.

Danny Abbott had been the first one to pick up scraps of intelligence hinting that Leung was involved in financing drug deals. Then Drexel had received similar intelligence through the DEA offices in Thailand. That's what had brought them together and made them unlikely allies. In the past their intelligence had been at best third and fourth hand, veiled and ambiguous. Nobody was going to start World War III on the strength of it. But a great many operations had started with information that was no better: you began with an acorn and watched it grow. That's why both had been first irritated at the bureaucratic torpor when they suggested surveillance and then amazed at the backlash when they pushed it further.

Drexel had received most of the flack from his own Deputy Administrator. 'What are you pushing this for, Carl? Leung is a pillar of the Hong Kong community. He endows hospitals, he crowns beauty queens. The guy is so righteous his piss cures cholic. Sure, rumours have been drifting around. You make a fortune in this part of the world and somebody is going to accuse you of basing it on dope. This is not the first time the local cops have checked him out.'

'So he's smart. But the fact is, the guy is making more money shipping heroin to the States than General Motors makes in a year.'

'You don't know that.'

'Then let me try and prove it.'

'For Chrissake, Carl, they say the guy could be knighted next year.'

'What are you telling me, that gangsters, even Chinese ones, don't get knighted? You're getting political pressure, that's it, it has to be.'

'You know better than that.'

'Then what the hell is this about?'

'Priorities, Carl, that's what it's about. Man hours. Money. In a nutshell, we've got better things to do in this organisation than chase our tails.'

So that had been it. Leung Chi-ming, the philanthropist, had been declared kosher. But tonight, thought Drexel with relish, events might just change all that.

It was nine thirty when he came out of the Tsim Sha Tsui station on the Kowloon side. The streets off Nathan Road behind the Holiday Inn were still crowded with tourists, pink-faced Yanks in shorts and flip-flops bargaining for cameras. The New China was situated in a back street behind the Empress Hotel. It was too shabby to be patronised by tourists – no gold paint or carp in aquariums – so the prices remained reasonable, an important consideration for an impoverished young cop like Danny Abbott.

Danny had arrived before him and was seated at the back of the restaurant drinking Tsingtao beer.

The two men were a study in contrasts. Carl Drexel, near fifty, had a heavy, bloodhound's face and, without glasses, fell over his own feet. With his brown hair receding, double-chinned and thick round the waist, he looked his age. But then, as he joked, he had looked his age when he was eight, the only middle-aged infant on the block! His clothes sense didn't help either. He always looked dishevelled and if there were two colours that clashed, sure as God he wore them. Three things saved him – his intelligence, a wry sense of humour and most of all, an easy, unpretentious manner which made him popular with just about everybody from the top dogs down to the ordinary Joes.

Danny Abbott, on the other hand, just thirty-one years old, stood well over six foot and was proportioned with the lean elegance of a high-jumper. He was blond, blue-eyed, with a straight nose, cleft in his chin and perfect white teeth. He worked out every day with weights – not coffee and a novel like Drexel – and, as one adoring female put it, thereby improved upon perfection. If his looks, however, were celluloid perfect, his private life was a disaster.

Danny Abbott was woman crazy and money hopeless, a fatal combination. A New Zealander by origin, he exhausted eighty per cent of his modest police salary maintaining an ex-wife and two children back home. As a result he never had a penny to his name and made ends meet by living with various women, paying for his board and lodging in kind. Danny's sex life was chaotic but the more chaotic it grew – one woman in his bed, one paying his board and two trying to kill him – the more he seemed to flourish. Carl Drexel didn't know whether to pity the guy or envy him.

Seating himself at the table, Drexel poured himself a beer. 'Are we going to eat?' he asked.

'I've already ordered. A plate of chilli prawns, some spiced bean curd, smoked duck.' Excitedly, Danny handed Drexel a computer print-out. 'Have a look at this. It's a check on Leung's various cars. Look at the second one from the top, the Mercedes. Same model, same colour, same sequence of four eights in the registration number. There's only one car in Hong Kong that fits that combination.'

But Drexel remained dubious. 'What's to say Leung himself was driving it? Your man didn't see him.'

'No, but I told you, he heard the name, Ah Leung. He heard it at least a dozen times.'

Drexel shrugged. 'There must be half a million people in Hong Kong with the surname Leung. And they're all called Ah Leung by somebody.'

'Maybe, but not driving that Mercedes, Carl. And that's what nails the bastard. Before a jury I'd be home and dry!'

'We've got a long way to go before that,' said Drexel wearily.

'But we've taken the first step,' Danny replied stubbornly. 'That's what counts.' A series of bleep-bleep sounds suddenly emanated from the area of his crotch. He reached down and switched off the small paging device attached to his belt. 'Won't be a second,' he said and, getting up from the table, went across to the telephone on the wall near the cashier's desk.

Local calls are free in Hong Kong and he dialled Narcotics at Police Headquarters in Wanchai. 'It's Abbott here. Are you paging me? All right, just give me the message.' As he began to listen, Danny was leaning casually against the wall but then he suddenly stiffened. 'Are you sure?' A grim look came over his face. 'Yeah, okay, I understand. No, no, there's nothing I can do, not now . . . just log the fact you spoke to me.'

Returning to the table, he slumped down. 'Ah, fuck it all,' he muttered in a tone of disgusted exasperation.

'What's the problem?'

Danny Abbott gave a long hard sigh. 'About an hour

ago Marine Police fished a body out of the harbour. Both hands had been chopped off, like pig's trotters, and shoved into a polythene bag. Then the bag was tied round the corpse's neck before it was dumped into the water.'

Drexel had no need to be told. 'Your informer?'

Danny Abbott nodded. 'Yeah, my supergrass.'

'There's no doubt about his identity?'

'None whatsoever. The bastards who murdered him stapled his identity card to his skull. Nice guys, really nice. Sweet as candy.'

Carl Drexel said nothing. He had been in the DEA since 1973 when it was first formed. He had seen it all before: New York, Miami, Mexico, Bangkok. It was a re-run of the same old scenario. With a depressed grunt, he sat back to drain his beer. As he did so he glimpsed three men enter the restaurant.

Normally he wouldn't have given them a second look. They were Chinese, in their late teens or early twenties, manual labourers by the look of it, long-haired, tough, dressed in T-shirts and denim jackets – strange, he thought, considering the heat – and standard blue jeans. But instead of coming straight in and taking a table, these three hung back at the entrance. One of them caught Drexel's eye and imperceptibly nudged his two companions. They all looked across.

Don't be stupid, Drexel thought to himself, this isn't New York or Miami. The Chinese don't touch foreigners, especially Westerners. It's unheard of. But instinctively he knew there was something wrong, very wrong indeed. 'Danny,' he murmured, 'just look round.'

But Danny Abbott was lost in his thoughts. 'Sometimes I wonder why we bother, Carl. We're fighting these bastards with our hands tied behind our backs . . .'

Drexel saw one of the Chinese reach slowly into his jacket. A word was spoken and they began to weave their way through the tables towards them. Drexel half rose from his chair. 'Danny,' he hissed, 'for God's sake look round.'

Only then did Danny Abbott glance up. 'Why, what's the problem?'

In that instant Carl Drexel saw a glint of metal as the first blade was drawn clear. 'Oh God, no, no . . .' he murmured, the blood draining from his face. Then he shouted. 'Danny!'

His scream pierced the restaurant. For an instant the sheer force of it stopped even the three Chinese in their tracks. But then, shrieking like wild men, they came at him and Danny, their meat cleavers held high, barging over tables.

Drexel saw waiters fleeing, guests falling to the floor. He heard the screams of terror and he staggered back against the wall looking desperately for an escape. But there was none. And in Hong Kong he didn't carry a weapon. 'Danny!' he yelled. 'Your revolver!' He grabbed a chair, anything to try and protect himself.

Dimly, through the miasma of his own shock, he saw Danny fumbling in the small of his back to pull his service revolver from its holster. But Danny was too late, too slow. And they were upon him like wild dogs, hacking and howling and snarling. A beef knife scythed in and Danny screamed, throwing up his arms. Another blow caught him in the ribs with a sickening crack of bone and Danny spun away in a spray of blood.

Then two of them turned on Drexel. He tried to use his chair as a shield but it did no good. Using their body weight, the attackers slammed into him, pinning him against the wall. A knife blow came in low, sweeping in under the protection of the chair, carving a great wedge into the back of his knee. And down he went.

Half on his belly, half on his back, he tried to scramble away. But they wrenched the chair from him and the blades came arcing in again. He tried to ward off the blows with the open palms of his hands and felt the shock as sinew and bone were severed. He was screaming incoherently, kicking out at them. He tried to roll clear, banging into tables. But it was hopeless. Their denim jackets were splattered with his blood. They were butchering him. 'You bastards!' he sobbed, unable to defend himself. 'You bastards, bastards!'

Then, as suddenly as it had begun, it ended. Dimly, he heard them shout to each other and turn to flee. But he didn't have the strength to look up. And there followed a calm, a dreadful eerie calm.

He found himself kneeling like a man in prayer. He felt no pain only a cold, clammy numbness. He looked for Danny across the shattered restaurant. He was lying against an overturned table with a tablecloth twisted round him like a shroud. He was in a terrible state, lying in a pool of maroon blood that spilled slowly out across the floor.

But it was his face . . . Merciful heaven, from the scalp down to the chin it had been splayed open, the wounds so deep that Drexel could see white bone. In a daze, he crawled towards him. When he was almost close enough to touch him, Danny reached up with a shivering hand. 'Help me,' he pleaded in a thin voice. 'Oh God, Carl, help me, please, I'm dying . . .'

Chapter One

HONG KONG – NEW YORK

Into the Year of the Snake

Nobody seeing them enter the departure hall of Kai Tak Airport that Saturday night could have guessed they were brothers, albeit half-brothers with different fathers. It would have been difficult in fact to imagine any blood relationship. Physically, in the manner of their dress, even in their spoken accents, they were as different as any two men could be.

Harry, the older of the two, was pure Chinese. Lee Wai-hong was his given name but he liked to call himself Harry Lee and that's how he was known by Chinese and Westerners alike. Fat and jovial, dressed in a cream-coloured Italian silk suit with a diamond and gold Rolex on his wrist, Harry was the image of affluence; a dimpled, fast-buck entrepreneur typical of Hong Kong.

Adam was just the opposite. Tall and spare, with his Asia-black hair greying at the temples, he was so much the product of his European father – quiet, understated in his dress, with a cool, controlled English accent – that people automatically assumed he was British. The dark, wide-set eyes and the high Mongolian cheekbones were puzzling to some, indication perhaps of Mediterranean roots. But few ever saw the Oriental in him.

Harry liked to tease him about it. 'You even hold your chopsticks like an Englishman,' he would say. 'Why don't you bend over the bowl and shovel it in, for God's sake. Enjoy it!'

It was an old joke and Adam would always smile. But sometimes it needled. The truth was that he spoke Cantonese with barely an accent, understood both the Hakka and Chiu Chow dialects and was proud to consider himself very much a fusion of East and West.

'What airline are you flying on?' asked Harry, carrying Adam's briefcase and rolled-up blueprints.

'Down that way - Cathay Pacific.'

'Club Class of course.'

'Sorry to disappoint you, brother - tourist.'

Harry rolled his eyes. 'You're going to Zurich to win a commission worth millions. How can you go tourist?'

'Simple,' said Adam with a quiet smile. 'I'm broke.'

'There's no such thing as broke, not in Hong Kong. A hotshot architect like you, with a little creative accounting, you should have the banks begging to extend your overdrafts. That's your problem, Adam, you know that - too much integrity. You're riddled with it. You're going to be a rich man soon. So what the hell.'

Adam laughed, shaking his head. 'I haven't won the commission yet, Harry. And the odds are I won't.' But he knew that Harry, who won and lost money with the speed of a demented gambler, would never understand. In that way, too, they were poles apart.

They reached the economy-class queues for the Zurich flight, two chaotic lines of trolleys and luggage and grim-faced travellers.

'Only two people in Club Class, the Marco Polo line,' said Harry. 'See what I mean.'

Adam just smiled. If Harry had two cents to his name and the flight was only an hour long he would still travel first class – even if the only person he impressed was the air hostess.

The family at the front of the queue, loaded down with boxes containing their Hong Kong purchases, appeared to be arguing with the airline staff. Nobody moved. After a couple of minutes had passed, Harry glanced at his gold Rolex. He was beginning to agitate.

'It was good of you to drive me out but you don't have to stay,' said Adam. 'I appreciate you've got things to do.'

Harry hunched his shoulders in a shrug. 'You know what it's like in my line of business, Adam. When you're trading, it never stops. No such thing as office hours. I've got to meet a guy at a hotel in Tsim Sha Tsui. He flew in tonight.'

'What is it this time?' Adam grinned. 'Last time, if I remember, it was digital watches to Nigeria.'

'I made a killing on them, too,' said Harry. 'There are now a quarter of a million Ibo tribesmen who can tell the time, the date and the temperature at the same time, Adam. Think of that.'

Adam laughed. 'I'm sure they're eternally grateful. Civilisation – "Made in Hong Kong" style.'

Harry shrugged. 'They're happy, I'm happy.' He

glanced at his watch again. 'When is Nicky getting here?'

'She had a last-minute meeting at the office so she said she'd come by taxi. Should be here any minute.'

'She's got business in Zurich, too?'

Adam smiled. 'She had to juggle a few dates to get it to dovetail with my trip. But it's going to be good to have her along.'

'Good?' Harry shook his head as if despairing. 'There you go with that British understatement of yours. It's not going to be good, it's going to be a medical necessity! If it wasn't for Nicky you'd have had a nervous breakdown weeks ago. I've never seen you so jittery over a commission before.'

Adam gave an uncertain smile. 'Maybe that's because I've never had so much in the balance before.'

Four months earlier Adam had been asked to present a design in a limited competition for the Swiss Federal Bank's proposed Hong Kong headquarters. The site had already been purchased in Central close to the waterfront on reclaimed land. For any architect it was the chance of a lifetime. If his design was chosen it would stand with three of the most architecturally important buildings in Asia: Foster's brilliant, high-tech space station that housed the HongKong and Shanghai Banking Corporation; Rudolph's dramatically sculptured twin towers; and, towering above them both, built for the Bank of China, Pei's glittering seventy-seven-storey silver obelisk.

Adam had appreciated from the beginning that he was the rank outsider. Two other architects had been asked to submit designs, one Swiss, one American, both men in their fifties, both with international reputations. In comparison, Adam was a novice. Although he had done work for the Swiss Federal Bank over the past couple of years, it had been bread and butter stuff. He had nothing of any real architectural note behind him. But no matter how slim the chance of success, he had to take it. An opportunity like that might never present itself again.

It had been four months of his life, however, that he never wanted to repeat – a financial and emotional nightmare: bigger offices, better equipment, new computers, half a dozen more staff to help with the load and eighteen hours a day of nerve-shredding work.

Unlike Harry, Adam was no gung-ho extrovert. He was a perfectionist who, at the best of times, agonised over his designs. But this time, knowing how much rested on the concept, he was plagued with doubts. It was too revolutionary, then too derivative, then too Asian, then too bland. 'Look at it,' he once exploded to Nicky. 'Look at the damn thing – a fifty-storey, post-modernist, chop-suey emporium. And I expect them to choose that!'

Yes, Harry was right. If it hadn't been for Nicky he would have fallen apart at the seams weeks ago. She had been the one who had kept him sane, cajoled and pushed him when it was necessary, encouraged him when he was low, the one person always there when he needed somebody most.

The queue hadn't moved. The family at the counter were still arguing with the airline staff. 'Look, I'm sorry,' said Harry, studying his watch again. 'If I don't make a move now, I'm not going to make this meeting.'

'Don't worry about it, go.'

Harry, a good head shorter, smiled up at his brother. 'Best of luck in Switzerland.'

'The best of luck to you, too – for whatever deal it is.'

'This time it's rice cookers for Indonesia,' said Harry with a pudgy grin. 'Two hundred gross and I can get the stock way below factory price. You nail those Zurich gnomes to the wall, you understand – just make sure first that it's the wall *you* designed!'

And with a quick handshake he was gone.

In New York, thirteen hours behind Hong Kong, it was not yet nine in the morning.

The weekday stampede of traffic down Manhattan's Fifth Avenue had been reduced to an intermittent weekend amble when the yellow cab pulled up at the corner of East 69th and a fresh-faced Chinese teenager alighted. He didn't look more than sixteen, a nice respectable kid dressed in a jacket and tie, grey slacks and black leather shoes. He stood for a time on the pavement in front of Hunter College consulting a hand-drawn map. Then, lifting a suitcase peppered with airline stickers, he set off along East 69th and across Lexington.

It was late February, a raw white morning, brisk and cold. Small groups of joggers in designer tracksuits, paunchy businessmen mainly, with their minds on the Dow Jones, ran past him. The Chinese teenager stopped at the junction of East 69th and Third and solemnly consulted his map again. Then he walked on for another fifty yards until, opposite a small brownstone synagogue, he came to an apartment block set back off the street behind flowering shrubs.

Hesitantly, the young man entered the black-marbled lobby. He approached the reception desk and put down his suitcase. 'I wish to visit apartment 601,' he said politely. 'My name is Chan.' An attendant, liveried in burgundy and grey, telephoned the apartment then nodded his head. 'Okay, take the elevator up – 601 is on your right.'

Picking up his suitcase, the young man entered the elevator. The attendant watched him press the button for the sixth floor. When the doors hissed shut he picked up a small portable radio transmitter and spoke into it. 'The mouse is here,' he said.

From the bedlam of Kai Tak Airport, Harry Lee drove in his leased BMW to a nightclub in Tsim Sha Tsui East called the Go-Go Paradise. That's where, amid the neon lights and the lobbies of the smart hotels, he picked up his lover of the moment, a hostess called Lilly Choi.

He and Lilly had been going together for six months now. Harry appreciated that a hostess like Lilly had to sleep from time to time with her customers, mainly Japanese and Korean businessmen. That was okay. Business was business. Just so long as she did what he wanted and – on nights like this – asked no questions.

The meeting was to take place in a small hotel in Yaumatei near the Typhoon Shelter. Harry parked the BMW in a nearby underground garage, then he and Lilly walked to the place.

'You remember what you have to do,' he said when they arrived at the entrance.

Lilly nodded, her eyes wide and nervous.

'Okay then.' He kissed her on the cheek, smelling her perfume above the sour stench of the street drains and the hawkers' offal cooking on nearby carts. Then he entered the small, dark lobby and, puffing with exertion, climbed the concrete stairs to room 410.

The door was opened by a short, wizened Vietnamese, a man Harry had dealt with before. Tac Long was his name; at least, that was the name he gave. 'Come in,' he said. 'Come, sit.'

Harry did so. The room was small and shoddy but the air-conditioning at least was cold and the sweat from the effort of climbing the stairs in the oppressive humidity began to dry on his face.

Tac Long shut the door and locked it. He went to his chair and picked up a case, tartan red in colour, which he placed on his lap.

A wooden coffee table separated the two men. An old-fashioned black telephone stood on it next to a bowl of plastic flowers.

Harry checked the time. It was 10 p.m. So it would be 9 a.m. in New York. His stomach muscles contracted in a sudden spasm of nerves. It should be happening right now, he thought.

As if reading his thoughts, Tac Long grinned, showing brown-stained teeth. 'No problem, no problem,' he said in broken English. 'Telephone ring any second. No problem, you see.'

Harry Lee tried to smile. Despite the air-conditioning, he was sweating again and dabbed at his plump features with a handkerchief. His stomach muscles contracted once more and he let out a small involuntary groan.

Tac Long gave him a quizzical look. 'You sick?'

Harry shook his head. 'Shellfish for dinner, under-cooked crab. It'll go away.'

'Crab no good in Hong Kong. Everybody shit in the sea.'

Harry looked at the red tartan case that Tac Long guarded on his lap. 'The place is polluted to hell. You're right, I should leave crab alone.' Not that he had had any crab for dinner. The truth was he hadn't eaten since lunch. He wouldn't have been able to hold it down. Too much rested on this deal, far too much. Everything.

The past six months had been hell on earth for Harry Lee. He had experienced bad times before but nothing this disastrous. Financially he was at breaking point and if this deal went wrong, he was as good as dead. That's what caused the stomach cramps and the sweating – pure nerves.

Not that Harry Lee looked like a man two cents away from perdition. The sun-desiccated Vietnamese opposite him could have been a coolie during daylight hours, a labourer on some building site in Kwung Tong, and probably was. But everything about Harry spoke of money – the Rolex, the ruby signet ring, the Italian suit, the pink tailor-made shirt with his initials embroidered on the cuff. At thirty-eight, good living had larded Harry as sleek and fat as a circus seal.

He stared across at the case on Tac Long's lap, trying to visualise the seven hundred and fifty thousand US dollars inside, all of it cash, crisp and green – the redemption of his soul.

Traffic sounds drifted up from Ferry Road which ran

alongside the typhoon shelter. The shelter was jammed with sampans, junks and lighters; if he sniffed deeply, Harry could smell the water. Tac Long was right, he thought, in Hong Kong everybody did shit in the sea.

Suddenly, with an abrupt jangling sound, the telephone on the table between them rang. Harry took a deep breath, hesitated, then picked up the receiver. And, with a dimpled smile of pure relief, he heard the New York buyer say: 'The stuff is in order. Let me speak to my man.'

The buyer, a Vietnamese by the name of 'Market Place' Trung, was in good humour. The suitcase that was open in front of him contained five units – three and a half kilos – of China White. He was paying Lee two hundred thousand dollars a kilo but here in New York it would retail at over one and a half million. Even a miserable refugee like him could figure out the profit, he thought smugly. America was an amazing place.

The courier, the Chinese kid, was out on the balcony recovering his nerves. This was his first job as a mule. But he had done fine, just fine.

In rapid Vietnamese, Trung spoke to his man in Hong Kong. 'Everything is okay,' he said. 'Give the fat boy his cash.'

Harry Lee opened the red tartan case and, in front of Tac Long, counted the individual bundles, each of fifty thousand dollars. 'It's been a pleasure doing business with you,' he said as he clicked the case shut.

Tac Long nodded. 'We buy more stuff soon, sure. We do business again. What you say?'

'Absolutely. This is just the beginning,' said Harry. 'I can see many profitable months ahead for us all.' He reached out to open the door – and in that instant his world exploded.

The hammering of fists on the door seemed to come out of nowhere, bursting his brain. 'Open up, police!'

Mouth agape, Harry stumbled back.

'We have a warrant! Open up!'

It couldn't be happening, he thought. Oh God, what did he do? He looked at Tac Long but the Vietnamese stood in the centre of the room, paralysed too.

'Police, we said! Open up or we break in!'

Frantically, Harry looked around. There had to be some way of getting out. But they were trapped there, like rats in a cage.

With a splintering roar, an axe smashed into the door. Outside, voices shouted excitedly, 'Smash it down!'

Tac Long had collapsed into a chair and sat there, eyes glazed, catatonic.

Harry's worst nightmare – the unthinkable, black dimension of every dream – was happening. He knew he was lost. But the money, somehow he had to save the money. His life depended on it. Spinning round, the case under his arm, he stumbled towards the room's single tiny window.

In the New York apartment the door flew open and agents were all over Trung before he could rise from his chair. But out on the balcony, the teenager, Chan, saw what was happening and, in a blind panic, scrambled over the balcony railings.

A DEA agent rushed out, training his .38 on him. Chan was trying desperately to claw his way along the face of the building. 'Don't be stupid, kid,' said the agent. 'You've got nowhere to go. Just stay right there.'

The young courier stared back, terror in his eyes.

'It's all over, buddie,' said the agent in a softer voice, trying to calm him. 'Why don't you climb back now, huh? It's not the end of the world.'

But the teenager didn't seem to hear. His mouth hung slack, his face was bloodless.

'Come on, kid, easy does it . . .'

Chan glanced down at the ground six floors below. He looked back at the DEA agent. 'I'm sorry,' he said, just once, distinctly. Then he dropped.

Half hysterical, Harry Lee wrenched at the window. But it was rusted shut. It hadn't been opened in years. Swinging the case like a club, he smashed the glass then hacked frantically at the jagged shards in the frame. 'Lilly!' he screamed in Cantonese as he thrust his head out of the window. 'Lilly, where are you?'

His eyes weren't accustomed to the gloom and for a moment the alley four floors below appeared deserted. But then, half hidden by an awning, he saw her. 'I'm up here, to your right! The fourth floor!' he bellowed.

She looked up. Their eyes met and hesitantly, frightened too, she waved.

'I'm throwing down a case!' he shouted. 'You've got to get out of here! It's the cops!'

Behind him, Harry could hear the door splintering open. He had a couple of seconds more, that was all. As he squeezed the case through the window, glass cut his wrists. Blood ran down between his fingers. But nothing mattered, nothing, only the money. He gave the case a final shove and watched it cartwheel down, bouncing off the drains. It hit the iron girders of a neon sign and then plunged into the darkness of the alley.

Lilly ran across, scooping it up. From what Harry could see, it still appeared to be intact. Lilly looked up at him. 'Run!' he shrieked. 'Go, go!' And, like a frightened rabbit, the tartan case clutched to her breasts, Lilly sprinted for the road.

Rough hands grabbed at Harry's shoulders trying to haul him back. But he resisted. First he had to be certain Lilly was clear. The last he saw of her was the swish of her dress as she turned into Ferry Road. Only then did he let himself be pulled limply back. The police – plainclothes cops from Narcotics – pushed him to the floor and handcuffed him behind his back. Somebody kicked him hard in the ribs. 'Bastard, trying to escape!' But Harry was in a daze. Thank God, was all he could think, thank God she got away.

A small group stood on the lawn outside the apartment block staring down at the broken body. They were all members of the thirty-man Asia Task Force that had been responsible for the bust: two New York City detectives, a Customs officer, a couple of DEA agents, a square-jawed woman from US Immigration. All of them, in their own way, were stunned that a young man could kill himself like that. 'He looks like the kind of kid who should be home helping his pa in the family store,' said one.

'That's just where he would have been,' Carl Drexel said as he came out of the lobby on to the lawn, 'except the store went bust. Do you know why he was acting as a courier? He was paying for his college fees, that's why. A goddamn holiday job.'

With the rank of supervisor, Carl Drexel had headed up the New York Asia Task Force, known in the DEA as 'Group 41', since his recall from Hong Kong eighteen months earlier. Nobody suggested it was easy co-ordinating personnel from the DEA, the City Police and three or four different Federal agencies, including the FBI, but he had managed it with more success than his superiors expected. A sense of humour helped, that and his easy way with people. Although he tolerated precious little bullshit, Drexel was an instinctive diplomat. He got things done without friction, that was the secret.

A couple of his men grinned affectionately as they watched him limp along with that portly battleship roll he had patented. 'The hazards of eating in cheap Chinese restaurants,' Drexel always said when questioned about his limp or the difficulty he had in using the fingers of his left hand. And those who knew would laugh. Because, when it came to his injuries, savage ones too, Drexel was pure John Wayne. Only a few of his closest friends appreciated the chronic pain he really suffered. But that's what the agents in the Task Force liked about Drexel. He was a 'character', a good old-fashioned professional.

'I've just heard from Hong Kong,' said Drexel. 'It seems the seller and buyer's agent were caught on the job there too – *in flagrante delicto*.'

There was a look of delight on the assembled faces. It had been a peach of an operation, slickly co-ordinated. There was no doubt about it, Drexel knew his business.

'What was the value of the seizure?' asked one of the newer, more bumptious DEA agents. 'How much junk did we get?'

But the others who had been on the Task Force longer only smiled. They knew from experience what Drexel thought about such statistics, what he thought about press photographs of agents standing around tables covered with polythene bags full of dope and headlines that read: 'DEA Make Five Million Dollar Heroin Bust'. Carl Drexel's philosophy was simple: on its own, heroin amounted to nothing. It was just a pile of white shit. You couldn't put it in jail. You couldn't push it back into the system and let it feed you information. That you could only do with people, people and the information they carried in their heads.

Lilly Choi was terrified. She had bolted the door, switched off every light. And now she huddled on her bed not daring to move. Harry Lee's case, the one he had thrown down, lay on the bed next to her. The tartan exterior was smeared with muck, one lock was shattered, the spine had snapped. It had taken all her strength to hold the suitcase shut. So there was no way she could avoid knowing what it contained: wad after wad of US $100 notes, hundreds of thousands of dollars, more money than she had seen in her life. And it was the money that made her appreciate the true enormity of her predicament.

She had managed to escape the police by boarding a taxi in Mongkok's crowded streets. But it was only a matter of time before they traced her. Everybody knew about Harry Lee and his nightclub hostess. The police would try the club in Tsim Sha Tsui first and when they didn't find her there, they would come to the apartment. And then what? How did she explain all this money? Harry had told her nothing about his business. 'Stay in the alley in case you're needed' – that's all he had said.

It wasn't fair, she thought, as the tears began to roll down her moon-shaped face. She might have suspected that he was dealing in white powder but she had had nothing to do with it. She hadn't received so much as a cent. But how did she convince the police of that? If they sent her to jail she would be an old woman by the time she got out. It just wasn't fair.

But then, in the depths of her misery, gazing at the case, an idea began to take shape in her mind. Harry was doomed. The police had arrested him, caught him red-handed. What chance did he stand? So why should she forfeit her life for him? What would it achieve? They weren't husband and wife. She was his lover, that's all, a woman for his bed. Loyalty only went so far. She had her own life to think of now, her own future. Survival, that's all that counted.

And quickly, before her resolve was lost, she began to pack her things . . .

It was 2 a.m. when they brought Harry Lee into the interview room, shoving him on to a chair and handcuffing him to it.

A European police officer, a big beefy man with freckles, walked round the chair, first one way then the other, in endless circles. 'So this is your first arrest, Harry, a new experience. What's it like? Feel like crapping in your pants, I bet.' He poured himself a cup of milky coffee from a thermos flask. 'So that we both know where we stand, Harry, let me explain a couple of things. First, we've had you under surveillance for the past two weeks.' He held up a sheaf of black-and-white photographs, fanning them out in his hand like playing cards. 'Second, your telephone conversations have been taped. We even bugged your car. And third, Harry, while we were arresting you here, DEA were seizing your shipment in New York. Do you understand what I'm saying, Harry? I'm saying we've got you cold.'

'I'm not going to say anything until I've seen a lawyer,' murmured Harry, his teeth chattering from nerves.

'You've got one chance, Harry.'

'Co-operate, is that what you mean?'

'Give us some names, Harry.'

'What do I get in return?'

'We'll see you right.'

'A full immunity?'

'Oh, a comedian! That's great. I like a laugh.'

'If I give names I'm a dead man.'

The European shook his head as if he was dealing with a stupid novice. 'Let's be sensible, Harry. With the evidence we've got, a retarded troglodyte could prosecute your case and win. You're looking at twenty years, Harry. But if you co-operate, if you give us some names, it could be half that. Then take a third off for good behaviour . . .'

'Easy to say, but I'll be dead long before that.'

'We can protect you, Harry.'

'Not against this man.'

The European looked direct into Harry's eyes. 'So that's it. You're running scared.'

Harry said nothing but he couldn't control his violent shivering.

'Who is he, Harry?'

Harry remained silent.

'Some Triad goon?'

Harry shrugged, his shoulders shuddering.

'What Triad society does he belong to, Harry? 14K, Wo Shing Wo, Sun Yee On? Just give us his name and we'll get him. We'll put him out of action soon enough. Come on, don't tell me you're prepared to spend the rest of your life in jail for some tattooed low-life?'

The European officer walked to his desk and sat down. He had a photograph of his wife and children on the desk, a big colour photograph in an ornate frame: wife, two red-haired children and a collie dog. He sighed. He looked tired. 'Think about it, Harry, that's all I say. When you've had some sleep and a meal, when you're not so frightened, think about it again. You'll see the sense in it. We can keep you here for forty-eight hours before we have to drag you before a magistrate. That's plenty of time to mull things over. You'll see the sense in what I'm proposing. It's no problem, we can protect you. You help us, we'll help you.' He poured himself more coffee. Then he said, 'Oh, by the way, your lawyer is here. Two fifteen in the morning – I wouldn't want to pay his fee.'

Harry was unmanacled from the chair and led down a passage to a room where his lawyer, a man called Au, was waiting.

Au was an unsavoury character, a homosexual some said. He spoke in a whine, had a pockmarked face and greasy hair. But he knew every twist of the law and how to take advantage of it. Au waited until the two escorting policemen had left the room before he put the first question. 'Have you made a statement?'

Harry shook his head.

'Good. Don't say a word, not until I'm able to work something out.'

That's what Harry liked about Au, he had the ethics of a pimp. 'How did you know I was arrested?'

'One of the police officers in the report room.'

'Does he get a cut of my fees?'

Au gave a thin-lipped smile. 'Don't you need my help?'

Harry forgot the sparring. 'Of course I do, you don't know how much. There's something you have to do for me, just one thing but it's crucially important.'

'What's that?'

'You've got to contact a woman for me.'

'What's her name?' asked Au.

'Lilly Choi.'

Seven hours later, shortly after 9 a.m., Au climbed from a taxi in Nam Cheong Street and entered the rundown tenement block at No. 32. He found the caretaker in his cubicle slurping his breakfast *congee*, a thin rice soup, out of an enamel bowl. 'I represent the landlord,' said

Au in his pompous whine. 'I require immediate access to apartment 2A. We suspect the tenant has been building illegal extensions on to the balcony.'

'Everybody builds illegal extensions,' grumbled the caretaker. 'Half of Hong Kong is illegal.' But it wasn't for him to query such things and, taking the keys to 2A, he led Au up the dark concrete stairs.

The apartment was typical and tiny, just a single room with a tiled floor, an alcove off to one side for the kitchen, and a toilet that doubled as a shower. The furniture remained – bed, table, chairs, a small fridge in the corner – but the apartment had been stripped of every personal possession.

It didn't take Au more than a few seconds to appreciate the obvious. Lilly Choi had fled – and she had taken the money with her.

Danny Abbott was a changed man. Everybody appreciated he had been through a tough time. For a couple of days after the chopping it had even been touch and go whether he would survive. But that had been nearly two years ago now and he was back on his feet, no permanent injuries, just the scarring. But somehow he didn't have the same drive, the same commitment to his work. At one time, you couldn't hold him back. If he wasn't bedding another of his fancy females, he was down in Wanchai with the lads. These days, however, he was a loner. Frankly, a pain in the arse.

Allowances had been made of course. Nobody had pushed him too hard. He had stayed on in Narcotics with the post of Research and Administration Officer, a steady desk job while he underwent the process of healing. But it was doubtful whether he would ever get back on the operational side. He was too passive these days, that's what they said. He had grown gun shy.

Danny Abbott knew what they thought. He heard them talk behind his back in the police mess. But what did they know? They didn't have to live with the scar tissue, the hard-ridged purple welts slashed all over his face and body. They didn't have to cope with the pain.

Well, to hell with them, he thought, as he stood that evening on the balcony of his apartment looking out over the grubby rooftops of Western. At one time women chased him all over the world. Now he had trouble getting one even if he was prepared to pay. Twenty floors below him, down on Conduit Road, there was another traffic jam: concrete mixers and Mercedes, nose to tail. If you had money in Hong Kong, you were fine. But if you were an expat police inspector with a face like Frankenstein's monster living on coolie wages, with no future and no options, the place was a dump.

Inside, above the drone of the secondhand dehumidifier, he heard the telephone ring. He had a fair idea who it would be – certainly not a woman – and drained the can of beer in his hand before padding back into the lounge.

The telephone rested on a pile of magazines, old *Playboys* and *Penthouse*. There were coffee cups on the carpet that hadn't been washed in a week. No more living with bachelor girls these days, smart chicks in commodity trading or law with their Saab convertibles. Now he was stuck with his government quarters. He flopped into an armchair: standard government issue, jungle green – the bloody thing deserved to be camouflaged, he thought – and picked up the receiver.

'Hi, Danny, it's Carl.'

'I was waiting for you to call.' Danny Abbott knew that Carl Drexel never had the patience to wait for official reports. He was like a kid in that respect, tugging at your sleeve, wanting to know everything the minute it happened. 'What time is it over there?' Danny asked.

'Six a.m.'

'Don't you ever sleep?'

Drexel laughed. 'I've been up since three. You know what it's like after a bust. Your mind won't stop buzzing. I've been listening to Bach on the CD and drinking ginseng tea. Great for the soul, Danny, great for the cholesterol.' Carl Drexel didn't mention the fact that he had also been lying in a warm bath trying to soothe the arthritic pains of his own scars. 'I phoned to see if your guys managed to get anything worthwhile out of those two arrests.'

Danny grunted. 'Nothing that I know of. Apparently the seller, Lee, is terrified what'll happen to him if he co-operates. He's staying tight as a clam.'

'What about the Vietnamese guy?'

'Tough as old boots. He says he was given the case full of money by an acquaintance and told to deliver it. Insists he had no idea he was part of a drug deal. Thought it was payment of a gambling debt. It's the standard bullshit. But who knows, a gullible jury might buy it.'

'What about the nightclub hostess, the one who got the cash?'

'Gone to ground, so I'm told.'

'Not too encouraging, is it?'

'What were you hoping for?' asked Danny with a hard edge of cynicism. 'Some lead to Leung Chi-ming?'

'Don't scoff, the time will come.'

'So will the next Ice Age.'

Drexel chuckled. 'You're a man of little faith, Danny.'

'Why should I have any at all? Christ!' Danny snorted with disgust. 'You and I get chopped like chickens in a Chinese market – two law enforcement officers right in the middle of Hong Kong. Every person in that restaurant must have seen who did it. Add to that the fact that we've got more informers in this town than Manila has massage parlours and you would have thought we could at least have managed a couple of arrests.'

Danny Abbott was right. The investigation had drawn a blank. Cheng Tak-shing, Dai Ngan, the one who had hired Danny's informer as a chemist, had been hauled in. Cheng had a known history of violence. He was an office bearer in the Sun Yee On, perfectly able to order the hit. He was obviously the one behind the attack. But, although he had been grilled for days, with some strong-arm stuff used, too, he made no admissions. Without the informer there was just no evidence against him and he had to be released.

A reward had been posted: three quarters of a million Hong Kong dollars. Money normally moved mountains in Hong Kong. Triads betrayed their Dragon Heads, fathers sold their sons. But this time nobody came forward.

The police had even mounted a three-month surveillance on Leung Chi-ming. But Drexel had known from the beginning that it would be a useless exercise. Leung was far too shrewd to show his hand in that critical period. And, living up to expectations, the tycoon had gone about his daily business with a demeanour pious enough to qualify for beatification.

'Our friend was on the cover of the *Far East Economic Review* this morning,' said Danny sardonically. 'Another coup. He's put together a consortium of companies for some multi-billion dollar redevelopment over in Kowloon. To the Chinese – your average taxi driver and the middle-class punters on the stock exchange – Leung is a legend. He's made himself bulletproof. Tell me, how do we ever get to a man like that?'

And Drexel replied, 'With persistence, Danny, that's how, infinite, painstaking persistence.'

Thirty-six hours after his arrest, Harry Lee was conveyed to the Central Magistracy in Wanchai to be remanded in custody pending trial.

When he was brought up from the cells, unwashed and dishevelled, Au, his lawyer, was waiting. Harry hadn't seen him since the night of the arrest and called him across to the dock. 'Why haven't you contacted me?' he asked anxiously. 'Did you find Lilly?'

Au shook his head. 'I'm afraid your lady friend has fled.'

'What are you talking about? That can't be right!'

'Sssh, keep your voice down. She's gone, Harry, she's fled Hong Kong.'

Harry couldn't believe it. Lilly wouldn't desert him. 'How can you be sure?' he muttered. 'She could be in hiding.'

Au gave an irritable sigh. 'I spoke to her travel agent, I checked with the airport. She flew to Taiwan on the first flight she could get.'

'Then she must have left a message,' said Harry with the fierce conviction of disbelief. 'She's got to have left some way of contacting her.'

'Nothing that I could find,' said Au flatly.

'Did you check her apartment?'

'Of course I did.'

'The nightclub? Her friends?'

'Credit me with some common sense, will you.'

Harry's head began to spin. He had to grip the bars of the dock so tight that his knuckles turned white. 'The bitch,' he mumbled and slumped down onto the prisoner's bench. 'What about the money?' he asked despairingly.

Au gave a supercilious smile. 'What do you think?' And he returned to the lawyers' benches.

The magistrate came into court, a middle-aged European woman dressed in black with her hair done up in a bun; polite and precise and as stern as a Victorian matron.

Listlessly, Harry studied the faces in the public gallery. His mother obviously hadn't been told about his arrest or she would have been there. Thank God for that, he thought. It was difficult enough trying to hold himself together without the burden of looking into her face and seeing the hurt. But she would find out soon enough. Tomorrow morning it would be splashed all over the newspapers. The criminal courts held a fascination for the people of Hong Kong. The colony didn't have any politics or foreign policy to talk of. After trade, the only thing left was crime. He knew what his mother's reaction would be. She would grieve but she would stand by him until the end. But what about Adam? he wondered and felt his stomach knot. What about his half-brother, how would he react when he found out?

Harry's name was called by the clerk and in a daze he climbed to his feet. Au made an application for bail but with the promise of a fat fee gone, there was no heart in it. In any event, with three and a half kilos of heroin involved, any hope of bail was illusionary. The magistrate didn't even glance up from her papers as she made the order.

Harry turned to Au. 'Do me one last favour,' he said as a warder took his arm. 'Phone my mother, will you? I don't want her to find out from the newspapers. At least I want to spare her that.'

That night at Lai Chi Kok holding prison, the pains returned. At first they were grumbling pains deep in Harry's gut but soon they crept up to his chest, sharp, muscular pains that made it difficult to breathe. It was nerves, he knew, all nerves. In the prison hospital on the far side of the yard he was examined by a Burmese doctor. Harry's blood pressure was high. It would be necessary to do tests if the pains persisted, the doctor said. Yes, it probably was tension. Not unusual, he said fatuously, for a man in his position. Harry was given medication and told he could return to the main block.

Outside the hospital a prison warder waited to escort him back. He was different from the one who had brought him across, much older and slower, close to retirement by the looks of it, his face heavily wrinkled like an old elephant.

As they walked across the open yard, dwarfed by the high walls around them, the old warder suddenly stopped. He glanced at Harry and seemed to smile. Then he said. '*Fai Chai* – Fat Boy – I have a message for you from Dai Ngan.'

Harry's mouth fell open in astonishment. How could Cheng have got to him so soon? He had only been here a few hours, not even time enough for one meal.

'You were given credit to buy merchandise because of your reputation,' said the warder in a slow, pedantic fashion as if he had learnt the words off by heart. 'But now there is talk that your woman has run off with the money, disappeared in Taiwan. Dai Ngan wishes to know your intentions. He is very concerned.'

Harry could hear his heart thudding in his chest. 'He'll be paid,' he blurted. 'I promise he'll be paid.'

'You owe him three quarters of a million United States dollars. It is a great deal of money.'

'But I can pay it, I promise.'

'What about the interest, Fat Boy? Remember that interest is accumulating every day.'

Harry had no need to be told. He knew all about the usurious rates charged by Hong Kong's loan sharks. A

Triad debt could double in a couple of months.

'In eight days, on the twenty-eighth of February, it is the New Year,' said the warder, 'the Year of the Snake. You know the tradition, Fat Boy. By New Year a man's debts must be paid.'

'Don't worry, I'll get the money.' Harry spoke with the desperate sincerity of a cornered man. 'You can tell Dai Ngan that the police wanted me to co-operate, to give names. They said I could halve my sentence but I kept quiet. Surely he owes me something for that?'

'Is that a threat, Fat Boy?'

Harry blanched. 'No, no threat. I'm proving my good faith, that's all. Dai Ngan knows that I won't let him down. But he must give me time. He must have patience.'

'Patience?' The warder's heavily wrinkled face broke into a benign smile. 'Ah, Fat Boy, but patience is such an expensive commodity.'

Chapter Two

ZURICH – HONG KONG

Adam Blake's overcoat was still over his arm when he strode through the baroque bronze doors of the Swiss Federal Bank into a blast of arctic wind. All around him on the Parade-Platz the sturdy burghers of Zurich were wrapped up against the freezing February temperatures. But Adam had already crossed the stone-flagged square and swung into the Bahnhofstrasse before he paid the slightest heed to the cold. At that moment a Siberian blizzard wouldn't have dampened his spirits. It was one of those rare, exhilarating moments when the urge to dance in the street or shake hands with total strangers seemed entirely natural. He was light-headed with it, a giddy concoction of triumph and joy – and perfect, pure relief.

When he had finished his presentation to the board a few minutes earlier – the last of the three architects to do so – he had expected a businesslike handshake, nothing more. The Swiss were not noted for high emotions. So when Helmut Gasser, the bank's chairman, had come over accompanied by his deputy, Adam had been caught totally off guard.

'I must congratulate you. A perfect synthesis of Western and Asian forms,' Gasser, a big, beefy man, had said with almost boyish enthusiasm.

'Most impressive,' his deputy added, smiling, without a hint of guile. 'Radical yet elegant.'

'You cannot ignore it,' Gasser continued while Adam stood there speechless. 'And Hong Kong may possibly be the richer for it. Bravo, my friend, bravo – a *tour de force*.'

Adam had felt like hugging them both. He had no idea of course what Gasser had said to the other two architects, and anyway, the winning design had to be decided by the full board. That would take another month, maybe more. Until then he would have to sweat it out. But now at least he knew that his design had been taken seriously and he knew, too, that he was closer to winning than he had ever dreamt possible.

Excitement, the kind of fist-clenching excitement he felt, radiated itself and, as he strode down the Bahnhofstrasse under the bare winter trees with his greying hair wind-blown around his face, a tall, long-legged figure built as lean as a long-distance runner, a good few heads turned to watch him pass.

He was about to swing off the street to his hotel when, further up, near the central railway station, he glimpsed a petite figure determinedly jogging. The white tracksuit with the red maple leaf on its chest was unmistakable. Crazy Canuck, he thought, trust her to go running in weather like this. And, chuckling to himself, he watched

Nicky du Bois weave her way through the traffic, ignoring a couple of disapproving car horns, and sprint the last fifty yards.

'How was it?' she asked breathlessly as she came to a halt, puffing clouds of steam. 'How did it go?'

Grinning like a man who had just won ten million dollars, Adam shrugged. 'I think it went okay.'

Nicky looked up at him, hands on hips, eyes watering. 'Is that it, just *okay*?'

He shrugged again. 'How did your own meeting go, the negotiations on the syndicated loan?'

'Damn the syndicated loan!' Her face was scarlet. 'I want to know what the reaction was to your presentation. Why do you think I almost killed myself sprinting through the traffic when I saw you?'

Adam couldn't conceal his excitement any longer. 'The reaction was fine,' he said, 'just fine . . .' Then he started to laugh, his pearl-black eyes shining. 'In fact, if you want the truth, it was bloody marvellous!'

Nicky squealed with excitement. 'What did I tell you? I knew it, I just knew it!' And right there on the pavement, at the hotel entrance under the medieval flags of the Swiss cantons and the approving grin of the hotel commissioner, she flung herself into his arms. She was warm as toast, glowing with perspiration, and she kissed him full on the mouth.

Embarrassed – always the Englishman – but delighted, too, Adam blushed. Dear God, he thought, she was the best thing to have happened to him in years.

'So,' said Nicky, still in his arms, 'tell me all about it – and don't leave out a thing. How many were on the board? What were they like? What did they say?'

Entering the hotel with his arm round her, the commissioner still grinning, Adam gave her a blow by blow account. 'So, what do you think?' he asked as they entered their room. 'Any grounds for cautious optimism?'

Nicky was ecstatic. 'That's the chairman talking. What more can you ask for? I told you all along – and did you listen?'

He grinned. 'Of course not.'

Nicky began to pull off her joggers. 'We're going to celebrate tonight. For over four months you've been existing on a diet of junk food, coffee and hamburgers and cold pizza – and it's enough. So tonight it's going to be a restaurant, the best we can find. Then a piano bar afterwards, far too much schnapps of course—'

'I'll just fall asleep.'

She gave him a pert kiss. 'Not tonight, you won't, my darling. And I don't want any arguments, tonight is my treat.'

Adam fell back on the bed. 'My bank manager and I are profoundly grateful.'

'Champagne to start – we must have champagne – and then, as they say, something "typically Swiss".'

'Not cheese fondue,' said Adam watching her take off her tracksuit. 'I hate cheese fondue.'

'That's because you're a xenophobic Chinese. If it's not stir fried in a wok it's not worth eating.'

'True,' he said.

'I've got just the dish,' said Nicky. 'Papillote of salmon with lime and cayenne pepper.'

'Can't you Canadians think of anything but salmon?'

Adam admired her hair. It was layered and wispy with a deep reddish tinge like the best teak wood.

'I love salmon,' she said. 'So do you.'

'I don't have any choice.'

'Wild strawberry mousse to follow, with cognac and coffee. Even to a decadent Chinese palate like yours that's got to be perfection.'

'I was educated at an English boarding school. Stewing steak with less than eighty per cent gristle is perfection.'

She smiled at him, teasing. 'Are you that easy to please?'

'Depends which way you want to please me,' he said languidly.

'Chauvinist!' And, naked now, leaving her running gear in a damp pile on the carpet, Nicky went through to the bathroom.

Nicky's full Christian name was Nicolle-Marie. But Nicolle-Marie du Bois, she said, was a ridiculous name for a West Coast Canadian, raised in Vancouver, who spoke about three words of French. So Nicky it was.

She and Adam had been together for just over four months now. The development of their relationship and the preparation of Adam's design for the Swiss Federal had run in tandem. It couldn't have made the going too easy for her, he knew that. Over the past four months, if he hadn't been obsessed with his work, agonising over every aspect of it, he had been dead on his feet. Just as Nicky said, their meals together had consisted almost entirely of late-night hamburgers or something she cooked up in the apartment while he flopped out, exhausted, on her sofa. It was still a constant source of amazement that she had stuck with him. But now that a little normality was returning to his life, he intended to change all that.

Dropping his jacket on the bed and pulling off his tie, Adam walked to the bathroom door to watch her shower. She was only a fraction over five foot, with a slim dancer's body. But she possessed none of the anorexic boniness associated with most ballet dancers. Her breasts, the hot water now splashing off them, were small but firm, her hips well rounded, and her skin had a texture to it, heavily freckled at the shoulders, as if she had never quite lost her summer tan. Autumn colours, he thought, soft brown skin, reddish hair and sparkling grey-blue eyes like Canadian water.

Rolling up his sleeves, Adam began to soap her back. 'Being as objective as possible,' he said, 'you probably have the best bum in the world.'

'I bet you smooch up to all your female creditors that way.'

Adam smiled. It was an old joke they shared. In purchasing new equipment, hiring new staff, Adam had been forced to borrow heavily and that's how they had met – across an office desk. Nicky was vice president of the Hong Kong branch of West Coast Equities, a Canadian finance company. She was a smart lady when it came to figures, an MBA no less. She had granted the loans to him but everything had been done according to the book. Bed and business, they agreed, had to be kept firmly separated.

'So that's the reason for your concern about the

presentation,' said Adam, bringing his hands around to soap slowly and luxuriously over her breasts. 'Checking on your investment. You don't have to worry, you know. I'm good for it.'

Nicky pouted under the rush of water. 'You're good for a lot of things, my darling.'

Adam smiled. 'Keep saying things like that and your salmon is going to have to wait.'

She purred deep in her throat. 'Here in the shower . . . ?'

Adam pulled off his shirt. 'If I slip on the soap, I'll never forgive you.'

While she watched with a wet, enticing smile, he unbuckled his belt. The trousers loosened. He bent to pull them off—

The telephone rang.

'Oh, bloody hell!' He waited a moment hoping the ringing would stop. But it persisted and, hauling his trousers back up while Nicky giggled, he blundered back into the bedroom to pick up the phone.

The hotel telephonist said in perfect English, 'It's a call for you, Mr Blake. Hong Kong on the line.'

'Thank you,' said Adam, smiling to himself as he stared down at his distended Y-fronts. The call from his office had better be bloody quick.

'Hullo, Adam, is that you?'

His mother's voice surprised him. He knew she didn't like to phone when he was away on business. 'What is it?' he asked. 'What's happened?'

'It's Harry . . .'

The tone of her voice put him instantly on guard.

'He's not hurt, is he, he hasn't been in an accident?'

'No, it's nothing like that.'

'What is it then?'

His mother was silent for a moment, summoning up the courage. Then she said in a voice filled with pain, 'He's been arrested, Adam. Harry has been arrested.'

'What in God's name for?' He couldn't believe it.

There was another silence, longer this time. Then his mother said, 'It's something to do with drugs, that's what his lawyer said. Heroin.'

'That's impossible!' Adam was dumbfounded. 'There's got to be a mistake. Have you spoken to Harry himself?'

'Yes, I saw him today.' His mother tried unsuccessfully to stifle her emotion. 'He looked so sick, Adam, so frightened and sick. Please, you must come back.'

'Of course I will, you know that. I'll get back as soon as I can. But what did Harry tell you, what did he say?'

'He said he has to speak to you, Adam. You're the only one, that's what he said, you're the only one who can help him now.'

It happened so quickly, that was the stunning part. Twenty or thirty seconds - without a sound, nobody even noticed - and it was done; a life expunged. One moment the prisoner, an old drug addict, was next to Harry washing his face in a basin, the next, after the alarm was raised, they found him in the bath section dangling from a shower hook.

He had walked through while the warder had his back

turned and climbed on to the edge of a bath, twisted his shirt into a rope and tied it to the overhead shower hook. He had looped it round his neck and then stepped off. When they found him, purple-faced and inert, his toes hadn't been more than an inch from the bottom of the bath.

Harry had never seen a man die before and the experience shattered him. The image of that gaunt, sinewy body dangling from the twisted shirt haunted him for the rest of the day. And that night, as if the hanging had been an omen, the warder came, the one who had spoken to him before, the old elephant with the heavily wrinkled face and red-rimmed eyes. 'Remember, Fat Boy,' he said, 'Dai Ngan expects his money by New Year.'

'But I can't settle the whole amount in one payment. It's impossible. You've got to speak to him.'

'Dai Ngan can be a difficult man.'

'Tell him I'll do everything I can,' said Harry, visibly sweating. 'But he's got to give me a chance.'

The warder sniffed as if he had a head cold. 'I believe you witnessed the hanging this morning?'

'I was there, yes.'

'So you know?'

'Know what?'

The warder smiled. 'How easily it can be done.'

The following day, Adam and Nicky caught the first available flight back to Hong Kong. The Swissair flight took twelve hours, an endless time for Adam, trapped in his seat, to stew on the shock of Harry's arrest. Drug trafficking – it was an incredible accusation.

'It's got to be some kind of mix-up,' said Nicky. 'It's crazy. You know your brother better than that.'

Of course I do – that was his instinctive reaction. But on reflection, Nicky's words had a strange, unnerving effect. As close as he was to him, just how well did he really know his half-brother? He knew that Harry was an easy-going, jovial, good-natured man who didn't seem to possess an ounce of malice. But Harry was ambitious, too, obsessed with material things, and in order to get them, he was prepared to cut corners. Men who played that way were vulnerable. So perhaps it wasn't so crazy, perhaps deep down he did harbour lurking doubts.

To even think it was a kind of betrayal. What did he know of the facts? Nothing. Where was his faith? If the roles were reversed, he knew that Harry would believe implicitly in him, there wouldn't be a moment's doubt. And that's what made the betrayal worse . . .

In almost every respect, physically, emotionally, culturally, he and Harry were different men. And yet Harry, the streetwise fixer, had always played the big brother, the protector, the one who knew best. In many ways it was a strange relationship, often incomprehensible to outsiders, but all the closer for it.

Adam's thoughts began to wander back to a time five years earlier. Dear God, he thought, what would I have done without Harry then? How would I ever have coped? And sitting there, a cognac in his hand, an unread novel on his lap, Adam turned his head to one side in case Nicky saw the tears spring to his eyes.

Five years ago his life had been perfectly set. He had set up his own architectural practice in Hong Kong and was beginning to make a name for himself. He had a Portuguese wife, Sophia, member of an old Macau family. Sophia ran her own jewellery design business and they had a daughter, Anna, just six months old. They rented a rambling pink-walled villa on the south side of Hong Kong Island near Shek O. They travelled, they were successful. It was the perfect family unit, the kind idolised in glossy magazines. Five years ago there had been no such thing as vulnerability. And then, one Saturday afternoon in early summer, the unthinkable had occurred.

Even to this day Adam wasn't sure how it had happened. He remembered driving up to Tai Po in the New Territories to visit friends, he remembered the lorry coming in the opposite direction. But as to how exactly the crash occurred, nothing.

Several months later, in the court case, the prosecutor said the lorry had been going too fast and skidded. All he remembered was lying against the twisted metal of his car with little Anna in his arms, her tiny body broken, staring first at his baby and then across at the lifeless form of his wife, and howling into the hot blue sky.

The weeks that followed had been beyond endurance. Their deaths destroyed him. He fell into a kind of madness. Week after week he remained in the Shek O villa, interested in nothing, incapable of responsibility. The practice went to hell, he lost commissions. He even contemplated killing himself. He was blinded first by grief and then by self-pity.

And that's when Harry had moved in: fancy car, fancy clothes, latest tart on his arm. 'A brother has squatter's rights,' he had said. And he remained there for the next six months. He never sermonised, never pushed, just went about the day-to-day chaos he called his life. But his presence was enough: the bad jokes, the interminable wrangles with his women, the long hours with just the two of them, drinking and talking; and in all of it the implied assurance that one day, when Adam was ready, the sun would shine again.

Those few months had been proof, if proof were needed, that no matter how different they were in character the bond between them was unbreakable.

While Adam's life had been pre-set in that solid Western pattern of school, university, career and marriage, Harry's – totally Chinese in character – had been shot ragged with crises, ruled by the money-mad paradoxes of the Hong Kong dream. Poor Harry, he loved wild schemes – fur coats to Kuwait, toys to Timbuktu – loved to associate himself with everything that had made Hong Kong traders world famous.

His favourite story was how, back in the twenties, when communal lavatories were first built in Hong Kong, smart Chinese took to sitting on them until somebody desperate enough, hammering on the door, was willing to pay them to get off. 'Do you know the difference between a Hong Kong street sweeper and one in England or the States, Adam? In England or the States the man is thinking about a few beers after work, in Hong Kong he's wondering whether he should buy yen or stay in dollars. We're all the same, you, me, the whole five and a half million of us. Believe me, well before 1997 when Beijing takes over, I'm going to be a *Tai Pan* in my own right – the Celestial House of Lee, brokers to the world. And when the time comes to leave, wait and see, I'll fly out of the place in my own Learjet. Destination, Palm Beach, Florida – US passport in hand!'

Adam smiled to himself. Harry was incorrigible, the ultimate hustler. Give him two chances and he would be selling kangaroos to the Aussies! Like father like son, he thought with a sad wistfulness.

Adam had heard hundreds of stories – legends today – about Harry's natural father, Lee Kin-sang, 'KS' as everybody called him. He had been a talented, charismatic man, one of Chiang Kai-shek's officers – a captain or general, depending on how much drink he had had – who had come to Hong Kong and founded a multi-million-dollar real estate business. A notorious womaniser and obsessive gambler, he had then proceeded in two years to lose the lot. The day he fled to Taiwan to avoid his creditors he had wagered his last dollar in the slums of Mongkok on two crickets fighting in a jar – and lost, of course. But by then his *joss* made it inevitable.

To stay ahead of his creditors, KS reasoned it was necessary to travel light. So his wife and his two-year-old son, Harry, were left in Hong Kong. And that's how Adam's father, a quiet, kindly banker from Cornwall with the imposing name of Denys Tudor Langforth Blake, had come into their lives.

Before his premature death, Adam's father often recalled his first meeting with Lee Mei-ling, Rita as she was called. 'She had come into the bank for a loan,' he used to say, 'just enough to keep body and soul together, you understand. She was in a bad way but you would never have known it. She wouldn't lose face, oh no, not your mother. She epitomised everything I admired in Asian women. As perfect as a flower, serene and dignified. I was enchanted from the moment I met her.'

And enchanted he remained. The courtship began in earnest and within a year the newly divorced Mrs Rita Lee and he were married. One year later Adam was born.

It hadn't been easy back then for an English banker to marry a Chinese woman. White men didn't marry Chinks. That had been spelt out in clear enough terms. But it was advice Denys Blake ignored and he paid the price. His promotions at the bank were niggardly and he was shunned by the pink-faced bourgeoisie who made up the elite of colonial society. Never once, however, did he appear embittered. Until his sudden death of a stroke, he had remained a caring, ideal husband.

In only one small way perhaps had he exhibited some of the prejudice that had been shown to him, and that was in respect of Harry. While he never directly shunned his stepson, he nevertheless managed over the years, politely and very correctly, in his English way, to distance himself. While Adam had been despatched to boarding school in England, Harry remained in Hong Kong to be educated in his own tongue. Harry, Denys had said, didn't have the academic bent for university. He was the kind of boy best left to practical things, trading and the like. Adam, on the other hand, had been guided and coaxed all the way to Cambridge.

Only in later years did Adam come to understand the reason. Although KS Lee never returned to Hong Kong, never once tried to contact his ex-wife or son, although nobody even knew for sure whether he was dead or alive, his legend endured – the brilliant, brittle, self-destructive entrepreneur, the old warrior, the womaniser, the kind of man Denys Blake could never hope to be. Denys had spent his life consumed with jealousy. that had been the motive for the discrimination, jealousy of a man he had never even seen.

Harry, who had tried so desperately to gain his step-father's approval, never realised that it wasn't what he did that mattered, it was who he was. Harry was the mirror of his father, and that Denys Blake could never forgive.

Poor Harry, he had grown up trying to emulate the deeds – mostly fictional – of a father he had never known and to seek the unobtainable approval of the one he did know. Harry was pure Han, Chinese down through the generations. It was Adam who had the mixed blood. Yet Adam knew that Harry was a more divided soul than he would ever be.

Harry was in a line of two hundred prisoners queueing for lunch when he received Dai Ngan's response. The warder with the heavily wrinkled face pulled him out of line. Nervously, Harry followed him across the canteen to the windows that looked down over the central yard.

'Dai Ngan has agreed to a deal,' said the warder. 'He'll accept half of what you owe by New Year. You'll have two months after that to find the balance.'

Harry tried to calculate what that meant in money terms and failed. He was too confused and too frightened to sort out the jumble of figures cartwheeling around in his head.

The warder clarified the position. 'With interest, the total debt is now one million.'

Harry felt giddy. 'Do you mean he wants five hundred thousand by New Year?'

The warder nodded.

'That's impossible! I just can't do it, not in a week. You'll have to talk to him again!'

'Dai Ngan can be a crazy guy, not easy to talk to.'

'But I can't perform miracles.'

The warder gazed down at a group of prisoners playing volley ball in the yard. 'We understand your brother is returning to Hong Kong. He's an influential man. Let him arrange it.'

'But half a million,' protested Harry, choking with panic, 'half a million in a week! It doesn't matter how influential he is.'

The warder shrugged. 'Nothing in life is easy, Fat Boy. If it was, there wouldn't be any prisons.'

When the Swissair flight touched down at 11.50 local time, Adam's mother was waiting for them in the crowded concourse of Kai Tak.

To a stranger, Rita Blake looked much younger than her sixty-five years. She was always impeccably groomed, dressed that morning in a linen suit of mint green with white accessories, a small, neat woman who still retained her serene good looks. But as Adam came through the sliding glass doors and saw her at the bottom of the ramp, squeezed in among the jostling crowds, he was shocked at how Harry's predicament had aged her. His mother looked tired, he thought, tired and drawn and frail.

After the initial greetings, inhibited by the throngs around them, they took the elevator up to the car park in virtual silence. It wasn't until they were in Adam's Volvo, a big silver 740 GLE, crawling through the chaos of Kowloon traffic towards the Cross Harbour Tunnel, that anything was said about the matter foremost in all their minds.

'How is Harry?' asked Nicky from the rear seat. 'Is he holding up okay?'

Rita Blake answered with a thin, brave smile. 'He'll be relieved now that Adam is back.'

'When can I see him?' asked Adam.

'Visiting hours are until four every afternoon.'

'Good. I'll have a shower, get changed and go straight out. What about the case against him? Have you found out anything more?'

His mother shook her head. 'Only what his lawyer told me, some man called Au. And he doesn't seem to know too much. Harry is charged with smuggling drugs into America, to some Vietnamese people in New York.'

'What sort of quantities are we talking about?'

'Five kilos, that's what Au told me.'

Christ! thought Adam. In Malaysia they hanged you for anything over ten grams. 'What about Harry himself?' he asked. 'Has he been able to tell you anything?'

'He says he'll explain everything when he sees you, Adam. He says the two of you will be able to sort it out. That's why I'm so pleased you're back. Harry wouldn't deal in drugs, he just wouldn't do such a thing . . .' His mother faltered, her emotions welling up. 'I'm sorry,' she murmured, taking a tissue from her bag.

Adam reached across to squeeze her hand. 'Don't worry,' he said. 'You're right, Harry and I will get it sorted out. This is just some horrible damn mix-up. Harry will be out within a month, you'll see.'

But he knew how hollow it sounded.

That afternoon at 2.30 he took the MTR to Lai Chi Kok. The prison was five minutes' walk from the subway, a great square monolith of a building painted cream and grey. From a distance, in among the clutter of buildings, with a bus station adjacent, it could have been just another factory block. Only the guard towers gave it away.

Lai Chi Kok was designed to hold less than a thousand prisoners awaiting trial or going through the process of appeals. In fact it held half as many again. Facilities were stretched to the limit and Adam had to wait nearly an hour before a warder escorted him into the long, narrow visiting room. Adam was taken to a chair which faced a large plate-glass window.

'Your brother will be here in a minute,' said the warder. 'When you want to speak to him, pick up the telephone in front of you. Visits are restricted to fifteen minutes.'

The warder departed and Adam sat on the chair. The plate-glass window was so thick that everything on the other side appeared distorted. And, as if the glass wasn't enough, there were iron bars, too, painted a battleship grey. My God, he thought, I wouldn't last more than a week in a place like this. He felt suddenly very unsure of himself. What would he say when Harry came in? Should he encourage him with brisk talk about lawyers and evidence? Should he try and console him? Emotionally, he was totally unprepared.

When Harry was led in, dressed in a faded brown smock, brown trousers and plastic sandals, he was trying hard to maintain a grin. He sat on the other side of the plate glass and gestured to Adam to pick up the telephone. 'How was your trip?' he asked as if this was some garish joke not to be taken seriously.

'Fine, fine, but, more to the point, how are you? God, Harry, how did you get yourself into this mess?'

Harry shrugged. 'It's complicated.'

'We've got to get you out of this place.'

Harry just smiled, his eyes glazing.

'I spoke to your lawyer before I came here.'

'Au? Not too impressive, is he?'

'He's a small-time scheister, Harry.'

'You get what you pay for . . .'

'We've got to get rid of him, get somebody who knows what he's doing.'

But Harry just shrugged again.

Adam gazed at his brother's haggard face. Only days ago Harry had been plump and smooth with fine clothes to wear and fine gold jewellery. The flesh seemed to hang on him now, sallow and sickly, and his forced air of nonchalance was so patently strained.

'You're obviously impressed by the weight loss,' said Harry, his grin persisting. 'I call it the "deep in the shit" diet. I'm working on a few gourmet recipes – diarrhoea duckling, gastric goose, terrified teriyaki. If I published them I could make a fortune. You know how people are about health fads.'

Adam smiled. But the gallows humour was getting them nowhere. He spoke into the phone. 'If we're going to get you out of here, Harry, we've got to seize the initiative. As I said, the first step has to be a better lawyer, a top criminal specialist. What do you say?'

But Harry just looked into his brother's eyes.

'Well, do you agree or not?'

'I think it's a waste of money,' said Harry.

Adam couldn't believe it. He had never known Harry to act so passively, so defeated. 'Come on,' he said. 'You can't give up on yourself. We've got to fight this thing.'

Harry gave an enigmatic smile. 'I'm not giving up on myself, Adam. I'm being practical, that's all.'

'Practical about what, for God's sake? If it's a question of money—'

Harry shook his head. 'The evidence against me is overwhelming, Adam. Don't waste your money on some pompous windbag of a lawyer.'

Adam was stunned into silence.

'I'm going to do the only sensible thing,' Harry continued. 'I'm going to plead guilty.'

Adam's mouth fell slack. He was appalled.

Harry laughed softly, the dimples showing in his drawn and pallid features. 'Don't look so shocked, Adam. Be honest, didn't it pass through your mind – just once – that I might be guilty?'

Adam had no answer.

'A plea will take five years, maybe more, off my sentence. With an extra third off for good behaviour, I could be out in ten.'

Still trying to come to terms with the numbing shock of it all, Adam asked, 'Was this the first time, your first deal?'

Harry shook his head. 'I've been involved in the business about eight years. Indirectly at first, as an investor. But over the last eighteen months I've been dealing direct.'

Adam was lost for words. 'How could you do it, Harry?' he murmured. 'I mean, drugs . . .'

The smile evaporated from Harry's face. His eyes glazed. 'I'm a China boy, Adam, remember that. I wasn't brought up with your expensive English ethics.'

'Even if that's the case, what difference does it make?'

Harry gave a limp shrug. 'You can afford the morality, Adam, I can't.'

'That's bullshit, Harry, and you know it! You might have had your schooling in Hong Kong but it was the best available. What you chose to do with your life is your business – don't blame it on anybody else!'

Harry blinked, seeming to sag into himself. Through the thick plate glass it seemed to Adam that his brother was trapped in some kind of terrible, airless aquarium. Oh God, Harry, he thought, how could you do this to yourself? How could you end up here?

'What do I tell Mum?' Adam asked.

'Tell her the truth.'

'It will break her heart.'

'She's got to find out sometime.' Harry said the words

with an off-hand curtness but for the first time there was a look of real pain on his face.

For a while they were silent, both lost for words, until Adam gave a short sigh. 'I don't understand. I came back because I thought you wanted my help, that somehow this was just some terrible mix-up which we were going to sort out. But it seems it's all been decided. You don't need a lawyer. You want to walk into the courtroom and plead guilty. What else is there left?'

'What else . . .?' Harry gave a low, dry laugh but it was shadowed by an emotion Adam hadn't sensed before, a sudden, almost panicky, fear. 'Believe me, brother, prison is the least of my worries.'

'Then what is it? Tell me. What other kind of trouble are you in?'

'I owe money, Adam, a very large amount of money.'

'Who to?'

Harry looked at him through the glass, suddenly paler. 'My heroin suppliers.'

Adam blinked. 'Are you telling me you got credit on a drug deal?'

The shock in his brother's voice prompted Harry to give a thin, mirthless laugh. 'Do you think buying and selling dope is different from buying and selling any other kind of commodity – cement, cars, houses? Business is business, Adam. Dealers owe each other money all the time.' Harry tried to maintain his air of supercilious humour but it quickly withered. 'My suppliers knew I had a secure line of supply into the States, that's why they advanced me the credit.'

'If it was so secure, what went wrong?' asked Adam in a flat, hard tone tinged with disgust.

'The first time, you mean?' Harry shook his head as if still incapable of believing his own bad luck. 'My courier had a car smash, that's what happened – Saturday afternoon in the middle of Brooklyn. He was unconscious – cracked skull, God knows what else – and the stuff was right there with him in the car. That was five units lost. Just the legal fees to represent the guy almost bankrupted me. Have you got any idea how much those American lawyers charge? But I had to do it. If the courier goes down, you have to do what you can.'

'And even after that, you still continued?'

'I had to make up my losses, Adam. What else could I do? My suppliers knew it was bad *joss*. It happens to us all. That's why they supplied more credit. And if that last shipment had got through, I would have been back on my feet, up and running again. I was so close, Adam, so damn close . . .'

'But even if you do owe money,' said Adam, 'what difference does it make? You're in jail now. You're facing ten years. You took a risk, they took a risk. You all lost out. To hell with the money!'

Harry's eyes widened. 'Don't tell me you're that naive, Adam. Don't you know the way Triads operate in this town?'

'What are you trying to say?'

'Do you think jail makes any difference?'

'Then if you're in danger, ask for protection.'

'Protection?' Harry gave a hoarse, mocking laugh. 'Do you know how they protect you in this place? They put you into solitary confinement, that's how. Some crappy cell, four foot by six. They let you exercise for half an hour a day – I've seen guys exercising up there on the roof – and even that's in a cage. I'd go mad, Adam, raving mad. I couldn't take it.' There were bubbles of spittle on Harry's grey lips. 'All I need is time. I can raise the money, I know it. But I've got to keep them happy, Adam – keep their goon, Cheng, off me – keep feeding them cash, just a bit at a time, until I can get the capital.'

'Who is this Cheng?'

'They call him Dai Ngan,' Harry answered. 'He's Chiu Chow, the front man for the investors. He supplied me the heroin. But he's a madman, crazy in the head when he gets angry.'

'The investors, who are they?'

'I don't know, I never learnt.'

'One or more?'

'I just don't know.'

'But you do know about this Dai Ngan. You know he's the front man. So do some sort of deal with the police. Point the finger at him. If he's threatening you, then put the bastard away. You could halve your sentence.'

'No, no.' Harry shook his head as if the very thought of it was a nightmare looming. 'That's suicide. It still means five years, Adam, maybe more. And how do I survive that, tell me? Don't you realise, we're talking about drug money here, this is business, big business. It's not just Dai Ngan, it's the men behind him. If I go to the cops I'm a dead man.'

'The police will protect you. For God's sake, they've got to have some sort of system.'

'Yeah, just as I said – solitary confinement.' The fear and cynicism flowed together in Harry's voice. 'Five years of eating alone, sleeping alone, waiting for somebody to stick a knife in me. Think about it, Adam. Five years! Don't you think I've been over all of this a thousand times already? There's only one way – I've got to pay the debt.'

Adam slumped back. 'How much do you owe?'

'The full amount? Close to a million.'

'Hong Kong currency?'

'No, US.'

'My God.' Adam closed his eyes. The amount was staggering. 'But how can you ever hope to raise that sort of money?'

Harry's eyes lit up with a wild hope. 'When the police broke into the hotel room, Adam, I had the cash payment for the drugs in my hand – three quarters of a million stacked into a suitcase. I ran to the window and threw the suitcase down. My girl friend was there. I had her waiting in case of trouble. And I saw her pick it up, Adam, I saw her get away. Three quarters of a million . . . and Lilly Choi has it.'

But Adam knew there had to be much more to it. 'Then why hasn't she paid this man Dai Ngan? Surely that solves everything?'

'Because she's gone to ground, she's fled Hong Kong.' Harry saw the reaction on his brother's face but, before Adam could say anything, he rushed on. 'I don't blame her, really I don't. She must have been scared out of her wits. I know she's in Taiwan, Adam. She's got family there. My lawyer is sure he can find her. All he needs is a deposit – twenty thousand US dollars.'

'Twenty thousand US? Christ, Harry, he's ripping you to shreds.'

'He's got to act fast, Adam, don't you understand? He's got to drop everything else. But it shouldn't take more than a few days to track her down, that's what he says.'

Adam didn't reply immediately. He remembered Lilly Choi, a nightclub hostess and part-time whore, good-looking but fickle, the sort of woman Harry seemed to have a fetish for. If Lilly Choi had to choose between Harry, a man facing ten years in jail, and three quarters of a million, Adam had a fair idea of the result.

'All I want you to do,' Harry went on, 'is help me until I can find her, help me keep Dai Ngan at bay.'

Adam gave a grim nod. 'And how much will that cost?'

Harry leant forward, his face almost touching the plate glass. 'He's asking a huge amount but if I can show good faith, if I can put some hard cash into his hands—'

'How much is he asking for, Harry?'

'Half a million, that's what he's demanding.'

'But I can't raise that sort of money, nothing like it!'

'No, no, I appreciate that. That's why I say, if I can just pay him something to keep him sweet—'

'And how much is that? You know the man, I don't. How much is going to keep him sweet?'

Harry hesitated, chewing on his lip. 'Do you think you could raise half that, say quarter of a million?'

'Quarter of a million, as a sweetener? Christ, Harry . . .'

'Please, Adam, my life depends on this.'

Adam's jaw muscles worked as he made feverish calculations in his head. His face was bloodless now, as pale as Harry's. 'You know my position,' he said. 'I'm already into the banks up to my neck. I've had to expand the office, get new equipment. But a quarter of a million . . . maybe, yes, if I stretch myself to the limit.'

Sweat began to dribble down Harry's temple. 'I swear to God, Adam, I'll pay every penny back even if it takes me the rest of my life.'

'How much time do I have to raise it?'

'The sooner the better.'

'What's the outer limit?'

'The first day of Chinese New Year.'

Adam nodded. 'And in addition you want me to pay this lawyer of yours to try and find Lilly Choi?'

'If you would . . .'

A prison warder drew close, tapping on the face of his wrist watch. The visit was concluded.

Like an exhausted man, Harry climbed to his feet. He gave one final grin and Adam smiled back, attempting to reassure him. Then, to the sound of doors clanging, they were parted.

There was a nullah outside the prison walls, an open watercourse that ran down to the sea. It was fed by effluence, and the water, smelling of yeast, was a dazzling indigo blue from nearby denim factories. Crossing the road, Adam leant for a long time on its concrete parapet staring down at the bright tide, lost in his thoughts.

What shattered him most was the fact that for the past

seven or eight years Harry had been dealing in heroin and yet, during that entire period, although they had seen each other constantly and even shared the same house for a time, he hadn't suspected a thing. He had always known that Harry played loose with the truth when it came to Customs declarations or tax returns but heavy crime, the trade in *pak fan* – good God, no, not in a million years. Was I so blind, thought Adam, or did Harry just disguise it well?

Poor Harry. The phrase kept coming up whenever Adam thought of his brother. Harry was his own worst enemy and Adam felt a bewildered sadness for him. But at that moment he felt anger, too, he couldn't deny it, a deep, burning resentment. Damn you! he thought. You betrayed me, you betrayed Mum. You destroyed our trust in you. And now you want me to pay a quarter of a million dollars – money I can't afford, money that will keep me in debt for years – just to keep some psychopath of a Triad happy for a few days. Why should I? Why should I compound your crime by dirtying myself with it, too?

But no matter what feelings of anger churned inside him, it made no difference. Harry was his brother, his own flesh and blood. And that, Adam knew, spoke more profoundly than any feelings of betrayal. He could raise the money. It would hurt badly but he could do it. If it was just a question of cash and Harry was harmed in some way because he held it back, he would never forgive himself.

So the decision was made, his course was set. And, still deeply brooding, Adam walked slowly back to the MTR.

* * *

It was early evening when he drove to his mother's small apartment on Conduit Road. He didn't relish the prospect of telling her but his mother accepted the news with a quiet, compelling dignity just as she had accepted the news of so many other tragic events in her life. After Adam had told her, she sat for a while, her face deathly pale. Then, with the barest quiver in her voice, she asked, 'So there's no doubt, his mind is made up?'

'Yes, he's going to plead guilty.'

'Why did he wish to see you, was it to help him make the decision?'

Adam avoided the question. 'It wasn't an easy decision to make . . .'

'No, of course not.' His mother took a deep breath and then, a little shakily, rose from her chair. 'Well, if that's his decision, we must give him all the support we can. There must be ways we can bolster his morale – regular visits, books and magazines, special food if they will allow it. I know he says he doesn't want a lawyer but, even if he's going to plead guilty, we must get him one, the best man possible. Every year the lawyer can cut off his sentence counts, every month, every week.' She turned to Adam. 'You must have many lawyer friends.'

'I'll see what I can do.'

'Good, good.' And his mother went through to the tiny kitchen to make tea for them both, Chinese tea in delicate porcelain cups, the way it had always been.

Adam stayed with her for an hour or more. But work was piling up at the office, clients were waiting, and in the end he had to leave. 'Nicky and I will call round later,' he said.

His mother put on a brave smile. 'That would be nice. But only if you have time. Don't worry about me, I'll be fine.'

Adam took the elevator down to the lobby and walked to his car. As a young woman, his mother had lived through war and famine in China. Her first husband had fled Hong Kong leaving her with a mountain of debts. The second, Adam's own father, had died before his time. And now she had to endure this. Why was it, he wondered, that those who deserved it least were so often visited with the greatest pain?

It took Adam two days to raise the quarter of a million plus the extra twenty thousand to trace Lilly Choi. Fifty thousand came from Nicky's Canadian-based finance corporation – on the lie that he needed extra cash for the office. Fifty came from friends, and the balance from the HongKong and Shanghai Bank. Achieving it had stretched him to breaking point. There was no more collateral left, no more friends to sign guarantees. How he would ever repay it, he didn't know. But the cash was there, that's all that mattered. Harry could breathe again.

On the morning of the third day, Adam returned to Lai Chi Kok. Harry, looking even more haggard and chewed up with nerves, was pathetically grateful. 'You've saved my life,' he said.

There was a shop in Sham Shui Po called So Kee that sold snakes for the cookpot. That's where the money had to be delivered, said Harry. Adam made the trip that evening, wrapping the money in a brown paper bag. He found the shop, a dirty place stacked high with boxes containing torpid, grey-scaled cobras. He spoke to the owner and left the package with him.

The matter was now out of his hands. He just hoped to God that was the end of it.

Seventy-five per cent of Hong Kong's business – legal or otherwise – is conducted in the ten thousand restaurants squeezed into the territory's overcrowded buildings and neon-cluttered streets. Property deals are struck in the steam of freshly boiled perch, conspiracies hatched to the taste of sweet and sour pork. Drug traffickers and police have paging devices buckled to their belts, businessmen in their Italian silk suits carry cellular telephones, all for the purpose of being contacted at the dinner table. That is the way of it. Life and death in Hong Kong, fortune and poverty, sit on the rim of a rice bowl.

One such meeting took place a few hours after Adam had delivered the money. Two men met in a Kowloon restaurant, a huge place that seated two thousand or more. They drank jasmine tea and shared a plate of steamed pork with salted cabbage. The first of the two men was the old prison warder from Lai Chi Kok, the other was Cheng Tak-shing.

The warder chose his words carefully. He always addressed Dai Ngan with deference. 'He says that the first payment, the quarter of a million, is to show his good faith.'

Cheng slurped loudly at his tea. 'Good faith? Fuck his mother, he's wriggling on the hook, that's what it is.'

'He needs more time, Dai Ngan, that's what he says. He must have an additional two weeks to track down his woman, the one who got the plane to Taiwan.'

Cheng rested his frying pan of a face in the cup of his hand. 'What does he think, that his bitch – his ex-bitch – will cough up the money?'

The warder smiled.

Cheng spat out a bone. 'The Fat Boy has eggs for brains. We've done some checking of our own on Lilly Choi. She stayed in Taiwan for two days, that's all. Then she flew to Thailand and from Thailand to Singapore. After that we lost her. Has the Fat Boy got his lawyer on the job, that guy Au? If so, he's wasting his money.'

The warder chewed at his food.

'What did Harry Lee say about paying if he couldn't find Lilly Choi?' asked Cheng.

The warder knew he was the bearer of bad tidings and hesitated before answering. 'He says that without Lilly Choi he has nothing. The best he can offer is five thousand a month through his brother.'

Cheng's frog-like eyes bulged. 'That won't even cover interest! Fuck his mother, who does he think he's dealing with, some two-bit loan company? He didn't buy a Datsun car, he bought *pak fan*. There are other ways to raise the money and he knows it. He's playing for time. Anyway, what about that brother of his?'

The warder replied through a mouthful of food. 'The two hundred and fifty thousand has come from the brother.'

'So why can't the balance? I've got pressure on me too. Unless I make good to my investor I get chopped to bits. Harry Lee is laughing in my face. I know the brother, he's an architect. He drives a big fancy Volvo, I've seen it. He can raise more than quarter of a million. The Fat Boy will have to see to it.'

'So what do I tell him?' asked the warder.

Cheng drained the last of the tea from the pot. 'Tell the son of a bitch not to joke with me.'

The last three days had been in vain – Adam knew it the moment he was escorted into the visiting room and saw Harry's face through the plate glass. Adam had never seen his brother look so terrified. The sweat was shining on Harry's forehead, his lips trembled.

'Cheng wants the full five hundred thousand, Adam, and he wants it by New Year.'

Adam sighed, shaking his head. 'That's in two days. I'm sorry, Harry, I just can't do it. You might as well ask me to fly to the moon.'

'But you've got friends, rich friends.'

'I've already borrowed everything I can from them. I can't raise any more. I'm sorry, it's just impossible.'

But Harry was in a frenzied panic. 'What about the deal in Switzerland, the bank thing? Can't you get an advance on that?'

'I don't even know if I've won it yet!'

'When will you know?'

'I don't know, three weeks maybe.'

'Can't you push them for a decision?'

'Even if I get the commission, Harry, I won't see any

money – not cash into my pocket – for months.'

'But there's got to be some way,' said Harry, tears brimming in his bloodshot eyes. 'Christ, people can raise millions if they put their minds to it.'

'I can't wish the money out of thin air, Harry.'

Harry cast him a grieved, petulant look. He was burping with nerves. 'So that's it, you're not prepared to help any further?'

'Are you listening to me?' It took all of Adam's will to control his temper. 'I just don't have the money, Harry. I can't raise any more.'

Harry didn't reply. Suddenly his mind seemed to wander and his eyes rested vacantly on a spot about two foot to the left of Adam's head.

Adam tried to bring some sense back into their conversation. 'Let me speak to the police,' he said in a quiet, rational tone. 'If this man Cheng wants to harm you, then pre-empt him, get in first. There's no other way, you've got to fight back.'

Harry blinked, refocusing on Adam's face. 'Attack is the best defence, is that it?' His eyes narrowed into an intense stare. 'You've got no comprehension, have you, Adam? You've lived all your life like some rare bird's egg in a box, cushioned and isolated. If Cheng wants me, he'll get me. Today, tomorrow, it doesn't matter. He's Sun Yee On, don't you realise that? Not the Dragon Head, maybe, but influential. People fear him. He's got power. More power than you'd believe. Do you know how many Sun Yee On there are in this prison? There's got to be four hundred. And probably half the warders too!'

'So what are you going to do, curl up and die? You've got to protect yourself.'

Harry snorted. 'There's only one way to do that – that's to pay the bastard his money.'

Adam sighed, despairing. 'We've just been through that. You don't have the money, I don't either. And there's no news of Lilly Choi. You still owe this man Cheng and whoever backs him three quarters of a million. How on earth can you hope to raise anything like that?'

Harry didn't reply, not immediately. But there was a sudden, nervous animation in his face. He smiled weakly, half muttering to himself. 'There is one way . . .'

'To raise the full amount?'

Harry nodded. 'Capital and interest, all of it.'

'But that could take years.'

'No, just a couple of months . . .'

An instinctive warning bell sounded in Adam's brain. But the danger it signalled seemed so farfetched, so lunatic that he ignored it. Harry had to be leading to something else, some solution that was rational, feasible. 'What are you talking about?' Adam asked in a dry whisper.

Harry's eyes darted from side to side, ensuring nobody could overhear. Then he leant across the table until his face almost touched the plate glass. 'I'm talking about merchandise, Adam.'

His brother looked at him in dismay. 'Drugs? Are you mad?'

'Two or three runs, that's all it'll take.'

'I don't want to hear this.'

But Harry wouldn't be stopped, not now. 'I've worked it all out. It'll be no problem. I've got the necessary contacts, I know the supply routes. I've even got new buyers, people I've been negotiating with for months now. But first I have to have more money, Adam. Just a hundred thousand, that's all I'll need to buy the first consignment.'

Adam couldn't believe he was hearing this. 'You want me to raise money to buy drugs? Are you completely out of your mind?'

'I'm as sane as I'll ever be,' Harry hissed between gritted teeth. 'But I'm fighting for my life.'

'Do you have any conception of what you're asking me to do?'

'I know exactly what I'm asking you to do.'

'You're asking me to finance a heroin shipment.'

There was the slightest pause. For a moment Harry's face appeared frozen behind the plate glass. Then he said in a hard, flat voice, 'No, Adam, I want you to do more.'

Adam stared at him. 'What are you talking about?'

'Just listen to me for a moment. I can organise things from in here. But I can't physically carry them out. I have to have somebody working with me, somebody on the outside, somebody I can trust with my life.'

Adam felt the blood draining from his cheeks. 'I can't believe I'm hearing this.'

But Harry wouldn't let go. 'Please, Adam, you're the only one left who I can trust. You won't be in any danger. You won't have to physically handle the stuff, I promise. You won't have to go near it.'

Adam gave an involuntary gasp. What his brother was asking him defied comprehension.

'Please, Adam!' Harry was begging him. 'If I can get a

message to Cheng that you're prepared to help me organise just a couple of runs, that's all, no more than two or three, then I know he'll hold back. I never wanted to get you involved, it's the last thing I wanted. But I've got no choice. What do you expect me to do? Unless I can work out a way, they're going to find my body one morning hanging from a shower hook. They'll call it suicide but it'll be murder. Don't you understand, Adam, unless you help me, I'm finished!'

Adam tried to think of a reply but he was too shocked to formulate anything coherent. 'I can't believe you're asking me this,' was all he could mumble.

'I've tried to think of alternatives, Adam, but they just don't exist. This is the only way.'

Shaking his head like a badly mauled boxer trying to clear his brain, Adam staggered to his feet. The telephone fell from his hand, cracking onto the concrete ledge. 'This whole thing is insane,' he muttered. 'My God, Harry, what's happened to you?'

But without the telephone neither could hear the other. All that remained was the silent image of Harry through the thick plate glass, and the sight of those pathetic begging eyes.

As he left the prison, out amid the traffic and everyday noise again, Adam tried to rationalise what had just happened. But it was impossible to focus his thoughts. He was lost in an incredulous stupor.

Forty minutes later, when he reached his office in Central, he was still in a daze. He told his private secretary he wasn't to be disturbed and slumped down in his high, leather-backed chair, staring through the smoky glass window at the office blocks around him. There were schedules and drawings on his desk, telephone messages to answer. His staff wanted urgent decisions. But he felt totally paralysed.

Whether he realised it or not, Harry had created the perfect dilemma. In a mad sort of way, Adam had to appreciate the symmetry of it, just as he would appreciate the lines of some outrageous radical new building. To save the brother he loved, he was being asked to commit a crime he despised. The ancient Greeks would have relished a moral equation like that, he thought with bitter irony, all answers leading to tragedy.

The telephone chirped on his desk. He was about to tell the receptionist to take a message when she said it was Miss du Bois on the line. In many ways Adam was a loner. He bottled up problems and this was one he could never share, not with Nicky, not even with his mother. But Nicky was the one person who could shake him out of his punch-drunk lethargy.

'Good news,' said Nicky when she was put through. 'I've tied up that syndicated loan, the one I was in Zurich to negotiate. Twenty million US, not bad for a week's work.'

'Not bad at all,' said Adam, sounding vacant and preoccupied.

Nicky laughed. 'I've heard you sound more interested when I've waxed my legs.'

'Sorry,' said Adam. 'I had my mind on other things.'

'The other little titbit,' said Nicky brightly, 'is that I'm being interviewed this afternoon for one of Hong Kong's glossy magazines. Business person of the week – sounds grand, doesn't it? How on earth they found me, some poor little expat lady locked away in her office, I don't know. But the PR can do me no harm. Come on, Mr Hotshot Architect, admit it, aren't you just a wee bit envious?'

Adam smiled. 'Green with it.'

'I'm in next week's edition, they say. Wedged in between adverts for cognac and Ferraris, no doubt.'

'Sounds like yuppie bliss,' said Adam in a distant voice.

'Don't look a gift horse in the mouth, that's what I say.' Nicky paused for a moment. 'Are you okay?'

'Fine.'

'You sound distracted.'

'Preoccupied perhaps.'

'Is it Harry?'

'Yes, it's Harry.'

'It was his decision to plead guilty, Adam. You're giving him all the moral support you can. What more can you do?'

'Sure,' he echoed. 'What more can I do . . .'

'Climb out of that swamp you call a mood, that's the first thing,' said Nicky. 'Why don't you come to my place tonight? We'll have a little spaghetti, a lot of Chianti and, who knows, the business person of the week might just end up seducing you. How does that sound?' She gave a quick laugh. 'On second thoughts, don't answer that. In your present mood it'll sound a little less exciting than a glass of warm milk and cookies.'

Adam chuckled. 'Am I that bad?'

'Worse.'

'Then I'll just have to prove it to you tonight.'

'Prove what?'

'That actions speak louder than words.'

'Is that a promise?'

'Absolutely.'

'Then don't be late,' she purred. 'Oh, and one final thing.'

'What is it?'

'I love you.'

A broad smile broke on Adam's face. 'I love you, too.'

Adam put down the telephone, sat for a while and then, getting up from his desk, stood at the window, his hands deep in his pockets, staring out over the city. Just when his life was knitting back together again, when he had found a good woman and the future held out so much promise, Harry's problem had to be thrust upon him. And it angered him, filled him with a bitter resentment. He had lived in Hong Kong long enough to know the results of the drug trade. It was a filthy, obscene business. Damn you, Harry! he thought. You've no right to demand this of me. Staring out at the crowded buildings that made up Hong Kong's financial heart, he imagined his own design for the Swiss Federal Bank being built there, transformed into a three-dimensional thing, into steel and glass and concrete. In his mind's eye he saw it soaring up from the yellow clay, workmen swarming over the bamboo scaffolding. For every architect it was a life's ambition.

No, he thought, he had too much to live for now. He couldn't dwell on this any longer. There was only one decision he could make. Because every instinct told him that there was no way, no way on earth he could be forced to deal in drugs.

The following morning Adam returned to Lai Chi Kok. Seated on a long bench in the waiting area, memories crowded his mind: Harry buying him his first drink, teaching him the odds of gambling, marching through the back streets with him, teaching him everything about Hong Kong that there was to know. Harry with his fast cars and fancy clothes, his expensive brandy and cheap women.

When Harry was escorted into the interview room, he took one look at Adam's face through the plate glass and gave an embittered shrug. 'I should have known better, shouldn't I?'

'To ask me for money, Harry, even to ask me to put my life on the line, that's one thing. But to ask me to deal in heroin – there's got to be some other way.'

Harry gave a cold, tortured smile. 'I heard from my lawyer this morning. More good news. He says Lilly Choi has disappeared. He managed to trace her to Singapore but, after that, nothing. The little cow has been flying first class, though, that much he did learn. Amazing how people stand by you in times of need, isn't it, Adam?'

'So what do you intend to do now?'

'What can I do?' A sour look came to Harry's face. 'You and Lilly have combined to make it impossible for me.'

Adam's temper flared. 'Don't blame me for this,

Harry,' he hissed. 'You got into this mess, not me! I'm doing everything I can to help you – everything legal. You're sitting there wallowing in self-pity. There are still options open to you and you know it. Good, sound options. Let me speak to the police, let me try and work out some sort of deal. They can protect you.'

'For how long? Three months, maybe six? And in the meantime, until some warder is bribed to poison my food or I get a knife shoved into my liver, I live like a rat in a hole. Is that the way you want it? Thank you, brother, thank you for nothing!'

Harry climbed to his feet, his hands shaking. He stopped, looking at Adam through the warped glass, and a kind of hopeless half-smile came to his face. 'Don't start looking for sops to your conscience. You've washed your hands of me, Adam. Why don't we just leave it at that?'

Chapter Three

THAILAND – HONG KONG

On the second day of Chinese New Year, suffering from a bad attack of gout, Carl Drexel flew into Bangkok. As usual the weather was hot and sticky and the traffic so badly snarled up that it took him three hours to get from the airport to his hotel. But Drexel enjoyed being back. Asia was his stomping ground. And, just two hundred miles north of the city where Burma, Thailand and Laos merged, in a span of desolate mountains, lay the Golden Triangle.

It amazed Drexel that in an age of heart transplants and satellite communications, a land like that, lost in a time warp, could still exist. He had been up there only once, that was three years back to try and bring a Shan chieftain into the DEA camp. But it was a time and a place he would never forget. Travelling by mule and guarded by Lao mercenaries, he had passed through a wilderness of mountains and jade-green swollen rivers, a land inhabited by aboriginal tribes and ruled over by warlords, medieval men answerable to nobody but themselves. Drexel would always remember it as a haunted place, a kind of doomed Shangri-la. A dream-like place, almost unreal. And yet real it was, too damn real. It was up there in the Golden Triangle that China White was cultivated, the purest, the very best heroin in the world.

Since he had joined the DEA back in the founding days of 1973, Carl Drexel's main sphere of operations had been Asia. But back in those days heroin from South-East Asia hadn't been considered anything more than a minor nuisance, the habit of a few US servicemen who had become addicted during the Vietnam War. The real threat – so the official thinking went – came from Mexico, from the brown heroin that poured across the Rio Grande, and, to a lesser extent, from the mountain fields of the Hindu Kush in Pakistan.

But all that had changed with a mighty bang back in June 1985, the day two Chinese businessmen had been stopped by Immigration officers at Tacoma International Airport, Seattle. They had been carrying business samples: silver ice buckets for sale to Chinese restaurants, they said. And they might just have got away with it if one of the Immigration officers hadn't thought the buckets were a bit too heavy. X-rays revealed a double wall in the buckets, and a hole drilled into the first of them brought forth a trickle of powder – ninety nine per cent pure, the very best grade of China White. Just short of a hundred million dollars' worth was recovered, up to that date the biggest single seizure of heroin in US history. And official thinking had changed overnight. It had taken nearly five years to get the mastermind, a high-living Hong Kong fur trader named

Johnny Kon, five years of painstaking work involving police forces stretched as far as Thailand, Hong Kong, Bolivia, Japan and the US. And with each month the realisation of just how immense the threat truly was had grown.

FBI and DEA operations against Chinese smuggling rings proliferated, culminating in Op Whitemare, the interception of a shipment secreted in rubber tyres, enough heroin in that one consignment alone to keep every addict in New York supplied for a year. The drug lord whose reign had ended when the rubber tyres were intercepted had been seventy-three years old, a respected member of New York's Chinatown community; he was a liquor store owner named Peter Woo, and all his contacts were Hong Kong Chinese.

US racketeering laws may have snapped the spine of the Mafia but Drexel knew that crime, like nature, abhors a vacuum and the Hong Kong Chinese moved in, monopolising the wholesale end of the trade, acting as brokers, suppliers, financiers. A better product sold at a cheaper price; tight business procedures, no fuss and the minimum of violence – no wonder the Cantonese and the Chiu Chow had it all sewn up.

Drexel knew that within a couple of years more than sixty per cent of the heroin hitting the US market would come from the Golden Triangle, brokered through Hong Kong. The New York judge who had sentenced Johnny Kon had described the size and sophistication of his operation as 'mind-boggling'. But Johnny Kon had come from the horse and buggy era. The dope smugglers today, linked through the Triads, the secret Tongs, were ten times smarter, ten times stronger. A new war had erupted. Maybe they didn't publish the casualties in the newspapers this time, but the fact remained that South-East Asia was America's front line again.

Drexel shaved and showered at the hotel and put on fresh clothes, the first garments he found in his suitcase: blue checkered slacks and a clashing green sports shirt. Then he caught a taxi to the DEA office in the American Embassy. After nineteen hours in the air, however, from the Eastern seaboard of the US all the way across the Pacific, his body clock was way out of synchronisation. Like a good wine, he thought ruefully, he didn't travel well. When he made it to the office of the DEA, the gout in his left foot inducing a semi-crippled limp, he wasn't too receptive to Benny Barack's suggestion of a hot night on the town.

Benny Barack, just turned forty, was head of station in Bangkok. Of Lebanese extraction, he had sharp Semitic features. Since Drexel had known him, he had always worn a full beard as thick and black as his hair. As a result, he looked more like a terrorist than most terrorists. 'Motor Mouth' they called him and he didn't suffer fools gladly. Abrasive, self-opinionated and fast talking, he was one of the brightest men in the DEA; if he could just learn a little diplomacy, he was headed for the top.

When Drexel limped into his office, Benny Barack was smoking one of his cheap Filipino cigars. 'You know your problem, Carl? You don't exercise enough,' he said as Drexel shuffled over to a chair.

'I don't exercise at all, Benny. Bad for my health.'

'Take up golf, I keep telling you.'

Drexel laughed. 'Leave me alone. Does this look like a body that can go under par? Last time I swung a club was up in Chiang Mai – at your insistence.'

Benny Barack gave a black-eyed smile. 'Yeah, I remember. Pity you put your back out. Beginner's bad luck. But you've got to persevere, Carl. No gain without pain.'

'Bullshit.' Carl Drexel put his foot up on a coffee stool to ease the pressure on it. He didn't smoke, didn't drink heavily and, although he had a weight problem, he watched his diet with the hawk-like ferocity of a Greek mother chaperoning her only daughter. The result of all that? Heartburn, a bad liver and gout. Life wasn't fair, he thought.

Benny Barack ordered coffee. 'So you've decided against a visit to Pat Pong Street tonight?'

'Sorry, Benny, the body is shattered and the mind isn't too willing either.'

'Nobody says you have to dance. Just limp in and park your butt on a chair. There's this one act I've found, you wouldn't believe it. The girl couldn't be more than sixteen. She's magnificent, a body on her like a snake. She fires darts out of her pussie, real darts! I've seen her burst a balloon at thirty feet. She brings the house down, Carl. How she gets muscle control like that, God only knows.'

Drexel smiled. Benny Barack never changed. 'Tell me, what news have you got on Tinko Chaiwisan?' he asked.

Benny puffed his cigar. 'I wondered how long it would take you to get round to him. You're turning this into a personal crusade, Carl.'

The smile left Drexel's face. 'Sure as hell I am. I think I've got the right to.'

Benny walked to the centre of the office and, with the cigar still clenched between his teeth, began to practise golf shots with an imaginary club. 'Chaiwisan is still up in Laos, still running his refineries. He pays his opium taxes to the Pathet Lao and they protect him. Business as usual.'

'How often does he leave the country?'

'Impossible to say. He's a cagey old bird. They don't call him Uncle Chicken for nothing.'

'But he's got to make trips, Benny. He's got to sell the stuff. He can't stay holed up in the jungle all his life.'

'Nobody says he does. We know he crosses the border. But by the time we can act on it, he's back across the line. Same applies when he flies out. Nothing big deal, just tourist class. But always on a false passport, always disguised – hair dyed, different glasses, you know the sort of thing.'

'How much priority are you giving to him?' asked Drexel.

Benny sucked at his teeth. It wasn't a question he was keen on answering. 'I'm stretched to the limit. You know the situation. It's not a question of winning this war, it's a question of how slowly we can lose it.'

'So you're giving him none at all?'

'Chaiwisan is just one of fifty, Carl.'

'Please, Benny, I'm asking a personal favour.'

Barack returned to his desk, stubbing out his cigar in an ashtray fashioned out of the base of an old mortar shell. 'So you still believe Chaiwisan can lead you to Leung Chi-ming?'

Drexel nodded. 'Business partners stick together, Benny. Yeah, I do.'

A slow smile came to Barack's dark features. 'Okay,' he said jauntily. 'Then let's blitz the old bastard.'

It was 3 a.m., two nights after Chinese New Year, his first night duty in the Year of the Snake, when Sergeant Wai Ka-keung, patrolling in a police Land Rover with three of his constables, received the radio alert. A red Porsche, registration number RD 8080, had been involved in a hit and run. It was heading up Stubbs Road towards Wong Nai Chung Gap. A police motorcyclist was in pursuit but Wai should try to intercept, those were his instructions.

The Land Rover was a big, heavy, cumbersome vehicle and, as the sergeant would later testify on oath, he and his three constables only reached the Stubbs Road roundabout in time to see the Porsche climb the centre island, skid wildly and then accelerate away at a lunatic speed. The police motorcyclist remained in pursuit about fifty yards behind.

Wong Nai Chung Gap Road climbs up into the hills, a broad, straight, three-lane highway, and, swinging into it, the sergeant was able, so he later said, to see clearly what happened despite the lingering mists.

There were road works ahead, partially blocking the way, and it was the sergeant's impression that the driver of the Porsche must have had second thoughts about his wild banshee ride because the car seemed to slow right down. The sergeant remembered seeing the police motorcyclist in his white crash helmet and orange and silver reflector vest draw alongside the Porsche and signal to the driver to pull over. And the Porsche appeared to be doing just that.

But then suddenly, without warning, the Porsche accelerated and swerved violently to its right to avoid the road works – straight into the path of the motorcyclist.

The sergeant, who was closing fast now, saw the motorcyclist fall under the wheels. Then, in the confusion and blur, he lost sight of him. But he remembered his driver, Constable 95778, Lam Siu-ping, shouting out, 'Our *foki* – colleague – is down. The car is dragging him! Why doesn't the car stop?'

The sergeant couldn't see the police motorcyclist, he could only see the twisted wreckage of the bike as it was dragged under the Porsche and see sparks flying so bright they could have come from a welder's torch. He expected the Porsche to stop, he was so certain that it would, but instead it ploughed on, swerving and bucking, its engine screaming, for another fifty yards. The sergeant searched for the body of the motorcyclist on the road, terrified of running over him. But all he saw in the beam of his lights was a long black slick that ran up the road. At first he thought it had to be oil, until he saw the tatters of clothing.

Unable to control the Porsche, the driver had mounted the pavement next to the Urban Council tennis courts, smashing into the iron railings. And there the car stalled, its front wheels spinning. The sergeant stopped the Land Rover a few yards behind, straddling it across the road to block traffic, and jumped out. He didn't think to radio back, not at that moment. He presumed that one of his constables would do that. His only concern, he said, was for his *foki* trapped under the Porsche.

Falling to his belly, the sergeant looked under the car. The face of his colleague was only inches away. But he was clearly dead. His helmet had been smashed in, the white enamel stripped away. His face was all blood. His back had been snapped backwards at an impossible angle. But what would remain with the sergeant all his days was the sight of the dead man's intestines pulled from his belly, silvery blue and dangling all wet, hooked round the wheel of his bike.

The sergeant admitted that after such a sight he was in a state of shock, 'high emotion', one of the lawyers later called it. He remembered, as he climbed to his feet, that the woman passenger in the car had been pulled out. She was screaming hysterically before she bent over and vomited on the road. The sergeant recognised her immediately. She starred in local Cantonese costume dramas, Kung Fu movies in which she always played the princess. Her name was Mimi Tse.

The sergeant didn't recognise the driver of the Porsche: Chinese, mid-thirties, about five foot six, gold spectacles, a little fat. But he stank of wine, he didn't miss that, and his eyes were glazed. 'Stupid cop,' the man kept mumbling, 'why did he get in my way?'

Yes, the sergeant admitted he was angry when he searched the driver. Wouldn't any man? A police *foki* was dead, his blood was spilling across the tarmac, and yet the driver – rich, drunk, spoilt – didn't show a moment's remorse. The sergeant admitted that when he saw the identity card and realised who the driver was, he shouted to his constables, 'Do you know who this murderer is? It's Teddy Leung, that's who, son of the great Leung Chi-ming. What is it, rich guy, do you think you can kill who you like? Do you think your father can rescue you this time?'

But he never assaulted the man, said the sergeant. Despite the provocation, he never laid a finger on him, neither he nor his constables. And, as God was his witness, he saw what he saw.

Carl Drexel's forty-eight-hour stopover in Hong Kong was purely personal; no work, nothing official, no more than a way of breaking his journey back to the States and seeing old friends. But all that changed the minute he landed.

Danny Abbott was waiting for him at Kai Tak Airport. As they took the elevator up to the car park, he asked, 'Have you heard the news?'

'What news?'

Danny handed Drexel that morning's edition of the *South China Morning Post*. 'Leung Chi-ming's son got involved in a hit-and-run last night, along Queen's Road East. Nothing serious, apparently, nobody injured. That's what makes the whole thing so bloody asinine. Instead of stopping, he set off like a bat out of hell. Ended up smashing into a cop and dragging him under his car. Killed the poor bastard.'

'Jesus.' Carl Drexel scanned the front-page headlines. 'What in the hell possessed him?'

'What do you expect from an over-indulged brat who thinks he owns the world? Never done a decent day's work in his life other than attending Daddy's board meetings.'

'Drunk, I suppose?'

'Pissed out of his brain,' said Danny venomously. 'Only on the best Tattinger of course. He was at one of those ritzy discos, all mirrors and strobe lights, where the yuppies go. Apparently he got into an argument over his fond papa's problems with the local broadcasting enquiry – great loss of face – and decided to wreak havoc on the world with his—'

But Drexel interrupted. 'What problems?'

'You mean the old man?'

'You said something about a local broadcasting enquiry.'

A smile flickered on Danny's badly mauled face. 'Haven't you heard about that either?'

'Not a thing.'

'Then turn to the business section. This you're going to love.'

As they came out of the elevator, Drexel stood to one side, avoiding the mobs of travellers pushing trolleys, and rustled through the paper until he found the business section. He adjusted his glasses to focus on the headline and, as he did so, a huge grin lit up his normally lugubrious features.

TRIBUNAL REBUKES C.M. LEUNG
STINGING ATTACK ON 'GUTTER ETHICS'

'I don't believe it. But this is the guy destined for a knighthood.'

'I wouldn't hold my breath waiting for that, not any more.'

'Give me a couple of seconds, I've got to read this.' Walking over to a patch of sunlight, Drexel folded the newspaper, resting it on the concrete parapet.

> Entrepreneur Leung Chi-ming was yesterday accused of 'deliberate deception' and 'gutter ethics' by the tribunal considering the renewal of his Hong Kong television and radio broadcasting licences.
>
> 'We have found it proved,' said the chairman, Judge Yang, 'that Mr Leung, among other things, threatened to use his media power to institute a smear campaign against Oriental Investments, a company which had legitimately opposed one of his takeovers, unless that company desisted in its opposition. This was blackmail, there is no other term for it.'

Drexel chuckled. 'Holy cow, this is just great!' And his face was shining as he read on:

> Leung, whose business empire encompasses real estate, textiles, breweries and shipping as well as his entertainment interests, has until this time had an impeccable record. A personal friend of the Governor, he was last year awarded an OBE in the Queen's New Year's Honours list.

> Leung has fourteen days to make further submissions before the tribunal decides what action to take. 'There have been some grave misunderstandings,' said Leung's lawyer. But he admitted yesterday that his client was in danger of forfeiting his licences.

'Shit!' Drexel couldn't contain his delight. 'So there is some justice in the world after all.'

Danny gave a disbelieving snort. 'Guys like Leung always come up smelling of roses.'

'Not always, they don't! Can you imagine the humiliation, the loss of face. It's bloody fantastic! What could happen to the son?'

'If he's found guilty of manslaughter, he'll go away. No doubt about it.'

'How long?'

'Four or five years, maybe longer. A couple of drinks less, a little clearer intent, and it might just have been murder.'

Drexel let out a long, appreciative whistle. 'That's going to hurt the old bastard, hurt him bad.'

They walked on together through the carpark until Danny Abbott stopped, put down Drexel's suitcase which he had been carrying, and removed a bunch of keys from his jacket pocket. 'So,' he said, 'what do you think of the new chariot?'

'This?' Drexel stood gazing at a metallic blue Mercedes Sports.

'Absolutely. A beaut, isn't she?'

'Is this yours?' Drexel was flabbergasted. 'Bloody hell . . .'

Danny grinned. 'I can't screw around with women any more so I might as well do it with cars. It's ten years old, one of the old 450 SLCs. But it's in mint condition.'

Drexel shook his head. The best he had ever managed was a four-year-old Chevvy. 'How can you afford it?' he asked.

Danny smiled a bland kind of smile that made his face seem empty. 'What the hell, you're nobody in this town unless you owe your life to the bank.'

'What's the ex-wife in New Zealand got to say about it? Last I heard, she was driving a 1965 Ford with about half a million miles on the clock.'

'What the dragon doesn't know, the dragon won't worry about.' Danny gave a cocky smile and the scars that ran down his temples, giving him a sour, embittered look, suddenly lightened.

Carl Drexel laughed. Danny was right, he thought, what the hell, why shouldn't he blow money he didn't have on a car he couldn't afford. No amount of surgery was ever going to restore his good looks. His skin was stretched across his cheeks like hospital sheeting, starched and expressionless. His lips were split by a scar. More scars chewed into the sinew of his neck. For Drexel it was different, he had never had any pretensions to physical charm. Anyway, most of his wounds had been to the body. But Danny had grown up relying on his matinee-idol profile; the blond hair and those blue-sky eyes. Everything had sprung from them: character, courage, ambition. Adjusting to the way he was now was going to take a long, long time. Danny had a few hard years ahead of him. So, if a fancy car helped, good luck to him.

Driving the Mercedes with so much caution it might have been made of glass, Danny Abbott negotiated the curling ramps down to the ground floor. 'How would you like an afternoon on the water?' he asked.

Drexel laughed. 'Don't tell me you've acquired a boat, too?'

A grin slid between the scars of Danny's face. 'Cars, boats and females, Carl, they've always been my dream, you know that. She's a thirty-foot sloop, twelve years old and heavy in the water but a good teak hull and easy as pie to sail.'

'Hong Kong cops must have had a raise.'

Danny laughed. 'Either that or we're on the take. So, what about it? We could sail across to Lamma, a long lazy dinner, chilli prawns and crabs and plenty of beer.'

But Carl Drexel's thoughts had switched to more immediate matters. 'When do you reckon Leung's son is going to be remanded?' he asked.

'This afternoon, two thirty. Why?'

'I'd like to be there.'

'It's just a bail application, a simple remand,' said Danny irritably. 'It'll all be over in five minutes. What do you think you're going to achieve?'

'I've never seen the old man – do you know that? – not face to face.'

'So?'

'So, now that he's on the ropes, I'd like to see the look in the old bastard's eyes.'

* * *

At 2.25 that afternoon Leung Choi-lam, known to the English press as Teddy, entered the iron-bound dock in Court No. 1 of the Central Magistracy, the same dock that Harry Lee had occupied a few days earlier.

In the harsh light of sobriety, manacled, with a prison warder at his shoulder and knowing that he faced anything up to five years in jail, the rich kid with his Porsche looked very young, very vulnerable and very sorry for himself. Although he was in his mid-thirties, Teddy Leung had a round schoolboy face, double-chinned and podgy. His black, unbrushed hair fell in a scruffy fringe. He had been crying, that was obvious, and he still sniffed, dabbing at the corner of his eyes with his fingers.

The courtroom was crowded, a noisy crush of clerks and interpreters, policemen and journalists. Squeezed in at the back of the public gallery, Carl Drexel was to all intents just another foreign newsman; checkered jacket and striped tie that clashed, overweight, wearing glasses. Nobody would have taken him for a DEA agent.

On the dot of 2.30, a few seconds before the magistrate was due to enter, Leung Chi-ming himself came into the court. Guarded by a phalanx of lawyers, he made his way slowly to the dock to confer with his son. He placed his hand through the bars to grip his son's arm and Teddy Leung began silently to weep. If Leung Chi-ming had been any other man, thought Drexel, it might have been a touching sight.

After seeing so many photographs of him, Drexel was surprised how much older and more frail the man appeared. He was tall and stooped, almost bald, his skin a malarial yellow, his cheeks sunken, thin lips pressed tightly together. He moved very slowly as if each step was an effort. Somehow Drexel had imagined that power – commercial and criminal – demanded more obvious pride. But there was no pride, no arrogance. It was almost disappointing. For all his wealth and influence, Leung Chi-ming looked like a sad, sick old man carrying the weight of the world on his shoulder.

As Danny Abbott had forecast, the hearing took less than five minutes. Teddy Leung was represented by a barrister, a Queen's Counsel, as the British called them, some hotshot Chinese guy who spoke English like a lord and was probably earning more for that one appearance than Drexel earned in a year. The charges were stated: manslaughter; reckless driving; and a whole shotgun blast of lesser offences. There was a brief address by the QC and Teddy Leung was granted bail of one million Hong Kong dollars. The QC didn't quibble. Why should he? Together, the father and son were worth billions.

With the hearing over, one of the lawyers took Leung Chi-ming's elbow to guide him out of the court. Leung's expression hadn't changed. There was no evident relief that, for the time being at least, his son was free. He remained impassive, his face a death mask.

But, sitting there in the public gallery, watching him, Carl Drexel could see deeper than the external inscrutability. You know it, don't you, he thought with fierce satisfaction, you know your *joss* has run out. You're vulnerable now, you can feel it in that thin, anaemic blood of yours.

Their eyes met briefly, just a passing glance. Carl

Drexel knew that to Leung Chi-ming he was a total stranger, just another lumpy *gweilo* who counted for nothing. But you'll remember me soon enough, he promised. Because I'm the one who is going to put you away. In the States or here in Hong Kong, it doesn't matter a damn, my friend, just so long as you die behind bars.

Night rain streaked down, unseasonal rain. It came out of the South China Sea drumming against the window of his apartment in Ya Mau Tei, turning the people in the alley below into dream-time aqueous ghosts.

Cheng Tak-shing leant his head against the window. His breath misted the glass. His bulging, frog-like eyes were heavily hooded. He felt numb, barely aware of himself as if floating in and out of a trance. Fuck Harry Lee! he thought. Fuck the day he had agreed to give him credit! That had been stupid and now he was paying for it. Why were things always so complicated?

Noises drifted up from the crowded alley: old amahs haggling for *choi sum* and chicken, rain gurgling down open drains, a wife scolding her husband, the crackling wail of Cantonese opera played through cheap loudspeakers. But for him they were a melody, the sounds that had comforted him since childhood.

He knew he would have to make the call. He was already late, inviting more trouble to pour down on his head. He needed to consult. But the effects of the *pak fan* were wearing thin. His muscles were beginning to ache, his teeth to chatter. Just once more, he thought, let me chase the dragon one more time. Yes, just once more. Then I'll make the call . . .

The packet of white powder, the tin foil, paper and matches lay on the floor. Unsteadily, with a languid moan, Cheng squatted down. This was the traditional way the Chinese took heroin: no needles, no bruises, no blood, no disease.

With painstaking care, like a drunk trying to place a key in a lock, he took the paper, twisting it into a taper that would burn with a low flame. Then he sprinkled the heroin on to a square of tin foil. When the taper was lit and held under the foil, the heroin would melt, giving off vapours that curled like marsh fog. But to suck them in, Cheng needed a funnel and the simplest one, the one every *do yau* used was the outside portion of the matchbox.

Ready now, humming to himself, Cheng lit the taper. He placed the matchbox funnel into his mouth and, with dreamy expectation, held the burning taper under the tin foil. The granules of heroin, yellowy-white and rough in texture, began to melt and, hungrily now, suddenly alert, he pursued each twist and meander of the dragon's tail, sucking in deeply, until there was nothing left on the tin foil and all the sweet white smoke had been trapped in his lungs.

Afterwards, torpidly, he lay on his back on the carpet muttering to himself in dull delirium. Cheng didn't consider himself an addict. But when times were hard, he needed the white powder, he needed the complete surrender, the tranquillity it imbued. Harry Lee was a stupid man and he had been stupid to trust him. But it all seemed so simple now. Yes, he would make the call, he would get clearance. And whatever had to be done would be done.

It was near midnight. But in his state of heavy-headed

euphoria, time meant nothing. Grabbing the lead to the telephone, he hauled it across the carpet and dialled. It was a number he remembered even at times like this, the number of a cellular telephone, one that could be carried everywhere. Even if he had to wait, he knew there would always be an answer.

The phone rang for thirty seconds or more before a voice answered, sounding half asleep and irritable. 'Cheng, is that you?'

'Yes, it's me, Ah Leung.'

'What do you want?'

'The Fat Boy says he must have more time.'

'How much time?'

'He's lost his woman. He says he has no more money.'

'But there are ways to raise it. He's stalling.'

'Yes, undoubtedly, Ah Leung.'

'Then why are you bothering me with this?'

Cheng answered dreamily, 'It is a difficult matter, Ah Leung.'

'Don't you read the newspapers, don't you watch television? You know the kind of troubles I'm having. You were stupid enough to advance the credit in the first place. You deal with it.'

Cheng hesitated. 'But it may be necessary to use other methods.'

'What methods you use are your business. Do whatever is necessary. I'm only interested in one thing. I want to see my investment recovered. Do you understand?'

'Yes, Ah Leung, I understand.'

'It's a matter of principle, a matter of face. Harry Lee has to learn. There are no bad debts in this business.'

* * *

Down in the yard the accused murderers were playing volleyball. They were kept separate from everybody else. Like lepers, thought Harry Lee. Like me. With his hands shoved deep into the pockets of his brown prison-issue trousers, he shouldered open the door of the second-floor toilet. Every hour in this damn place lasted a century, he thought, as he headed for the nearest urinal – and suddenly they were all around him.

They must have numbered a dozen; stony-faced prisoners as grim as executioners. 'What do you want?' hissed Harry in a terrified whisper as they closed in on him. 'No, please, you can't do this . . . get away . . .'

One of them pulled a knife from under his shirt, a crude prison-made thing, the handle wrapped with insulating tape. But all Harry saw was the eight-inch serrated blade, blue-black like the skin of a shark. He staggered back against the tiled wall, opening his mouth to scream. But the only sound that came was a truncated gasp as a hand was clamped across his mouth.

Then, like wild dogs, they tore into him. Somebody punched him hard in the gut, bending him double. They grabbed his legs, up-ending him, pinning him to the concrete floor. Harry squirmed and kicked but he couldn't get free. A wad of cloth was jammed into his mouth. Harry gagged on it, spitting up bile. He couldn't breathe. I'm going to die, he thought, I'm going to die.

His left ear was seized, pulled so hard that he was certain it was going to be ripped from his scalp. His face was going purple, eyes bulging. He felt the serrated blade touch the flesh behind his ear and let out a silent shriek.

Oh God, no, please, no! His eyes were pleading. Please, please no! But nothing would stop them. The knife sawed in, three violent slashes, and away it came. Harry felt the blood, like jelly, dribbling down the side of his head. A brown hand waved the severed ear in front of him but it was unrecognisable, just a shred of limp gristle dripping gore.

Harry moaned deep in his belly, arching his back. He was lost in his own black universe of pain. He couldn't bear any more. But it wasn't over yet.

Hands grabbed at his trousers, wrenching them down around his knees. Mad with terror, Harry tried everything to free himself, twisting, wriggling, heaving. But it was hopeless. They had him in a vice. And, with a second explosion of agony, he felt his flesh begin to part . . .

Adam and Nicky had been on a pleasure junk that night, a long boozy cruise with a party of financiers and their wives. It was the standard Hong Kong junket from Queen's Pier following the Lamma Channel to Deep Water Bay and back, the pungent smell of sewage in the sea, Chinese boat boys serving Chablis and Singapore Slings, plenty of talk about 'home leave' and even more about money: pure Asia colonialism. It was a chore for both of them, Hong Kong's equivalent of the cocktail party. But when the junk moored back at Queen's Pier at last, that was it. A few hearty handshakes, the discreet exchange of business cards, and everybody dispersed.

Adam and Nicky drove up into the clouded halo of the Peak. It was 11 p.m. when they reached his rented apartment. As they came through the front door, they could hear the telephone ringing.

Adam's mother broke the news. 'Harry is in hospital,' she said. 'He was attacked in prison.'

'How bad is it?' Adam asked, dry-mouthed.

And, as his mother began to explain, his worst fears were confirmed.

When Nicky heard, she was appalled. The pure, primeval savagery of it turned her blood cold. She was flying to Vancouver the following day on a business trip and had hoped to spend the night but the news of Harry's attack destroyed any intimate intentions either of them had had. She thought of offering to stay just to keep him company but she knew Adam well enough to know that at times like this he needed to be alone.

'I'll see you tomorrow,' she said.

'Yeah, sure,' he answered absently, his thoughts on another plane. 'I'll drive you out to the airport.'

After she had gone, Adam tried to sleep but it was impossible. He opened a bottle of red wine, a heavy burgundy, but even that couldn't calm his churning emotions. All he could do was lie on his bed and stare up at the ceiling fan as it ploughed the warm, damp air, lie there and think and worry himself sick.

Harry was transferred to the custodial ward of the Queen Elizabeth Hospital, not to one of the beds in the open section of the ward but to a single bed in a small, single cell. Adam and his mother found him there the next morning. Ironically, it was for his own protection. It was just as Harry had said, solitary confinement was the only answer.

The orderly-in-charge said there could be only one visitor at a time so Adam waited while his mother went in. A few minutes later she came out, fighting back the tears. 'I'll wait downstairs in the car,' she said. 'I don't think I can bear to wait up here.'

Adam nodded. 'I won't be long.' Then he entered the tiny cell.

When Harry saw him, he attempted a feeble smile but otherwise there was no expression on his face. A blood-stained dressing covered most of his skull. His mouth hung slack. Saliva glistened on his chin. His eyes were lost in pouches of bruising. He looked like an old man.

'Who was responsible?' Adam asked.

Harry blinked. 'Who do you think?'

'Sun Yee On, Cheng Tak-shing's men.'

'Who else?'

'Did you recognise any of them?'

Harry gave a small sigh, as if despairing, and closed his eyes. 'Even if I did, what will that achieve?'

'I don't think you have a choice any more. You've got to fight back.'

'Fight back?' Slowly, painfully, Harry shook his head. 'You still don't understand, do you, Adam? Do you know what they did to me after they had sliced off my ear? They pulled down my trousers, that's what they did, and then they cut an arrow into my belly. And do you know where that arrow pointed?'

Adam had a good idea.

'Do you know why? Because that's what they're going to cut off next if I don't pay the debt.'

The obscene symbolism left Adam bereft of words. He

tried to imagine the agony and terror his brother must have experienced but it was way beyond his comprehension.

Harry was silent for a time. Then he said in a dry, croaking voice, 'If I try to fight them, Adam, I'm a dead man. I've told you. It's not a question of whether they can get to me again, it's only a question of when and where. Somehow, I've got to raise the money . . .'

Adam shook his head. 'No, Harry, I'm sorry, there's no way I'm going to deal in drugs.'

Harry strained to lift his head up from the pillow. 'For God's sake, Adam.' His head fell back on the pillow and he stared at the wall, breathing through his mouth in short gasps. Then, in a lower voice, he said, 'It's not just me, not any more.'

Adam looked at him, suddenly alarmed. 'What are you talking about?'

'You know things like this don't remain static. They grow, one thing leads to another. The violence expands.'

'What do you mean?'

'Come on, you're not that naive.'

'Just tell me! What do you mean, the violence expands?'

Harry hesitated. 'I mean that we both have a mother . . .'

The blood drained from Adam's cheeks.

'Relatives are an asset, Adam. Leverage. We're all the same family, that's the way they see it. You, me, Mum, it makes no difference. It's just one debt.' Harry coughed, bringing up phlegm. 'And if they don't get the money . . .' He fell silent.

'Then what?' Adam demanded.

Harry sighed. 'Then they'll get their pound of flesh.'

Driving back through Kowloon's incessant nose-to-tail traffic, Adam's mother could see how deeply preoccupied he was. But she needed answers, too. 'Why was he attacked, Adam? It can't have been some ordinary prison dispute. It had to be more, much more than that. Please, you're not helping by keeping me in the dark, you're just making it worse.'

Adam knew she was right. There was no way of sparing her feelings, not after what she had been through these last few days. She was entitled to know the truth. The only question was how much of the truth.

One thing was certain, he couldn't tell her anything about Harry's plea that he deal in heroin. To do so would place an impossible burden on her. The burden of that, the responsibility for whatever decision he might make, would have to be borne by him alone.

'What was the cause of the attack?' his mother asked again.

'A dispute over money,' he answered.

'Who does he owe?'

Adam hesitated. 'His heroin suppliers.'

She didn't flinch. 'How much?' she asked. 'Is there any way we can help him? You know I have some savings. It's not a great deal but—'

'I'm afraid it's more money than we could ever contemplate paying.'

'Then what's Harry going to do?'

'The police will protect him. He'll be okay now,' said

Adam, trying to sound emphatic. 'You saw for yourself, even in hospital they had him in isolation.'

They edged their way through the traffic, five lanes thick, towards the toll gates of the Cross Harbour Tunnel as Adam searched for the right words for what he had to tell her next. 'I think you and I are going to have to be a little careful, too,' he said. 'Just for a couple of weeks until this thing blows over.'

There was a look of alarm in his mother's eyes. 'Why, we're not in any danger, are we?'

'I'm sure it's nothing, just bluff,' he said in a tone calculated to dispel any fears. 'But apparently the men who attacked Harry made a number of threats. You know the sort of thing, about looking to the family if he couldn't raise the money himself.'

'So what do we do?'

'I'm going to ask the police to provide protection for you. A precaution, that's all, but it's better safe than sorry.'

'And what about you? If I'm in danger then so are you.'

Adam gave a smile of quiet bravado. 'Don't worry about me. I'm big and ugly enough to look after myself.'

His mother smiled, her face suddenly shadowed with memories. 'That's what your father always used to say. You're like him in so many ways. I can see it all the time, the same mannerisms, the same little turns of phrase.'

'You miss him still, don't you?'

She nodded. 'Every day.'

They arrived at her apartment on Conduit Road, an old block only five storeys high, weathered and grey, and

Adam parked the Volvo. A few years back, when his father had been alive, the apartment had had an uninterrupted view out over the harbour. The birds would glide by the balcony so close you could touch them. Now the view was gone, blocked out by a barricade of forty-storey apartment blocks. Any feeling for the environment had been sacrificed to the god of square footage years back. But that was Hong Kong, thought Adam, suddenly soured by everything about the place: profit, profit and more damn profit.

His mother's apartment was on the third floor. 'Would you like some coffee?' she asked as they walked in together.

'Just a quick cup, thanks. I have to rush, I'm afraid. I've got a long line of appointments at the office.'

'Come through to the kitchen,' she said. 'We can sit and talk for a few minutes.'

Adam, who was a couple of paces ahead of her, pushed open the kitchen door, and stopped abruptly.

His mother, who only caught a glimpse, gave a gasp, recoiling in horror. But Adam didn't move. He remained there, rooted to the spot, his eyes fixed on it.

The cockerel, a huge bird, black and red, had been hung by its feet from the ceiling. Then – still alive – its head had been sliced off and the blood had sprayed out of its neck as the bird spun and shuddered and gyrated. The kitchen table was awash with its blood, turning black now, half congealed. The kitchen cupboards were splattered with it, a fine spray speckled the walls.

The bird was just a mess of feathers now. It had been dead an hour or more. The nerves had ceased twitching.

But blood, like treacle, still oozed from its neck and dripped, drop by drop, on to the kitchen floor.

Within half an hour the police were there. They searched the apartment, checking every window and door. They searched the fire escape and stairs. But there was no sign of forced entry, that was the puzzling aspect. And sinister, too.

Forensic experts came to take photographs and check for fingerprints. But the decapitated bird was left dangling, a grizzly focal point around which all the work was done, until an officer from the Narcotics Bureau arrived.

His name was Davies. He was a chief inspector, a florid-faced Welshman, one of the old school of expatriate policemen who had marched the Hong Kong beat for twenty years and still spoke Cantonese with an accent so thick that only a Chinaman from Cardiff had the faintest hope of understanding it.

Davies examined the cockerel, prodding it with a stubby finger like a man examining a brace of partridge in a butcher's shop. 'Why doesn't your brother agree to co-operate with us, Mr Blake? It would make it so much easier. Maybe then we could stop this kind of nonsense.'

'My brother's intentions are his own affair,' said Adam. 'At the moment my main concern is my mother's safety.'

'All this Triad mumbo-jumbo is out of character,' said Davies. 'Your average Chinese drug dealer doesn't resort to this kind of stuff. He's a businessman, a pretty sensible bloke most of the time.'

'Obviously not in this instance,' said Adam with controlled politeness.

Davies lit a cigarette, a French Gitanes. 'It's as bizarre as old buggery,' he said, exhaling smoke through his nostrils.

'I'd like to know what you intend to do about my mother's protection,' said Adam.

'No problem there, we'll organise a guard. Twenty-four hours a day, Mr Blake.'

'Thank you.'

Davies walked to the kitchen door. 'You know the best way of helping your mum, Mr Blake? Speak to that brother of yours, get him to co-operate. He's a bloody fool if he doesn't.'

Adam didn't answer.

Davies shrugged. 'Well, it's his funeral. I just hope it's nobody else's too.'

Adam remained at his mother's apartment for the rest of the morning and into the afternoon. Once the last policeman had departed, she said she would be fine on her own. But he could see that she was still in a state of shock and even with a guard downstairs he didn't want to leave her.

Nicky was scheduled to fly to Vancouver that afternoon, departing at 3.15. Driving her out to Kai Tak was impossible now. The best he could manage was a phone call to apologise and wish her *bon voyage*. He said nothing about the incident in his mother's apartment, making some excuse about being kept longer with Harry than expected. Nicky, for all her bright, breezy ways, was a worrier, she let herself get emotionally involved. There was no purpose in sending her off with news that would simply depress her.

'Don't worry,' she said. 'I'll get a cab out.'

'I'm going to miss you,' said Adam.

'I'm going to miss you, too.'

'A whole ten days.'

'A lifetime.'

And they both laughed.

Why Adam had been dragging his heels proposing marriage he didn't know. Over the last couple of months he had been on the verge of asking her countless times. But, whatever the reason, once this nightmare with Harry was finished, once he could see further in his life than the next crisis, then it was going to be different, he thought, very different indeed.

Adam and his mother spent a lot of time talking that day. Despite the personal threat embodied by the butchered cockerel, his mother's main concern was still for Harry. In some ways she felt personally responsible for his troubles.

'You can't blame yourself,' said Adam. 'Harry knew the risks. It was a calculated gamble, just business – that's the way he saw it.'

But even so, Harry was her son, the child she had raised. Emotionally, deep down, she couldn't shake off the feeling that his wrongs were her wrongs, too. She talked about Harry as a boy, his wilful ways, his hero worship of the father he had never known. And from Harry, as the day wore on, she turned slowly to herself.

His mother was normally reticent about her past. There was not a great deal in her youth to look back upon with fond memories. But it was clear, as she recovered from her shock, that she wanted to talk, to share things with Adam that she had never shared before.

She spoke of her childhood in Manchuria, one of four sisters, their lives so well ordered and secure. She spoke of her father, a loving man, a prosperous rice merchant, and how she had been forced to witness his execution at the hands of the occupying Japanese army. When she spoke of it, even though the event was fifty years old and she had been only fifteen at the time, a sparkle of tears still came to her eyes. 'We all loved him very dearly,' she said. 'And to see him die . . .' She tried to finish the sentence but couldn't; a lifetime of the unutterable was lodged in her throat.

She told Adam how, after her father's death, all their property was confiscated; their house, their money. They couldn't remain in Manchuria and, in the war-ravaged years that followed, slowly worked their way south – Suchow, Nanking, Shanghai. One sister died of tuberculosis, their mother worked herself into an early grave.

'How did you live?' asked Adam.

'In Shanghai I worked as a house servant,' she said. 'It was in the house of a Kuomintang general, one of Chiang Kai-shek's aides.'

And that's where she had met KS Lee, Harry's father. He had been a young lieutenant then, an artillery officer, good-looking, charming, full of dash and bravado; in many ways larger than life, like a screen idol. And she had fallen head over heels in love. They had married after a whirlwind courtship, then travelled south to Canton.

In 1948, as Mao Tse-tung's armies encircled the city, she and KS had escaped, dressed as peasants, joining the great swell of refugees pouring into the tiny British colony of Hong Kong.

For the first time, too, she spoke of her life with KS, separating the myth from the man. She spoke of his constant gambling debts and his affairs. She spoke of how they argued, fierce, passionate clashes in which he would physically attack her, and how in the end all that passion had been reduced to nothing more than an indifferent contempt.

Adam's father, she said, had brought her life full circle, back to the security and contentment of her childhood. Those had been her happiest years, married to Denys Blake. He hadn't been a man of great ambition but he had been a true gentleman, caring and concerned, even for Harry, although it didn't always show. Denys Blake had taught her, she said, just how good life could be, what there was to be grateful for – most of all her children. Despite his death, that outlook endured.

Adam had never known his mother so forthcoming; he could have remained there listening to her indefinitely. But by five o'clock it was impossible to stay away from the office any longer. He had to leave her, driving down to Central, back into the mayhem of dictation, telephone calls and conferences. But at least it took his mind off other things.

It wasn't until near midnight that he was finally

through, exhausted but still hyped up. Far from ready to go home, Adam and a couple of his architects went down to Wanchai and propped up the bar at Joe Banana's, drinking Scotch on the rocks until 2 a.m. Only then did Adam finally drive home.

His apartment on the Peak was on the ground floor of a block built in the grand colonial fashion, with a dining room that could seat fifty and ceilings palatially high to let the tropical air circulate. After parking the Volvo, he let himself in and went through to the kitchen to grab something from the fridge.

But the moment he was inside, he detected an odour. It was strange and sulphurous, a smell that he couldn't define. At first, his head muzzy with alcohol, he ignored it. But the odour persisted. For a moment he thought it might be a gas leak. But no, the smell of gas was different.

The source of the smell was in the main bedroom. When he opened the door, it was so bad that he began to cough. He switched on the lights but could see nothing that would have caused the stench. The room was clean, quiet, undisturbed.

Worried now, not knowing what to expect, Adam went across to the cupboards where he hung his clothes. His eyes were beginning to water. He jerked open the doors - and the stench of acid washed over him like a wave.

His suits were still smouldering, reduced to skeletal tatters by the acid. The plastic hangers from which they hung had been liquefied into grotesque bubbled shapes. Everything, his shirts and ties, his jerseys and sports kit, had been burnt through. Even his shoes gave off the stench of acid, slowly disintegrating.

Coughing violently, Adam half turned his head. And that's when he saw the sheet of paper on his bed. There was a message on it written in Chinese characters. Adam picked it up. He felt strangely calm, almost detached. It was written in a formal style, awkwardly high-flown: 'Involve the police and there will be no more warnings. No warning for you, no warning for your mother, no warning for anybody upon whom we place our hand.'

At 5 a.m., gritty-eyed and angry, he was still clearing away the mess when the third blow came.

The telephone rang. It was Nicky on the line, phoning from Vancouver. 'I'm sorry to wake you,' she said, 'but I had to phone.'

Adam could hear the anxiety in her voice. 'What is it?' he asked.

She gave a perplexed laugh. 'I don't know what to make of it. It's really crazy. But when I got back to the house with Mum and Dad, there was a note lying on my bed, right there on my pillow. I thought maybe it was Wayne, you know what younger brothers are like. Kids of fifteen have warped senses of humour. But he swears it wasn't him. It's really weird, Adam, crazy but scary at the same time.'

'What does it say?' Adam asked.

'I've got it right here. Hang on, yes, here it is.' Nicky laughed again, a nervous, bewildered laugh. 'It's all too weird to be true. Okay, this is what it says: "Acid rain can fall anywhere at any time. Tell your boy friend that." '

The breath caught in Adam's throat. He didn't say anything, not immediately, but suddenly he was frightened, scared to hell. They had constructed it with all the drama of a play. He could still smell the lingering odours of acid in the apartment, and now this message from the other side of the world. It was all so terrifyingly clear: there's no escape, no protection; Canada or Hong Kong, there's nowhere to hide.

Nicky's voice intruded, sounding a million light-years away. 'This is to do with Harry, isn't it?'

Adam didn't know how to answer.

'I'm sorry, Adam,' she said, 'but nothing else makes sense.'

'No, no, you're right,' he answered in a dull voice. 'We've had similar threats here.'

'What kind of threats?'

Adam was vague. 'Damage to my clothing, notes warning me not to go to the police.'

'Who in the hell is making them? What's this all about, Adam?'

'It's a money thing. Harry still owes his suppliers and they're putting on the squeeze.'

'But why threaten us? What have we got to do with this?' Then suddenly the full implications of it hit home. 'God, are you saying we've got drug dealers on to us?'

'It's just tactics, Nicky, that's all it is,' said Adam, trying to calm her.

'But what do I do? Do I call the police?'

'I think that would be a good idea, yes, just to be on the safe side. I've got police guarding my mother's place now.'

'She hasn't been harmed in any way, has she?' asked Nicky, concerned.

'No, it was a threat, that's all.'

'So she's safe at least?'

'Yes, thank God, she's safe at least . . .' But, as he echoed the words, Adam's mind seemed suddenly to switch to another dimension. No, he thought, no, she's not safe! My God, that's where the pattern of threats had to be leading. There had to be one final gesture, absolute proof that they could get to anybody in any circumstances.

'Look, Nicky,' he said, 'I've just thought of something. I'm sorry, I have to go.'

She didn't question him. 'Yes, of course . . .'

'Make sure you contact the police.'

'Will you phone later?'

'Yes, I'll phone. I'm sorry, there's just no time—'

Slamming down the phone, forgetting to even lock the door, Adam rushed out to his car.

He came down through the dense mist that shrouded the Peak at breakneck speed. Skidding round the dizzy switchbacks, deserted at this Godforsaken hour, his brakes smoking, he made it down the precipitous descent and onto Conduit Road in five minutes flat.

He parked out on the road and ran into the lobby. The caretaker was asleep, slumped over his desk. But, as Adam punched the elevator button, a uniformed policeman stepped into the lobby. 'Good morning,' said Adam, speaking Cantonese. 'Has everything been quiet?'

'Nothing unusual,' the police officer replied.

Adam should have been reassured but he wasn't. When he reached his mother's apartment, he kept jabbing at her doorbell like a man firing a machine-gun, in short, persistent bursts until eventually she answered.

'Who is it?' she asked nervously from behind the locked door.

'It's me, Adam.'

When she opened the door, she was standing in her dressing gown, her skin as yellow as parchment, her eyes still puffy from interrupted sleep. 'What is it?' she asked.

'You've not heard anything during the night, nobody has disturbed you?'

'No, nobody, I haven't heard a thing . . .'

Adam barged past her as he made for the kitchen door.

'What is all this about, Adam?' his mother called as she followed him.

Adam said nothing. But, even before he opened the door, he knew – and there it hung, in exactly the same place as before, trussed up in the same manner, an exact replica: the decapitated carcass of a cockerel, proof perfect that even a police guard made no difference. That's what the symbol of the blood and the twisted feet and the broken feathers said: there's no shield that can protect you.

Adam glanced down at the floor and there, with a final Triad flourish, as bloody as some atavistic pagan ritual, he saw that the bird's entrails had been laid out to form a single Chinese character, *sai*, the character that signified death.

It was at that moment that Adam knew he had been stripped of all choice.

As he stood there, images flooded his brain: Nicky's autumnal face, her brown hair and soft grey eyes melting under a rain of acid; his mother dying. He knew that's what was intended, that he should react to the mutilated symbol with pure emotion.

At that moment he felt nothing for Harry, only an abiding resentment. Harry was the one who had brought all this upon them. But for his mother . . . dear God, hadn't she suffered enough already? And Nicky, the only wrong she had committed was to love him. If either of them was harmed, how would he live with himself? Moral righteousness was cold comfort.

Like any normal man, he hated the drugs trade. But it was an objective hatred, intellectual and distant. There was no passion in it. He knew he had only one choice now, between seeing those he loved killed or maimed – a prospect that turned his blood cold – and supplying drugs to anonymous people in a far-off country who craved them anyway. And for Adam that was no choice at all.

It was late afternoon, Hong Kong was shrouded in its season of mists with a dull drizzle falling, when Adam visited his brother.

When he entered the tiny cell, Harry was lying on his iron bed in a drugged half-sleep. His eyes opened and a smile flickered across his face. His lips were chalky white with the residue of medication. There were wires taped to his chest. 'They're doing some heart tests,' murmured Harry. 'As if I don't have enough troubles.'

'It's nothing serious, is it?'

'Just tension, that's all . . . tension.'

It was dark outside, with the rain, much heavier now, beating against the single grimy window. There was only one light in the cell, a small bulb set into the ceiling and protected by a mask of wire. They sat beneath it, not knowing what to say, trapped in the striated shadows like flies caught in a web of silence.

Harry knew why Adam had come. No words were necessary. 'I'm sorry . . .' he murmured.

Adam shrugged. Regrets were superfluous now. 'Will this keep them off our backs? That's all I want to know.'

'I'll get the message to them.'

'If Mum or Nicky are harmed in any way—'

'Don't worry, they'll be okay.'

'If they touch one hair on their heads, that's the end of their fucking money!' Adam put the full weight of his bitterness behind the words. 'And you can tell the bastards one other thing, too, tell them this can't be done overnight. I'm not going to be pressured into anything hasty.'

'They'll understand. If they know you're going for it, there'll be no more threats.'

Adam nodded. His stomach was churning. 'All right, so where do I get the stuff?'

Harry's eyes were half hooded as if a great effort was required to keep them open. 'One step at a time . . .

getting the stuff to supply will be no problem. But first you have to secure the buyers.'

'Who am I supposed to sell to, the Vietnamese you were dealing with?'

'No, not them . . . far too dangerous. The ones that haven't been arrested will be under DEA surveillance. But there's another group . . . I was negotiating with them before I was arrested. I've done all the ground work . . . they're very cautious but businesslike . . . good people to deal with.'

'Where are they?'

'New York.'

'Chinese?'

The slightest smile appeared on Harry's face. 'No, *gweilos* . . . your kind of people.'

'Are you sure I can trust them?'

'They'll be asking the same question.'

Adam took a deep, shuddering breath. He still couldn't believe he was doing this. 'How do I make contact?'

'You'll have to fly across, negotiate with them face to face. I can set it up for you. I have a contact. I'll give you his number. When do you think you can go?'

'As soon as possible. I want to get this over with.'

Harry murmured, barely audible, 'It shouldn't take more than a week to get the preliminaries done. Then you're on your way.' A threadbare smile came to his face. As always, he tried to make a joke of it. 'Welcome to the trade, brother,' he said.

But Adam's only reaction, as he got up from his stool, was a stonehard stare.

Outside, the rain was coming down hard, a full tropical storm that scoured the pavements. People huddled in doorways, waiting for the storm to pass, but Adam was oblivious of it. Leaving his car, he walked down the road, the rain beating against his face, his clothes sodden. And Harry's facetious phrase stayed with him all the time, no rain could scour that away: ***Welcome to the trade, brother***.

Chapter Four

NEW YORK – HONG KONG

Adam sat by the telephone for more than an hour before he made the call. His sense of disbelief – that this couldn't be happening to him – was only slowly diminishing. But, for all his hesitation, he knew he was committed. It was too late now. There was no pulling back. With leaden fingers, he dialled the code for New York City.

Harry had told him that his contact was a man called Slug Delaney and it was Delaney who answered the call. Adam had it all worked out in his head, what he would say, how he would say it. But, speaking to the man, trying to explain everything in a garbled impromptu code, he stumbled nervously over his words, certain he was making a total mess of it. Delaney said little. He was patently suspicious and clearly terrified of committing himself in case the call was some sort of police set-up. It was like a fool talking to a deaf man, thought Adam.

'Harry tells me that he negotiated a trading contract with you.'

'He offered me a line in fish,' grunted Delaney. 'No big deal . . . shark fins, that sort of stuff.'

'Harry wants me to honour that agreement, Mr Delaney.'

'You say your brother has been arrested. What's the charge?'

'Drugs.'

Delaney was taken aback by the bluntness of it. 'Yeah, well, I don't know . . .'

'This is very important to him, Mr Delaney, important to us both.'

There was silence at the other end of the line.

'Look. I tell you what,' said Adam. 'Let me give you my telephone numbers. I appreciate you need time to consider the matter. If you want to check out my credentials, please feel free.'

Delaney just grunted.

Adam gave him his home and office numbers and his fax number, too. The call, he knew, was a disaster. He had projected himself exactly as he was – a stumbling amateur. His nervousness could only have compounded Delaney's suspicions. In a strange way he was almost pleased, as if fate was pulling him back from the brink. One thing was certain, he never expected to hear from the man again.

Twenty-four hours later, however, he was proved wrong. At 10 p.m. the telephone rang in Adam's apartment. He picked it up to hear Slug Delaney's gruff New Yorker's voice at the other end. 'What do you want to mess in your brother's business for? Ain't you some kind of fancy-assed architect?'

'My brother needs my help,' Adam replied.

'What kind of help?'

'He has debts, Mr Delaney.'

'We all have debts.'

'Business debts, credit in the sale of shark fins.'

'Ain't you got enough to bail him out?'

'I wish I had.'

'So you've got to move into his business, is that it? Take over the reins.'

'Yes, Mr Delaney, that's it exactly.'

'Yeah, well . . .' There was a long silence as Delaney considered matters. 'Have you ever traded in the merchandise before?'

Adam knew there was only one way to prove his *bona fides* and that was by keeping deceit to a minimum. 'In shark fins? No, never.'

For the very first time the tone of Delaney's voice changed. He gave a gravelly chuckle. 'But you're willing to learn, is that it?'

'All I need is the opportunity.'

'Opportunity? Yeah, right. So tell me, do you see much future in the business, for yourself, I mean?'

Adam paused before answering. Too much sincerity would ring false. 'It depends on the incentives, Mr Delaney. If you and your associates are prepared to make worthwhile orders, then yes, I do see a future – for all of us.'

Delaney grunted. But he was impressed. 'Okay,' he said, 'give me a few days. I'll see if my associates are still interested.'

* * *

Over the next two days Adam did everything like a man under hypnosis. He was so deeply preoccupied, so much a prisoner of himself that friends and colleagues began to ask if he was all right. He needed a few days away, they said. He was looking rundown. When Nicky got back, the two of them should fly to Phuket or down to Bali. Just laze on a beach, take a break. Hong Kong could get to you, it was that kind of city; constant work, constant bustle. Christ, thought Adam, if only they knew.

On the third day Delaney telephoned. 'You're lucky,' were his first words. 'The present supplier of shark fins is a little less than reliable. You know what I mean? So we're looking to ease him out and ease somebody else into his place. Shark fin is a speciality dish, Mr Blake. Customers are disappointed if it's not on the menu. But they expect quality. Can you supply good quality?'

'As good as you'll get anywhere,' said Adam, who wouldn't know heroin from baking powder.

Delaney laughed. 'I like you, Mr Blake. You've got chutzpah. Okay, we'll see soon enough. But what about reliability of supply? Reliability is critical.'

'It's all in the pipeline,' said Adam.

'So's last month's cheque.'

Adam replied bluntly, 'There's no way I can talk about reliability until you give me some idea of quantity.'

Delaney saw the sense in it. 'First time around all we want is a sample. We need to test the quality of the product, the speed and assurance of delivery.'

'And after that?' asked Adam.

'After that, shit, the sky's the limit. We have a nationwide chain of restaurants. Maybe one day we'll even franchise!' And he laughed. 'So, Mr Blake, are you prepared to fly over and talk business?'

'When do you want me there?'

'As soon as you can make it.'

'Okay, I'll get back to you.'

'And Mr Blake.'

'Yeah?'

'One thing. Chutzpah we admire, bullshit we don't.'

When Harry heard the news, he let out a long sigh of relief, dropping his head back on the pillow. 'Thank God for that. I don't know how you did it, Adam. I was certain they were going to shy off.' Then he sat up, all smiles again; another hurdle jumped. 'So what sort of deal are they offering, did Delaney say?'

Adam cast his eyes around the white-painted cell. 'Are you sure it's safe to talk in here?'

'Don't tell me you're paranoid already!' Harry laughed, finding it immensely funny. For Harry everything was a joke.

But Adam didn't laugh. His life was on the line and he wasn't going to take careless risks.

'This cell is eight foot by four,' said Harry. 'You don't need a team of technicians to de-bug it.'

'Have you checked it out?'

'Don't look so worried, Adam.'

'I've got reason to be bloody worried! Have you or haven't you?'

Harry looked crestfallen. 'I've checked it out, okay?'

Adam said nothing, simply shook his head.

Harry tried to recover the situation, giving a limp grin. 'I've found there's only one way to deal with pressure, Adam, that's to joke your way through it.'

Adam muttered beneath his breath, having difficulty holding his temper. 'With respect, Harry, the last thing I need now is homespun advice. You want to help, then give me some facts and figures, not platitudes.'

Harry's cheeks were blotched pink and white. 'All right,' he said, his voice full of hurt. 'What do you want to know?'

'What units of measurement are we going to be trading in – pounds, kilos, what?'

'You're going to be dealing in units. One unit is about seven hundred grams.'

'And what's the going price for a unit?'

'In the US, wholesale, about a hundred and forty thousand. They're going to try and push you down but don't take less than a hundred and thirty.'

'That's in the States,' said Adam. 'That's selling. But what's it going to cost me here in Hong Kong?'

'Wholesale, between fourteen and eighteen thousand in US currency.'

'Delaney is talking about a sample shipment first. How many units would that be?'

'Probably just two.'

'So I've got to find around thirty-six thousand.' Adam was looking pale. 'But it doesn't end there, does it?'

Harry shrugged, trying to downplay the problem. 'You've got expenses, sure, everybody has expenses. But they shouldn't be more than another ten thousand, fifteen maximum.'

'So, in round figures, I've got to dig up another fifty grand. That's what you're telling me.'

Harry just looked at him, his face pale.

'Where am I supposed to get it from, tell me?' asked Adam in an icy voice. 'I've exhausted every source I have. I'm praying I can pay my staff salaries at the end of this month.'

'It's the last amount,' blurted Harry. 'I swear it! All you need is this first sale then the profits will pay for the next. It's a snowball effect.' He forced a weak smile. 'Think of it, Adam, a net profit of around two hundred thousand. And that's just for a sample run. Where else can you make profits like that?'

But Adam wasn't that easily impressed. In the best of businesses, expenses were like landmines dug into every pathway you took. But in a criminal enterprise like this . . .

A minimum of seventy-five or eighty thousand would have to be used to finance the next purchase. If he was lucky, that would leave around a hundred thousand to pay Cheng Tak-shing. But that was barely enough to meet the crippling interest rates that he knew Triads charged. At best – on this first run at least – they would be marking time.

With the financial side clarified, Adam turned to the most important matter of all, the one matter they hadn't spoken about yet. 'Assuming I can raise the cash,' he said, 'where do I buy the stuff? Who am I supposed to deal with here in Hong Kong?'

Harry gave a quick, jerky nod, acknowledging the question. But he didn't answer. He reached across for a glass of water on the bedside table, drinking a little. Only then did he reply. 'In this game, Adam, you have to realise one thing. If necessary, you'll trade with the devil.'

Adam slowly nodded. He knew what was coming was ominous. 'Then give me the devil's name,' he said.

Harry drank more water, gulping it down. 'Business is business, Adam. In our situation we've got to be blind to everything else.'

'Just give me his name.'

Harry chewed nervously at his lip. He took a small breath. 'It's Cheng Tak-shing.'

Adam half rose from his stool. In the dark recesses of his subconscious he had been expecting it but even so he was stunned. 'Are you mad? After what he's done to you, after all his threats, you expect me to deal with that animal?'

'Just listen a second,' pleaded Harry.

Adam whirled away. 'I just don't believe this. The bastard hacks off your ear, he threatens to slash away your genitals. He threatens my life, he threatens our family. And the next day you're trading with him! For God's sake, Harry, what sort of incestuous bloody world do you live in?'

Harry stared up at him, anguish on his face. 'Do you think I'm happy to do it? Don't you think I hate the bastard as much as you?'

'Then why, Harry, in the name of God, why?'

'Because I've got no other choice.' Harry's eyes beseeched him. 'He's my only source of supply.'

* * *

That same night, a few minutes before midnight, with half a bottle of Scotch in him but still cold hard sober, Adam telephoned New York. 'I'm booked to fly out tomorrow,' he said.

'There's a hotel in midtown Manhattan,' said Delaney. 'It's called the Madison Towers, corner of Madison and East Thirty-eighth. Book in there.'

'And after that?' asked Adam.

'Sit and be patient. That's the second rule of the game.'

'What's the first?'

Delaney gave a knowing laugh. 'The first rule, Mr Blake, is the only rule that counts – don't get caught.'

The following day Adam flew out of Hong Kong.

Exactly one week had passed since he had agreed with Harry to trade in heroin. But he remained in a daze. Seated on the plane, drinking too much wine, trying unsuccessfully to get into a novel he had picked up at the airport bookshop, he found himself possessed by the unnerving sensation that, although his physical body was involved in this thing, it was inhabited by another man's personality, another man's mind. It was him and yet it wasn't; the muted beginnings of schizophrenia.

On his arrival in New York in the early evening, he booked into the Madison Towers as Delaney had instructed. His room was small, the furniture old. The cream-coloured walls were scuffed and faded. An ancient air-conditioner growled behind the curtains. He was on the thirteenth floor – lucky or not? – with a view across a wasteland of red-brick rooftops towards the Pan Am building.

Superficially, New York and Hong Kong were similar: a jungle of skyscrapers, like concrete plants, clawing upwards for the light, streets clogged with traffic, neon signs, noise and exotica everywhere. Except New York was so much bigger, super-charged; ten times more threatening.

Adam showered and changed into fresh clothing. There was a deli across the road called Reubens where he had a snack of toasted bagels and coffee before returning to his room.

Be patient, that was Delaney's second rule of the business. Adam kicked off his shoes and flopped down on the bed. The room smelt musty: countless layers of dust and cigarette smoke and other people's body odours. He picked up the novel that had defeated him on the aircraft. He turned to page one. And the telephone rang.

'I trust you had a pleasant flight, Mr Blake.' The voice surprised him. It was Ivy League and cultured, theatrical and just a little effete. 'I've never had the dubious pleasure of flying that sort of distance without a number of convenient stop-overs. That's why we decided to give you tonight at least to sleep off the effects and discuss our business tomorrow. How does that sound?'

'I'm at your disposal,' said Adam, feeling his heart beat faster.

'I live out of New York, Mr Blake. I can't abide cities. They are all towers of Babel as far as I am concerned.' He laughed very gently, with an edge of self-mockery. 'I live in Connecticut, about two and a half hours north of the city. But the weather at the moment is splendid, spring at its very best. I'm sure you'll enjoy the drive.'

'I'm sure I will,' Adam replied.

'I'm afraid though that I have to impose upon you still further. As much as I would like to be able to supply a car and chauffeur, at the moment it's rather, well, shall we say inconvenient.'

There was more to it than inconvenience, thought Adam. What did they want to do, shadow him? Check that he didn't have police back-up? 'It's okay,' he said. 'I can hire a car and drive myself up.'

'Once you are out of New York, the route is very easy, very scenic, too. I'll arrange to have you met somewhere convenient, say Stockbridge. It's a delightful little town. You'll find it on any tourist map. How does two thirty sound? That will give you time to make the journey at leisure.'

'Two thirty sounds fine.'

'I would recommend that you lunch at the Red Lion Inn. It was built back in 1681 and has a great deal of charm. They do an excellent game pie.'

Adam found it hard to believe he was talking to a drug dealer. Anybody would think they were getting together to discuss antique furniture.

'All being well, my employee will meet you on the verandah at two thirty and bring you straight to the house.'

'Does he know what I look like?' asked Adam.

'Oh yes, Mr Blake, perfectly.'

Adam smiled to himself. Not only were they cautious

but they were thorough, too. 'Okay,' he said. 'Tomorrow, then, at the Red Lion in Stockbridge.'

'I look forward to meeting you, Mr Blake. It's not every day that one meets an architect who prefers to deal in fish rather than design those towers of Babel I referred to earlier.'

Adam measured his answer. 'Fate, they say, is a comedian.'

The man laughed, clearly amused. 'Oh yes, Mr Blake, absolutely.'

It was only after Adam had put down the telephone that he realised he hadn't learnt his name.

Overnight the weather soured. The following morning was grey and blustery with sleet coming down from Canada. Harlem Valley and Dover Plains drifted by in the gloomy shadows of scudding clouds. When he drove through the village of Sharon, a thunderstorm broke overhead.

But the countryside was still magnificent; hedgerows of hawthorn along the roads, white clapboard houses standing high on hills sheltered by waving oaks. It surprised him that so close to New York the country could be so rustic. It could easily have been England where he had been at school, Devon or Hampshire or the rolling hills of the Cotswolds.

It was one o'clock before he pulled into Stockbridge and parked his hired Buick across the street from the Red Lion Inn. As he climbed from the car a thin drizzle was still falling.

A war memorial stood close to where he had parked.

He noticed that a small vase of flowers had been placed in front of it, just a few gladioli and gardenia, their white petals fading into the colour of old ivory. A week before, Adam would have walked past the memorial without more than a second look. But today somehow the sight of those few wilting flowers touched an emotional chord and he lingered there, reading the inscription that was carved into the weathered granite of the memorial:

> To her sons, beloved and honoured,
> who died for their country in the
> great war of the rebellion,
> Stockbridge in grateful remembrance
> has raised this monument.
> AD 1866.

Adam took a deep breath, the feelings welling up inside. Beloved and honoured – such fine words. They had rallied to the flag, all bugles and patriotism, such an easy choice. Dear God, if only his had been that easy.

How would they honour him, he wondered, if he was struck down? With twenty years in jail, that's how. He looked up into the grey sky, letting the drizzle hit his face. Then suddenly, conflicting emotions tearing at each other, he swung away from the memorial. Maudlin contemplation wasn't going to get him anywhere. He knew why he was in this small Connecticut town. And honour had nothing to do with it.

If honour had been so important he would have refused to kow-tow to Triad blackmail, he would have gone straight to the police and to hell with Harry's wishes. He would have been a good citizen. He would have lived in hiding. He would have stood at his mother's graveside after the Triads had butchered her, he would have stood by Nicky's grave, too, courageous and dignified. That would have been the honourable thing to do. But damn honour!

Life – that's all that counted. That's why he was here. Life and love. He had made his decision. He knew the risks. If he was looking for inward peace, he was deluding himself. In the eyes of the world, he knew that the ends, no matter how honourable, could never justify the means. So there was no point in bitterness, no point in tearing himself apart. There was only one avenue open to him, that was to get on with the job and be done with it.

It was warm inside the inn with a log fire burning; cosy and hospitable. He sat in the bar and had a glass of the house red which calmed him. Then he went through to the dining room and ordered the game pie. He was served by a waitress in a blue gingham dress, a tawny-haired buxom woman who smiled at him a lot and asked how long he would be in town. 'Are you a travelling salesman?' she asked.

Adam was tempted to laugh. 'Yes,' he said, 'you could put it that way.'

Later he overheard her talking to a couple of the other waitresses as they gathered round the sweets trolley. 'I think he's cute as hell. Have you seen those dreamy black eyes? And that hair with the white streaks through it. Like snow on a bitumen roof. Do you know if he's staying overnight?'

'What is he, d'ya reckon? Italian?'

'I dunno, there's something Oriental about him.'

'Oriental? Naaw.'

Adam enjoyed the attention, the harmless flirtation. If nothing else, it took his mind off other things. He had a second glass of red wine with his food and, when he got up from the table at 2.30, he was more relaxed, better prepared for the encounter. Deep inside, like a trapped echo, a sense of uneasiness remained. Fear or conscience, call it what you will, Adam knew it would remain with him until drugs were just a distant memory.

He walked out on to the verandah. It had stopped raining. Shafts of watery sunshine cut down through the clouds, glinting off the puddles. He looked around. There was nobody on the porch but a Dodge truck was parked on the road in front of the Inn. It was a hard-used farm vehicle, mud-splattered and dented, with sacks of chicken feed in the back.

A man leant against the truck smoking a cigarette. He looked about fifty, well weathered and scrawny. He wore a lumber jacket, boots and a faded Mets baseball cap. The man looked at Adam then flicked the cigarette away.

'You that fella Blake?'

'That's right.'

'Got wheels here?'

'Across the street.'

'Follow me.' And, without a further word, he climbed into the Dodge.

For twenty minutes Adam followed him along curling country lanes until the truck turned off the tarmac onto a dirt track. Thick woodland closed in on either side casting the track into dappled shadow. The wheels of their vehicles churned up the mud. They descended a steep slope into a vale, following a stream with fallow ground on either side. They crossed at a ford, beginning to climb, and Adam could see the house.

It stood high above the vale against a backdrop of cedar and oak. It was a double-storey dwelling, painted white with a shingle roof and bluestone chimney as tall as a mast. It was symmetrical, sturdy, agelessly elegant, a perfect example of eighteenth-century country colonial architecture. To the right of the house, further down the hill, stood a couple of barns painted plum red; further down the hill still, on the far side of an apple orchard, he glimpsed a paddock with horses grazing.

They drew up some distance from the house, parking by an old ivy-clad wall, and Adam climbed out of the Buick.

The driver of the Dodge came over, a cigarette clenched between his teeth. 'Got to search you,' he said.

Adam smiled. 'I'm not carrying a gun.'

'Guns ain't the problem.'

'What then?'

'Recordin' devices, body tapes mainly. Suggest you open your shirt. Save a few buttons poppin'.' The driver conducted a brisk body search and, when he was finished, nodded towards the house. 'They'll be waitin' for you.'

'Thank you,' said Adam.

He realised how incongruous it sounded thanking a man for frisking him. But the driver simply grunted, returning to his truck where he began to unload the chicken feed.

Adam did up the last button of his shirt, adjusted his tie

and turned towards the main house. In the shadow of the entrance, he could see two men waiting for him, and one dog: a very large, magnificently regal Irish wolfhound.

As he drew closer, skirting the puddles in the dirt, one of the two men came forward to greet him. 'Ah, Mr Blake, so good of you to come all this way. What a pity the weather has turned inclement. But you're here safely, that's what counts.'

Adam recognised his voice from the telephone, the same cultured tone, airy and theatrical. The man looked to be in his late sixties, small-boned and pixie-like, his white hair fluffing up in the breeze. He was casually and expensively dressed, very much in the European style, very un-American.

'I'm so pleased you had the game pie at the Red Lion. Marvellous, isn't it? Toby Casement is my name. But please, no ceremony, just call me Toby.' He held out his hand and Adam noticed how truly that indicated his age; bony, sprinkled with brown liver spots.

'I trust you were able to ensure I wasn't followed,' said Adam with the flicker of a smile, more irony in it than mirth. 'For my sake as well as yours.'

Toby Casement laughed as they shook hands, a kind of bird-like trill. 'Security is a sad fact of life, Adam.'

Far off over the trees, low grey clouds trailed tendrils of rain. A few drops touched their faces, cold and prickly. Adam turned up the collar of his jacket.

'We'd best go in,' said Casement.

They approached the porch where the second man stood with the Irish wolfhound. 'This is my partner, Patrick Ryan,' said Casement and he called out,

'Patrick, meet our friend from Hong Kong!'

Ryan obviously wasn't as eager or outgoing. He gave a guarded nod, patently suspicious, patted the dog and then turned ahead of them to enter the house.

They made a strange combination, thought Adam. Ryan looked to be in his mid-fifties, younger than Casement by a decade or more, beefily built with the pouchy looks of an ex-pugilist. His face was florid, as if he liked the hooch too much, and he had gingery hair. The ballet master and the boxer, thought Adam, classifying them both.

It was Ryan's eyes, however, that attracted Adam's attention most, those sad, defiant Irish eyes that spoke of drink and hardship and endless vendettas.

They entered the house. Mozart's *Eine Kleine Nachtmusik* was being played. That was Casement's choice, Adam guessed. And the furnishings, too, all peach and pastels, pale polished wood and antique paintings. There was an air of lightness and contrast and perfect taste.

Adam hadn't anticipated anybody like Toby Casement and it was disconcerting. What induced a man like him to become a drug dealer? Back in Hong Kong, Cheng Tak-shing's menace had advanced before him like the boiling black curtain of a typhoon. But at least Cheng was predictable. With Casement, however, all of Adam's preconceptions had been turned on their head. How did he deal with the man? How did he react to him?

Adam was ushered into a spacious study with a view down over the vale. Ryan had already taken a corner seat, leaning forward to stroke the Irish wolfhound which lay at his feet.

'Would you care for some tea?' asked Casement.

'No thank you, later perhaps.' Again it seemed so out of place: tea and heroin, an afternoon in the country.

Above the fireplace hung a portrait in oils, so large that it dominated the room. It was of a man dressed in a frockcoat who stood in a pose of high Victorian seriousness. It had been painted in the grand manner with bold contrasts of light and shade, all blacks and browns, and heavily varnished.

'He was my great-uncle,' said Casement, his voice suddenly subdued, almost reverential. 'He passed on to a better life the year I was born. The exact date was the third of August 1916 in Pentonville Prison in London, that was the date the English hanged him.'

Hanged him! My God, thought Adam ludicrously, don't tell me he was a drug dealer, too!

Toby Casement stepped nearer to the portrait. 'The English attempted to despatch him as a common felon. But all they achieved was his immortality. I was present at the service in Dublin in 1965 when at last we were able to inter his bones in Irish soil. I can say honestly that it was the most moving movement of my life.'

There was a brass plaque at the bottom of the ornate gold frame. Adam stepped closer to the painting so that he could read it:

Sir Roger David Casement
(1864–1916)
Irish Patriot

Adam tried to drag what little he knew about the man out of the dim recesses of his memory. 'Wasn't he a British diplomat?'

Toby Casement seemed pleased that Adam should know even that much. 'A diplomat, and a humanitarian, too. He reported on the appalling conditions of the plantation labourers in the Belgian Congo and Peru. He was knighted for his services. But of course the English stripped him of all his honours before they hanged him – another futile gesture.'

'I remember something about him going to Germany in the early days of the First World War,' said Adam, wanting to sound out Casement a little more.

'The First World War was a stupid, senseless conflict,' said Casement with a bitter edge to his voice that was out of character. 'There was only one war that concerned my great-uncle – that was the struggle for Irish liberty. And if Germany was able to advance that cause, he would have been failing in his duty to have ignored the opportunity. Yes, you're right, he did go to Germany. He returned to Ireland in a German submarine just a few days before the Easter Rising. But he was betrayed and arrested—'

'Mr Blake didn't come here for a history lesson,' interrupted Ryan. 'If we've got business to do, let's get on with it.'

Toby Casement flushed high on his cheeks. He smiled apologetically. 'Yes, of course. Do forgive me.'

Adam retreated to the sofa near the window. Slug Delaney, Patrick Ryan, both clearly of Irish extract. And now Casement with his impeccable Eire pedigree.

One thing was obvious, he wasn't dealing with an everyday group of traffickers, in it for the profits and nothing else. There was more to these men.

Adam looked up and saw that Ryan had anticipated his thoughts. Those scowling Irish eyes were staring at him intently. 'Are you looking for motives, Mr Blake?'

Adam smiled disarmingly. 'It's not my business to look for motives, Mr Ryan.'

'A nice pat answer, I'm sure. But pat answers tend to hide more than they say.'

'Then let me put it simply,' Adam replied. 'I'm here to talk about three things – price, quantity and delivery dates. Your motives are your business. And mine are mine.'

Ryan gave a small sniff. 'But you've made your motives clear, Mr Blake. They're to help your brother, that's right, isn't it? Pay off his debts, stop somebody cutting his throat – those are your motives.'

'That's right.'

'And when you've achieved them, when your brother's as safe as an egg in cotton wool, what happens then?'

Adam knew what he wanted to hear. 'All being well,' he said, 'I'll keep delivering the merchandise.'

'Why?' Ryan looked cynical. 'How does that serve your purposes?'

'Profit, Mr Ryan. Profit. In eighteen months, if all goes well, I could make enough to last me a lifetime.'

'What about your architecture?'

'Architecture isn't a priesthood, it's a job, that's all.'

'So you want to stick with it, deliver stuff on a long-term basis?'

'Yes,' Adam lied.

Ryan and Casement glanced at each other. Then Casement said, 'Mr Delaney made it clear, I hope, that the first delivery was to be in the form of a trial run only.'

'He did.'

'We would be interested in two units.'

'That's acceptable.'

'How soon can you deliver?'

'Give me a month,' said Adam.

'Two weeks,' snapped Ryan.

'Two weeks is too tight.'

'Two weeks will tell us if you're all wind or if there's some substance in you.'

Adam looked straight at him. 'Very well,' he said. 'Two weeks it is.' He just hoped to hell two weeks was feasible.

'As far as price is concerned,' said Casement, 'we consider that one hundred and twenty thousand a unit is equitable.'

Adam smiled. 'I'm afraid I can't go below one hundred and forty thousand.'

'Split the difference,' said Ryan. 'One hundred and thirty. That's a top offer for a first run. Take it or leave it.'

Adam simply shook his head. 'You seem to forget, gentlemen, that I have to deliver within two weeks. That places pressures on me. And pressures, as you both know, translate into costs.'

Casement conceded with a smile. 'Very well, Adam, one hundred and forty thousand it is.'

Adam remained politely impassive. 'Assuming the

first delivery goes through smoothly, what quantities do you anticipate after that?'

'Depends on demand,' said Ryan, picking at his teeth. 'No way we can committ ourselves.'

'Very well,' said Adam. 'But if I can't plan ahead, you can't expect assured deliveries. It takes two to tango.'

Toby Casement laughed his high canary-like trill. 'Absolutely right, Adam, it does take two to tango. So let's not beat around the bush – if you'll excuse the mixed metaphors. At the moment, as you know, we have certain arrangements with a Singaporean gentleman—'

'Gentleman? Two-timing little shit,' muttered Ryan.

Casement smiled thinly. 'We have had our differences with the man and are in the process of disentangling ourselves. However, we do have certain commitments to him. So, if you understand my meaning, Adam, as you walk up the steps, he walks down.'

'Just tell him,' grunted Ryan irritably.

'We are looking to an eventual minimum of ten units a month,' said Casement.

'But there will be a lead-in period?'

Casement nodded. 'It will be better for both sides, I'm sure.'

'So what size of delivery should I plan for next time?' asked Adam.

'Six, maybe seven units,' said Ryan.

'When would that be?'

'We're talking about thirty-day intervals.'

'And after that?'

'Eight to ten units.'

Adam absorbed the figures, making quick mental

calculations. The first delivery – the two units – would get him virtually nowhere. He would cover interest and chip a little off the capital. But the second delivery would gross a minimum of eight hundred and forty thousand, enough to clear the full debt. On that basis, if everything went according to plan, he could have this nightmare finished within the next six to seven weeks. Just two deliveries, that would be it.

Casement's pixie-like features were shining. 'So, Adam, we have an agreement?'

A dry smile flickered at the corners of Adam's mouth. 'Yes,' he said, 'we have an agreement.'

All the way back to New York it rained: cold, dark and depressing.

Perhaps, with the meeting over, with the quantities and prices agreed and the tension seeping out of him, the feeling of anti-climax was inevitable. But Adam had never felt more alone or more vulnerable. It was at times like this that he longed for Nicky. She had a way of dragging him out of himself, of making him laugh. 'There you go, lost in your own head again. You dream too much, Adam. If somebody paid you to design castles in the sky it would be a different story.' When he felt defeated by the world, Nicky had a way of giving him new courage. She was a practical woman, she got things done. And, oh God, courage was what he needed now. An agreement to supply heroin was one thing but the physical delivery of the stuff was something else entirely.

Forty-eight hours later, punch drunk after the flight across the Pacific, Adam was back in Hong Kong. He landed at Kai Tak under slate-grey skies on a warm, humid evening and drove straight to his apartment on the Peak.

He spoke to his mother on the telephone. She was holding up well, she said, and, yes, she had been to see Harry. She was amazed how much stronger he was, physically and psychologically. 'He relies on you so much, Adam,' she said. 'You mean a great deal to him.' Adam didn't answer.

He telephoned his secretary at home. He wanted to know if there was any news from Switzerland. But she said there was none, just a brief letter from Helmut Gasser to say that regrettably the board's decision might be delayed a week or two due to illness. So he remained in limbo.

Last of all, he telephoned Nicky. But there was no reply from her apartment, none from her office and when he contacted one of her associates, he learnt that she was still in Canada. Something new had come up, in Ottowa this time. She wasn't likely to be back for at least another week to ten days.

'Isn't there any chance she'll be back earlier?' asked Adam.

'Afraid not,' said her associate. 'In fact there's a chance she may even have to go on to Montreal. I'll give you our Ottowa office number if you like. You can try speaking to her direct.'

'What's the time difference?'

'Give it four hours or so and then try phoning.'

Four hours. Adam looked at his watch. That would make it one in the morning. There was no way he could stay awake that long. He went to the fridge, cracked open a can of beer then flopped onto his bed. His mind was whirling, full of doubts, self-pity, full of dark foreboding. Damn it, he thought, why wasn't she here? He needed her so badly. And, when eventually he fell asleep, it was for twelve straight hours.

It was late afternoon when he made it to the Queen Elizabeth Hospital. He had just quarter of an hour to spare before the custodial ward was closed to visitors.

As his mother had said, Harry was looking better. His cheeks were filling out, dimples reappearing. Adam had to admire him. Harry was a survivor. 'So what did you think of them?' Harry asked. 'Casement, I mean, and Ryan.'

Adam still wasn't sure. 'They make an odd pair, not what I expected.'

Harry grinned. 'And what did you expect, Italian-Americans who have to shave six times a day, guys with broken noses and bulges under their jackets?'

Adam couldn't help smile. 'Something like that.'

'They're businessmen. Brokers, facilitators, that's all,' said Harry expansively as if Ryan and Casement dealt in nothing more threatening than car exhausts or avocado pears. 'Casement is a very cultured man.'

Adam gave a sceptical shrug. What in the hell did culture have to do with it? Even here, facing half of his life in jail, Harry didn't seem to appreciate what an immoral, filthy trade the drugs business was. He was oblivious to it, bereft of conscience. Brokers, facilitators – no, they were more than that, they were criminals, all of them. And Adam knew that included himself. Now, no matter what his motives, he was no better than they were.

'I've got to get the first consignment to them within two weeks,' he said in a toneless voice.

'Two weeks? Why in hell did you agree to a crazy time limit like that?'

'I had no choice.'

Harry looked distinctly unhappy. 'I don't like it.'

'Like it or not, I'm stuck with it. I need some way of contacting Cheng Tak-shing.'

'Okay,' said Harry, 'I'll give you his pager number. But for God's sake, Adam, as much as you hate him, remember you've got to do business with the man.'

It wasn't until the following morning that Adam was able to make contact. He expected Cheng to be guarded and suspicious but, over the telephone at least, he exhibited an almost eerie good nature.

'Did you have a profitable trip to the States, Mr Blake?'

'That's what I would like to see you about.'

'When?'

'Today if possible.'

'Do you know the Shang City Restaurant?'

'Across in Tsim Sha Tsui?'

'Come at noon. Speak to the captain on the third floor. He'll bring you to my table. I think maybe we can do some business, Mr Blake, good business for both of us. What do you say?'

Adam answered with acid in his voice, 'You got me into this, Mr Cheng. You tell me.'

The Shang City Restaurant did a roaring trade in *dim sum*, the day-time eating of the Cantonese. The third floor was the bottom one of three, each seating over a thousand people, and by 12.30 each day every table was taken.

Dim sum in Hong Kong, especially in establishments like this, wasn't the polite Oriental smorgasbord that it had been transformed into in New York or London. Here it remained a brash trough-guzzling jamboree. The waitresses, with voices like crows, pushed trolleys from table to table screeching out their wares - spring rolls, shrimp dumplings, barbecued pork buns, chicken's feet, noodles, pig's intestines, custard tarts - every colour, every smell. All of it was consumed to a cacophony of sound, shouting and laughter and the squealing of kids, that even a Neopolitan fish hawker would find unbearable. Most Westerners were appalled by it, the noise, the food, everything. But the Chinese lived to eat and *dim sum* was the heartbeat of each day. Adam loved it all. Only his purpose for being there soured the occasion.

He arrived purposefully late. It was a futile gesture, he knew it. But he didn't want to be seen to be openly grovelling to the bastard and it was 12.20 when he took the crowded elevator to the third floor. The restaurant captain, undoubtedly a Sun Yee On Triad member, led him through the crush of tables and jostling waitresses to a far corner table with a view out over the harbour. A man sat at the table nibbling irritably at a bowl of steamed dumplings.

'You're late,' said Cheng Tak-shing.

'I'm a busy man,' said Adam.

Cheng grunted irritably. 'And do you think I have all day to sit here?'

Cheng was younger than Adam had expected; in his early thirties. He was squat and heavy, bullock-like, with a round unattractive face and pockmarked skin. He was almost bald, the last few strands of his hair brushed sideways across his scalp in lank rat's tails. The nickname, Dai Ngan, suited him, thought Adam. His bulging eyes gave him an air of constant, cold-blooded menace; physically, he mirrored his reputation: crude, aggressive, shrewd.

'So, tell me, how much stuff do you want?' grumbled Cheng as he picked with his chopsticks into a mess of noodles.

'First things first,' said Adam.

Cheng looked up. 'And what's that?'

'I want to know exactly how much my brother owes. I want to know exactly what I've got to repay – capital and interest.'

Cheng gave a casual shrug. 'About nine hundred thousand.'

'Nine hundred – that's ludicrous! What about the quarter of a million I paid?'

'Interest . . .'

'How much interest do you charge, for Chrissake?'

Cheng chewed at his noodles, long strands of pasta dangling from his mouth. 'Normal rates for this business.'

'And what,' Adam asked 'are *normal* rates?'

'You'll have to ask my investor that.'

'I don't have access to your investor. That's why I'm asking you.'

Cheng wiped the grease off his chin. 'Difficult to say. Anywhere between five hundred and a thousand per cent.'

Adam gave an incredulous gasp, almost a laugh, of sheer disbelief. 'You're mad. I'm not paying anything like that.'

Cheng cast him a quick baleful look. 'Then, Mr Blake, we go back to square one.'

Adam's temper snapped. 'Don't you threaten me,' he hissed. 'If I have to, I'll call this whole thing off. I'll go to the police, I'll fight you all the way, you bastard. Then your investor won't get a thing, not a bloody rupee!'

Cheng looked at him, eyes glazed. 'Except blood.'

Adam stared straight back, filled with loathing for the man. 'Blood doesn't pay the bills. Your investor knows that. Blood just dirties the linen and puts men like you behind bars. I hear you got away with it once. Don't push your luck. So I suggest you go talk to your investor. Tell him I'll pay a reasonable rate but nothing like the figures you've quoted. Tell him that compromise is the name of the game. Otherwise we have no game. Do you understand?'

'Your brother, Fat Boy, he knew the rates.'

'My brother isn't paying, I am.'

Cheng hesitated, not sure what to do. He raised his hand, calling for a waiter to refill the teapot on the table. Then, without warning, he gave a broad, malicious grin. 'Okay,' he said, 'I'll talk to him.'

'When will you get back to me?'

'When I can. Like you, Mr Blake, my investor is a busy man.' He scooped a basket of chilli tripe from a passing trolley and placed it in the centre of the table. 'Now, Mr Blake, why don't we stop threatening each other and talk about the real business. How much stuff do you want?'

Adam exhaled, trying to relax. In his own crude way, Cheng was right. He remembered what Harry had said, too; as much as you hate him, remember you've got to do business with the man. 'For the first shipment,' he said, 'just two.'

'And after that?'

'In the second delivery, six, maybe seven.'

Cheng scratched his ear. 'When do you want delivery of the first two?'

'I have to ship them within ten days.'

'So soon?'

'That shouldn't be any problem for you, not two units.'

'What do you think we're dealing with here,' said Cheng, 'a consignment of cameras? You've got a few things to learn.'

'Can you supply or not?' Adam asked sharply.

'Sure I can supply. No problem. Except it's going to cost.'

'How much?'

'In US dollars, twenty-three thousand a unit.'

Adam glared at him. 'I'm not a fool.'

Cheng shrugged. 'There are expenses.'

'I'll pay you twelve.'

'Fuck your mother.'

'Then give me a realistic price.'

'Seventeen thousand.'

'Fourteen is my highest offer.'

Cheng stared down at his food. He burped. 'I want to help you,' he said. 'Why are we arguing like this? Okay, fifteen thousand. But cash, no credit. I don't deal like that, not any more, not since your brother.'

Adam knew he wouldn't be able to push him any lower. 'All right,' he said. 'I agree.'

Then Cheng smiled as if they were the best of companions. Emotionally he was like a yo-yo. 'That's fine,' he said. He took a mouthful of the chilli tripe, swallowed it, decided he had eaten enough and lit a cigarette. He leant back in his chair, smoke curling round his pitted moon of a face. 'Tell me, brother of Harry Lee, how do you plan to get the stuff into the States?' he asked. 'Have you worked that out? What are you going to do, carry it yourself?'

It was a point Adam hadn't considered. Up until now he had just been taking one tortuous step after another. 'I don't know,' he answered. 'Maybe.'

'Then you're as dead as your brother. Fuck your mother – deader! At least the Fat Boy can survive behind bars. But you?' He shook his head. 'Do you think your brother is the first man to continue trading when he's in jail? Where do you think bail money comes from? How do you think those fancy fat lawyers get their fees? And do you think your brother is the first man in history to get his family to help out?'

'What are you trying to tell me?' asked Adam.

'I'm telling you that the local cops and the American DEA might want to know why you're travelling to New York so much. I'm telling you that maybe next time they'll search your bags.' Cheng gave a rough, throaty laugh. 'Look at you – your face is a book. What chance do you think you stand? Maybe the cops are suspicious already but they've got nothing on you, not yet, not until you put the stuff in your briefcase and present them with a gift. This time maybe you'll get away with it, maybe. But after that –' And he drew a slow finger across his throat.

What he said made sense. But Adam remained suspicious. 'So what do I do?' he asked.

'You need a mule.'

'A what?'

'Somebody to carry the stuff.'

'And how do I get one?' asked Adam, knowing the answer.

'People can always be found, Mr Blake, even at short notice.' Cheng smiled. 'For a suitable commission, of course.'

Her name was Polianna Kim. She was a Korean air hostess employed by Cathay Pacific and, according to Cheng, was one of the very best. Cheng set up their meeting which took place the following evening, just the two of them, in a room at the Wanchai Ramada. It was like visiting a high-class whore, thought Adam.

She had got there first and came to the door when he knocked. She was tall and slim with her black hair pulled tightly back in a bun. Her skin was pale, pearl-white. She had a broad Korean face, her eyes wide-set, and when she smiled her mouth opened a little, showing the red bud of her tongue.

After he had entered, she latched the door then walked over to the bed, her hips swaying. She was very physical, very aware of herself. She sat on the bed, curling her feet up beneath her. When she spoke, it was in fluent English and her voice was low, full of timbre. 'I must warn you that my prices are not cheap.'

Adam smiled. 'How much is not cheap?'

'I charge five thousand dollars a unit – greenbacks, not Hong Kong. But I guarantee safe delivery.'

'What gives you that kind of confidence?' asked Adam.

She looked at him and smiled. 'I have a boy friend in US Customs stationed at San Francisco Airport. Every time I fly in he meets me.'

'Are you saying your baggage is never searched?'

She stretched her long legs like a cat stirring from its sleep. 'Sometimes, of course . . .' And she gave a languid, very sensual smile. 'His friends hold up my panties and wink and joke a lot, you know the sort of thing. It is never serious.'

Adam nodded. He understood. 'Once you've cleared Customs, how do you get the stuff to me?'

'That is no problem,' she answered. 'I have a friend who works at the Hertz car hire counter. She is Korean, like me. I always go to see her there, we always talk. I will carry my suitcase to the counter and place it down next to me. You will have a suitcase, too, the same colour, the same shape.'

'So we swap?'

She smiled again. She was constantly smiling. 'As you see, it is very simple.'

'Who organises the cases?'

'When Dai Ngan supplies the stuff, he will supply two cases.'

But that still left the question of timing. 'When are you next scheduled to fly to San Francisco?' asked Adam.

'I am afraid it is the day after tomorrow,' she said. 'After that it will be another three weeks before I fly the same route. Can you organise things in so short a time?'

Adam's only concern was his ability to raise the cash in time, forty thousand dollars – thirty thousand for the stuff and ten thousand for her fees. 'It should be okay,' he said.

She handed him a card. 'This is the address and telephone number of a friend's apartment where I'll be staying tomorrow night. When you have the stuff, ring me.'

Adam took the card from her, noting that it was on the island at Jardine's Lookout; reasonably central. 'Until tomorrow then,' he said, moving towards the door.

But she remained seated on the bed, watching him with a smile in her eyes. 'You don't have to go immediately,' she said. 'The room has been hired for the whole night. You seem like a very nice man, very gentle. Two hundred and fifty dollars – greenbacks – is all I charge.'

Adam was momentarily flustered. Christ, he thought, on her back or standing up – she's making it every way. 'Maybe another time,' he said with an embarrassed smile.

She pouted. 'Don't you care for me?'

'No, it's not that . . .'

'What is it then?' And there came that smile again. 'You'll see I'm very good. Have you ever done it with a Korean woman, a woman like me?'

'I'm afraid I'm strapped for cash right now,' said Adam, not wishing to antagonise her.

'If you cannot afford two hundred and fifty,' she said, teasing him, 'things must be very bad for you.'

Adam grinned foolishly. 'Believe me, they're even worse.'

Later that night, after leaving the Ramada, Adam used Cheng's pager number to contact him. The two units were to be handed over the following night. The agreed place was the car park on top of Ocean Terminal, the agreed time was 9.30 p.m. Adam had one working day in which to raise the cash.

The following morning he was in his office early, contacting friends in the financial world, people he hoped would be able to bend the rules a little in his favour. He knew it was hopeless going to his bankers. He had reached the limits of his overdrafts and had no further security to offer. Shares and insurance policies had been pledged. There was even some kind of notarial bond securing the office equipment and his car. About the only things he owned outright were the clothes he stood in and his wristwatch.

A number of friends in finance companies agreed to see him but the visits turned out to be fruitless. They couldn't make a decision without statements of assets and liabilities and, as soon as Adam supplied them, they could see just how deep in debt he already was. If the

Swiss commission had been confirmed, or something equally big, it would have been different. But, without major work on the drawing boards, it was the same old story: no further assets, no further cash.

Nor could he approach any of his close friends on a purely personal basis. He had already milked them dry raising the first amount and not repaid a penny.

It appeared that all his options were exhausted, all except one.

It saddened him to have to take it. He held back as long as he could. But by mid-afternoon he knew there was no other way. So he left the office and drove up to his mother's apartment.

He couldn't tell her the real reason why he needed the money. Apart from anything, it would make her an accessory to trafficking in drugs. At the very outset, when he had first agreed to Harry's proposal, he had resolved that his mother must never know the full truth. He knew how she would react, he knew it would tear her apart. So, when he reached the apartment that afternoon, he said something suitably ambiguous, a lie wrapped in a truth. He needed the cash to 'satisfy Harry's creditors', that was the way he expressed it.

Forty thousand dollars amounted to almost three quarters of her savings. But, of course, she didn't hesitate for a moment. Adam drove her into Central to the bank and, as she climbed out of the car, she pressed him for the third or fourth time. 'Is that all you need? Are you sure? Because, if you need any more, please, just tell me.'

'No, that's all,' said Adam, his heart going out to her, his insides churning with guilt.

His mother saw the look on his face and smiled. 'What's the matter, do you feel you're letting me down? Do you think because I'm retired and live on a pension that I'm incapable of helping?'

'It's not that,' he answered lamely. 'I don't know, it just seems all wrong.'

'Why?' asked his mother. 'What does the money mean if I can't help my children? Don't you see, Adam? I'm happy to pay. I'd be happy to pay my last cent. Just so long as Harry is safe, that's all I worry about. So long as they don't harm him any more.'

Adam kept his 9.30 p.m. appointment. Cheng was waiting under the huge neon signs that shone across the harbour from the roof of Ocean Terminal. When Adam parked the Volvo, he saw Cheng pacing up and down, chain-smoking; a squat figure drenched in electric blue from the 'Yashica' sign above him.

Adam handed him an envelope. 'It's the equivalent in Hong Kong dollars,' he said. 'I didn't get the chance to change it into US currency.'

Cheng gave a quick shrug, shoving the envelope into the pocket of his nylon windcheater. 'Somebody will come up from the shops carrying two suitcases,' he said. 'Both cases will have labels on them like they've just been bought. When you see the guy carrying the cases, go to your car and open the boot. He'll put both suitcases inside. Tip him, make it look natural. Then drive away.'

'Okay,' said Adam. But he noticed that, as Cheng spoke, he appeared agitated, much more so than when they had last met at the Shang City Restaurant. He kept sniffing and rubbing his forehead as if he had a migraine. There was a look about him, too, that Adam couldn't quite place: distracted, almost feverish.

'Which suitcase contains the merchandise?' Adam asked. 'Is it marked in any way?'

'Yeah, the one with the price tag on it contains the stuff.'

'Is the stuff hidden inside?'

'Yeah, I've had a false bottom built.' Cheng glanced anxiously at his watch, then looked towards the distant door that led up from the shopping mall. 'Your guy will be here any minute, I don't want to hang around.'

'Why, what's the problem?' asked Adam. Cheng's behaviour was beginning to spook him. 'What's going on?'

'Nothing is going on, everything is fine.' Cheng stubbed a cigarette out beneath his heel, immediately lighting another. 'The stuff is your property now. That means it's your risk. Why should we both stand here like dummies?'

Adam looked at him, trying to find the cause for his agitation. And, instinctively, as soon as he realised, the question came. 'You use the stuff yourself, don't you? You chase the dragon?'

Cheng looked startled. He curled his lips back, glaring at him with those green-black chameleon eyes. 'That's my affair,' he muttered. 'Fuck you, Mr Architect, you're a dealer now – you've got no right to judge.'

'I'm not judging,' said Adam quietly.

But Cheng just spat at Adam's feet and swung angrily away, muttering beneath his breath.

Adam watched him leave. The overdeveloped chest on the stocky legs gave Cheng a clumsy, top-heavy look. He seemed almost to waddle. So he was a *do yau*, an addict. That explained a great deal.

Adam walked to the parapet that looked out over the harbour. There was a stiff breeze blowing. The night air smelt of brine and diesel. A million lights were reflected in pyramids of gold off the shining black water. Such a beautiful sight, he thought.

He was waiting for his first consignment of heroin, enough to put him away for fifteen years, and had expected to be palpably afraid. But it was all too unreal, he was just a character in a pantomime, a charade. Even now he couldn't bring himself to accept the harsh reality of it. How could he, an architect, an honest man, be involved in anything so outrageous?

He checked his watch. Three minutes had passed since Cheng's departure. He was becoming anxious. 'Come on,' he muttered into the teeth of the wind, 'come on, come on, where are you?' Then, to his relief, in the distant doorway he saw the slim silhouette of a figure dragging two suitcases.

Walking over to the car, his heart thudding in his chest, Adam opened the boot and waited. He expected the deliverer of the two cases to be one of Cheng's Triad street soldiers, some tattooed low-life from the alleys of Mongkok. But, as the small figure drew closer, stepping into the green and electric-blue glare of the neon signs, he saw that he wasn't a man at all, he was just a boy; no more than thirteen or fourteen.

The boy came up to the car, checking the registration

number, and grinned, totally unconcerned. He spoke in Cantonese. 'I've been told to bring these two suitcases to the owner of the silver Volvo. Is that you?'

Adam gave a grave nod. 'Yes,' he murmured, 'that's me.'

The boy placed the suitcases in the boot. They were Samsonite, both mushroom in colour, both with combination locks; expensive pieces of luggage. Adam confirmed that only one of them had the price tag still tied to the handle before he closed the boot. He didn't have any loose change on him so he gave the boy the only change he had, a twenty-dollar note.

'Thank you,' said the boy, clearly delighted, 'thank you very much.' And off he jogged, whistling snatches of some local Cantonese pop tune.

Adam watched the boy until he had disappeared through the doorway. Either he's the best little actor in the world, he thought, or he doesn't have the faintest idea what he's just delivered.

He had borrowed a portable telephone for the night and, standing by the car with the wind tugging at his hair, he dialled Polianna Kim's number. 'I've got the stuff,' he said.

'I'll be waiting,' she answered.

'When should I come over?'

'Come now.'

He drove carefully, almost too carefully, terrified of being stopped by the police. He was so acutely aware of the two blocks of Number 4 heroin lying in the boot that they seemed to radiate an energy of their own, burning into his back.

He returned to the island, driving through the Cross Harbour Tunnel and up to Jardine's Lookout. The traffic was thin and he made it within twenty minutes. He parked opposite the apartment block where Polianna Kim was spending the night, got out, opened the boot and removed the suitcase with the price tag tied to the handle.

A young Chinese couple, walking a poodle, went past. The man saw the suitcase and asked pleasantly, 'Going on holiday?'

Adam smiled. 'Yes, a few days away . . .'

He let the couple walk on, took one deep breath and crossed the road to the apartment block. The block was called Blissful Heights. He had to smile at the unintended irony of it.

He took the elevator to the eighth floor and rang the bell of apartment 8B. Polianna Kim came to the door. She was wearing a dove-grey tracksuit and white joggers. Her hair which, the night before, had been brushed back into a bun, now fell to her shoulders in luscious black clouds. 'Come in,' she said.

Adam stepped inside. The apartment was small and untidy, smelling of powder and perfume. An old Beatles album was playing 'It's a Hard Day's Night'. Appropriate, he thought.

He handed her the suitcase. She took it, feeling its weight. Then she lay it on the sofa and opened it, probing for the false bottom. 'They've done a good job,' she said, speaking with the calm, knowing confidence of a professional.

Adam made no comment, just handed her the envelope containing her fee.

She smiled at him, her lips parting. 'Would you like a drink? You look a little tense.'

'No thanks, I have to be on my way.'

'You're new to the game, aren't you?'

'Is it that obvious?' he asked.

She gave a gentle, half-teasing laugh. 'Remember that when we make the swap, you'll get my clothes and I'll get yours. I have clothes in my boy friend's apartment in San Francisco so it's no problem for me. But you'll have to take some extra in your hand luggage, either that or buy some more when you get to New York.'

'Thanks, I'll remember.'

'Are you sure you wouldn't like a drink?'

'Thanks, but it's getting late. I've still got a hundred and one things to do.'

An impish look came into her wide-set eyes. 'So you still don't like me?'

Adam smiled. 'I still don't have the extra cash.'

He drove up to his apartment on the Peak, up high into the wet, moisture-dripping mist that blanketed the mountain at this time of year. He threw a few items of old clothing into the second suitcase, the one that he would be taking. Then, switching off the lights, he lay on his bed, listening to the slow whirr of the ceiling fan. He tried to fall asleep. Sleep more than anything was what he needed now. But sleep, of course, was impossible.

* * *

At 10.05 the next morning, Cathay Pacific flight CX800 took off from Kai Tak for Vancouver and San Francisco. It was fourteen hours across the Pacific, a flight that seemed to drone on for ever. Physically, emotionally, Adam was exhausted but he could still only manage a short, fitful sleep. He watched one of the movies, listened to music on the headphones and tried to read. But most of the time he just counted the slow seeping of the hours like a condemned man waiting for dawn.

About halfway through the flight, when he went forward to the toilet, he glimpsed Polianna Kim dispensing drinks in the business section. By that stage the constant tension had knotted the muscles in the back of his neck but she appeared to be totally relaxed, in every respect the perfect cabin attendant; efficient, demure, attentive. Adam could only wonder at her.

They approached Vancouver in the early morning, dipping beneath the clouds. Adam looked north along the glacial coastline, over the silver sea to those endless ranges of stone-black mountains tipped with snow. Every time he flew in, he always marvelled at the sight. Nicky's birthplace . . . God, how he missed her now.

There was an hour and a half on the ground; time for a black coffee that he didn't need, more time to wait and worry, feeling the tension gnaw at him. Then they were airborne again for the final short leg south into the USA.

As the giant Boeing 747 lumbered in towards San Francisco Airport, Adam glimpsed the city shrouded in sea mist and experienced a sharp pang of fear. He felt like a soldier about to land in enemy territory, aware of all the dangers, knowing that all he could do now was grit his teeth and pray.

After landing, he collected his suitcase from the carousel, cleared Immigration and then took the Green Route through Customs. Never in his life before had he been stopped or searched.

'Open your suitcase,' said the official.

Adam just looked at him. He could feel the blood draining from his cheeks. His mind was racing. He's been tipped off, that has to be it. He's got information. Christ, he knows!

'Your suitcase, sir, open your suitcase please.'

Like an automaton, Adam obeyed. The palms of his hands were sweating. 'I've got nothing,' he said in a dry, croaking voice, trying to make a joke of it. 'Not even any Scotch.'

The officer rummaged through the suitcase, turning over his old clothing; so few items, so tatty and badly folded. That was suspicious on its own, Adam knew. The officer poked into the corners with an extra sense of purpose, obviously searching for hidden compartments. But he found nothing. With a shrug, he replaced the clothing and shut the case. He gave Adam a quizzical look. 'Are you okay? You don't look too good.'

Adam knew then why he had been stopped and his luggage searched. It hadn't been any intelligence, no tip-off, just the rank smell of fear. He tried to smile. 'It's been a long, tiring flight.'

The Customs officer nodded. 'Have a nice day.'

'Thank you,' said Adam. And he was through.

* * *

Not daring to look back, Adam lost himself in the concourse crowds searching for the black and yellow sign of the Hertz counter. 'Get a grip on yourself,' he muttered to himself between gritted teeth. 'Take it easy, stay calm. And for God's sake, act normally.' He found the Hertz counter easily enough but there was no sign of Polianna Kim.

There was a seat a little distance away which gave him a view of the counter. He took a magazine out of his hand luggage and pretended to read. Customers came and went: a group of Japanese tourists, each man with a video camera dangling from his shoulder; a Mid-west family with squabbling children; a couple of businessmen. He kept checking his watch. Five minutes had passed since he had been sitting there. He thought air crew always got through Immigration and Customs first. He was beginning to feel conspicuous. Where was she?

He buried his head in the magazine, forcing himself to read: 'Just look at it: tiny flat windshield, miniature running boards, weird bug-eyed headlights. The silhouette of a sea turtle, engine in the back, gas tank up front – that's what "Beetle" Mania was built upon.'

Adam couldn't keep his eyes off his watch. Six and a half minutes now. Panic began to grip him. Something must have happened to her. What if she had been picked up, what if they've found the stuff? He tried to push the thought out of his mind, turning back to the magazine article . . . 'Much as we hate to admit it, credit has to go to Adolf Hitler who decided that a "people's car" should be built. Ferdinand Porsche was commissioned to design the Volkswagen and on May 26th, 1938 –'

Christ, what was he doing reading about a bloody car?

Ten minutes had passed now. All things being equal, she should have cleared Immigration and Customs well ahead of him. He found himself clenching and unclenching his fists. Twelve minutes now . . .

She would have done everything to make sure she got here without delay. She wouldn't have left it this long. There just wasn't any other explanation – she must have been caught.

But where did that leave him? What in hell did he do? Wild thoughts began to spin around his head. Caught cold, with the stuff in her possession, her only option would be to put all the blame on him. He could hear her now: 'I promise I didn't know what was in it. You've got to believe me. My boy friend gave me the case. He said he had a lot of business papers he had to fly over. That's why he asked me to take the extra suitcase. I trusted him, he's an architect. I never dreamt it could be drugs. Yes, I know my clothes are in the case. He must have taken them from my closet. Of course I didn't check the case, why should I? I told you, I trusted him. Yes, he's out there now waiting for me. He's by the Hertz counter.'

Adam was seized by an overwhelming desire to get up and run, it didn't matter where, but he had to get away. He couldn't just sit here and wait to be picked up. Twenty years in a US penitentiary – oh God, no, he'd rather be dead. He stumbled to his feet, reaching for his suitcase. He half turned – and there she was.

Adam stared at her for a second and then, with a small grunt, like a man punched hard in the belly, he slumped back on his seat. Stupid, stupid, he thought, if only he had kept his head, he would have realised . . . so damn stupid.

He watched Polianna Kim walking arm in arm with a US Customs officer, a big brawny man with chestnut hair and freckled face. He watched her smiling up at him and he remembered that was why she could guarantee delivery – the boy friend. That was the reason for the delay; so simple – she had been with him.

As if she had all the time in the world, Polianna Kim walked up to the Hertz counter. She set the suitcase down next to her, putting her arm round her boy friend's waist, and greeted one of the girls behind the counter, her Korean friend.

Adam slung his hand luggage over his shoulder, picked up his suitcase and, with conscious slowness, walked up to the counter. He stood just behind Polianna, to her left, away from the boy friend. He put down his own suitcase. 'I'm sorry to interrupt you,' he said to the Korean girl behind the counter, 'but would it be possible to give me the weekly rate on your compact sedans?'

The girl broke off her conversation with Polianna and gave him a brochure. She pointed out the relevant figures. Adam didn't hear a word. He smiled vacantly. He glimpsed Polianna and her boy friend talking and smiling, kissing each other, lost in their own little world. Adam took the brochure. 'Thank you,' he said to the girl. 'I'll think about it.' He took half a step back, reached down and put his hand on the other suitcase, the one containing the heroin. Polianna and her boy friend were still fixed eye to eye. She was a professional, no doubt about it.

Adam lifted the suitcase, smiled at the girl behind the

counter, turned and walked slowly away. I've done it, he thought, dear God, I've done it!

Two hours later he was on an internal flight to New York. No more Immigration, no more Customs controls, all he had to do now was make the delivery and receive his cash. He could begin to relax.

He arrived in New York at 7 p.m. eastern seaboard time, bought himself a copy of the *Daily News* at La Guardia and caught a cab into Manhattan.

Sitting in the back of the vehicle, he flipped through the tabloid, reading a few stories, skimming through most. On page 3, bannered across the top of the page, a bold black headline hit him:

DEA SMASH HONG KONG CONNECTION

> DEA agents swooped on the Seattle docks this morning seizing four hundred pounds of heroin hidden in woodblocks shipped on a Taiwanese freighter.
>
> Five men caught unpacking the woodblocks drew weapons when confronted. Mike Pethes, head of the back-up SWAT team, responded: 'Make my day.' The five promptly surrendered.
>
> Seattle DEA chief, Joe Blanchflower, confirmed that the seizure, the biggest in eighteen months, was part of an international operation. In the past twenty-four hours

> there have been two major seizures in Hong Kong, with over three hundred pounds confiscated, and one seizure of a Thai fishing trawler on the high seas.
>
> 'We have destroyed more than one syndicate,' said Blanchflower, 'we've shattered a whole narcotics cartel, Hong Kong-based but with operations right across the Far East and here in the US from Seattle to New Orleans. So far, worldwide, there have been sixty-eight arrests. We've taken them boys to pieces and they're hurting bad.'

Adam let the newspaper drop on to his lap. His first reaction was shock. Which syndicate was it? Could the DEA somehow be on to him? But then, as he started to think it through, a desperate wild hope started to burn. What if Cheng Tak-shing and his investor had been among the ones arrested? If that was the case, it could be the end of it all. He and Harry would be free of the bastards.

As soon as he had booked into the hotel, Adam put through a long-distance call.

Cheng's gruff voice destroyed any hopes he may have had. 'What do you want?' he asked. 'Why are you phoning?'

'I've just read the papers.'

'And you thought it might have been me?'

'I didn't know what to think,' said Adam in a hard, cold voice. 'I wanted to find out what was happening.'

'Don't worry, Mr Architect, there's been a few

troubles but not with us. In fact, if you understand my meaning, we could do very well out of this. One less stall in the market place, huh? One less hawker on the street.' He laughed. 'So nothing has changed, not for us, nothing at all.'

Adam lay on the bed, his insides churning. What choice did he have in the matter? None. He had to continue. And with slow reluctance he dialled Slug Delaney's number. 'It's Adam Blake,' he said. 'I'm back.'

'Got the sample?'

'Yes, it's here with me.'

'Any problems?'

'No,' said Adam – except for myself, he thought.

'Are you in a hotel?'

'The Madison Towers, room 706.'

'Okay, give me an hour.'

'You'll bring the cash?'

'Shark fins is a strictly cash business.'

'Not always,' said Adam ruefully.

'In our books it is, Mr Blake. We prefer it that way.'

Adam wondered why they called him Slug, whether it related to his punching ability or his looks. But when Delaney walked through the door, there could be no doubt. The man must have weighed three hundred pounds. And all of it was white lard. Delaney looked as if he hadn't been in the sun for years. Even his hair had a subterranean greyness to it. His eyes were lost in pouches of flesh while around the waist he was huge. There was a smell to him, too, the constant sourness of sweat.

'Okay,' said Delaney as he came into the room. 'Let's have a look at the stuff.'

Adam handed him the empty, open suitcase. 'There's a false bottom to it.'

Delaney sat on the edge of the bed, the mattress squashing beneath him. His belly rested on his knees. He carried a sports bag, emerald green in colour, and from it he removed a fold-up knife. With a few deft slashes he cut away the false bottom. And there lay the two units.

It was the first time in his life that Adam had seen heroin in any shape or form. He didn't know why, but he had expected it to possess some kind of forbidden allure. But, once the brown greaseproof paper had been removed, the units looked like nothing, just two small blocks of white substance, foot powder or plaster of paris, they could have been either. Mundane and disappointing.

Delaney checked the labels on the clear polythene wrapping, peering at the small red and black logo that depicted a tiger leaping out of a circle of Chinese characters. 'Tiger's Claw? Never had this before. Normally it's Double Uoglobe or Lion Brand.' He smiled, his jowls puckering. 'I find it kinda funny how those guys up in the Golden Triangle, the warlords and the opium growers, try to foster a brand image. Who in the hell do they think they are, Coca-Cola? Tiger's Claw . . . well, shit is shit, I guess. It all comes from the same poppy.'

Adam had expected him to test the heroin in some way. But all Delaney did was pick up each block, weigh it in the palm of his hand and then drop it into the sports bag. 'Okay,' he said. 'It all seems in order.' He handed

Adam a small parcel wrapped in newsprint. 'There we go, two hundred and sixty thousand as agreed, all in used one hundred dollar bills.'

Adam put the parcel on the table next to him. Trust, he supposed, was a two-way thing. 'What about the next delivery?' he asked. 'How much do you require?'

'Have you got a drink in here?' asked Delaney. 'One of them little fridges with beer and stuff inside?'

'I'm afraid not,' said Adam. 'I can call room service.'

'No, don't worry. I'm out of here in a couple of minutes anyway.'

'So, how many units?'

'Five.'

Adam was surprised. And disappointed, too. The smaller each delivery, the more he had to make. And with each delivery the risks increased. 'Casement said six, maybe seven,' he protested.

'Yeah, well, we're moving a little slower than we thought.'

'You can't take more?'

'Afraid not, not on this second delivery. We're cautious people, Mr Blake, not too greedy, not too fast.'

'You moved fast enough with me.'

Delaney grinned. 'Yeah, but we checked you out every which way first. You were so clean you squeaked. To be honest, I was none too happy. Without meaning any criticism, you're an amateur in a world of professionals, Mr Blake. But Casement thought you were worth the risk. "Earnest and honest", those were his words.'

'So five units is the limit on this second run, you can't push it higher?'

Delaney shook his head. His jowls wobbled and ripples seemed to run down through his body. 'Don't be so anxious, Mr Blake. You'll pay your brother's debts and you'll make big bucks too, just give it time.'

'What about the price?' asked Adam.

'No change in the price, one hundred and forty as agreed – except we've got a proposition.

'What sort of proposition?'

'Did you read about them busts today, the one in Seattle and those over in Hong Kong?'

Adam nodded, pointing to his folded copy of the *Daily News* on the bedside table.

Delaney smiled. 'High-school economics, Mr Blake. When you've got a poor wheat harvest, the price of wheat is gonna rise. And in a couple of weeks, when present stocks are exhausted, that's exactly what you're gonna see. But the timing has got to be right, you know what I mean?'

Adam was already ahead of him. 'How soon do you want the stuff?'

'We figure that present stocks will be exhausted within fifteen or sixteen days,' said Delaney. 'By then prices will be near their peak. Two weeks after that, the market will be flooded.'

'Give me eighteen days,' said Adam.

'That would be good.'

'And if I make it within that time, what price do I get per unit?'

'I'm authorised to offer a bonus of twenty thousand per unit.'

Adam shook his head. 'That's not worth the risks, nor the extra costs involved.'

'Okay,' said Delaney, 'so give me a figure.'

'Two hundred thousand per unit, a bonus of sixty thousand.'

Delaney coughed. 'Fuck,' he murmured, 'some amateur.'

'You know as well as I do, prices are going to rise a minimum of thirty per cent,' said Adam, pushing home his advantage. 'All I'm doing is getting my cut.'

'Are you sure you've got no fridge, no cold beer?'

Adam smiled. 'Phone Casement, he'll agree that figure.'

'Not two hundred, he won't. Like I said, Mr Blake, we prefer to move cautiously. Okay, purely to prove our good faith, a hundred and ninety thousand. That's the highest we can go. Provided you get the stuff to us within eighteen days.'

'Agreed,' Adam replied. 'Five units at a hundred and ninety each – a total of nine hundred and fifty thousand.'

Picking up the sports bag, Delaney heaved himself off the bed and made his way to the door. He turned back to face Adam. 'You need a good night's sleep,' he grunted. 'You look like shit.' And with that he squeezed out of the door.

Adam sat on the edge of the bed, his shoulders slumped, staring down at the carpet. The room was very still, the air very thick. Silence, like a dense cocoon, wrapped itself round him. It was done. The first delivery had been completed. Thank God. But he felt no sense of achievement, no triumph, only an exhausted relief like a marathon runner at the end of a race who has come terrifyingly close to breaking himself.

Heavy-limbed, he went through to the bathroom. He stared at his face in the mirror. Delaney was right, he did look like shit. He was red-eyed and drawn, as haggard as Harry had been that first time they had met at Lai Chi Kok. But then they were the reflection of each other now, brothers in crime.

Adam's fingers began to tremble. He gripped the basin. The trembling reached up his arms and into his chest until his whole upper body began to shake. Reaching over the basin, grey in the face, he was violently ill.

Chapter Five

MACAU – HONG KONG

Police Constable Lam Siu-ping was not a happy man. Sometimes he thought it would be best if he just went to the top of a tall building and fell off. That way at least his troubles would be ended.

After fifteen years in the Hong Kong Police Force, he remained a constable with no prospect of promotion. He had a wife who was a drudge. He lived in a 300-square-foot pigsty and, to add to his woes, he had a son who was retarded. Other members of his family, one brother and several cousins, had emigrated to Australia. The life was good, they said. But he was stuck in Hong Kong. Who wanted a policeman? Policemen were two a penny, qualified for nothing. When he left school all those years ago, he should have become an electrician or a clerk. Life, felt Lam, had never been his friend.

No wonder, therefore, that once or twice a month he took the hydrofoil from Hong Kong across the mouth of the Pearl River to the scruffy little Portuguese enclave of Macau to frequent the casinos there. A man had to find some release from his frustrations or he would go mad. But luck, like life, had been no better friend.

Early that morning Lam had come to Macau, getting a taxi to the Lisboa Casino and going straight to the *pai kau* tables. He had five thousand Hong Kong dollars on him, nearly a full month's wages. But within two hours – to his stunned incredulity – he had lost the lot. There was no way he could return to Hong Kong with nothing. His wife would make his life a misery for the next six months. It had been a freak of fortune, he decided. His luck had to improve. So, rashly, he had done what he had never done before – he had found a loan shark.

His first loan had been ten thousand Hong Kong dollars. But by mid-afternoon, in a flood of high-blooded, disastrous betting, he had lost that too and was back again for a further ten thousand. If he lost that, his debt would be twenty thousand dollars plus interest, an impossible amount for a humble police constable to repay. Lam was in a fever. Other men had come back from the brink of disaster, why not him? By five that evening, however, the second ten thousand dollars had gone the way of the first.

Lam knew that the loan shark would find him soon enough. There was no point in hiding. In any event, he didn't even have money for the fare back to Hong Kong. So he walked outside the casino and slumped down on the steps watching the sun sink in a pink wash over the island of Coloane.

The loan shark was Macanese. Antonio Wong, he called himself. He was thin, hollow-cheeked, with a small moustache like a shadow on his upper lip. He wore a white suit and white leather shoes and smelt very strongly of eau de cologne.

'I must have time to pay,' said Lam, expecting the worst. 'It's no good pushing me.'

But Antonio Wong didn't so much as frown. 'Why don't we talk about this in my suite? You're a man of common sense, Ah Lam, and men of common sense can always work these things out.'

The suite was very plush with thick Chinese carpets on the floor, brocade curtains and ruby-red velvet furniture. Antonio Wong poured cognac into two ornate crystal brandy balloons, handing one to Lam. 'Here's to luck,' he said.

Lam was puzzled. Why no threats? Why no rough stuff? Why this expensive cognac and all this courtesy? 'I have no money,' he said defiantly. 'You have to realise that, none at all. I'm not some high roller with a Rolls-Royce back in Hong Kong.'

'I never thought that for a moment,' said Wong. 'I know how difficult things are for you. You police do a good job. But what do you earn? Hardly more than a coolie loading boxes onto a truck. Your wife works in a factory.'

'She sews dolls heads on to dolls. How much do you think that pays?' grumbled Lam.

Wong gave a sympathetic cluck, filling both their brandy balloons again. 'And with your son, of course . . . the poor retarded boy.'

Lam was surprised. 'How do you know about my son?'

But Wong just smiled. 'In Australia they have all sorts of schools for retarded children. Have you been to Sydney, Ah Lam? Have you visited your family there? I understand you tried to emigrate there yourself. What a pity the fools in Immigration don't recognise a worthwhile man.'

By now Lam was distinctly nervous. How did this man know so much about him?

Wong walked to the window. 'Luck doesn't always have to be bad for you, Ah Lam. If I pick up that telephone, I can have a woman here for you in less than five minutes, a very beautiful woman. What would you prefer, Chinese, European, Thai? And a woman is just the beginning. It's up to you, Ah Lam, all up to you.'

Lam coughed nervously. 'I don't understand . . .'

Wong lit a cheroot. 'I represent a certain person, a very powerful man, Ah Lam, the sort of man who can arrange things. And this guy wants to help you.'

'Help me?' asked Lam. 'How?'

'For a start, by cancelling your gambling debts. By helping to get you into Australia, to set you up in a little business in Sydney, maybe buy a house for you, too. And to pay for your son in one of those special schools. All these things and more, Ah Lam.'

Lam's face reflected a sudden rush of emotions: anxiety, hope, fear. 'But what must I do to earn these kinds of rewards?'

Wong drew closer to him. 'Do you remember that night when the unfortunate policeman, your *foki*, was dragged beneath the Mercedes and killed?'

Lam felt his throat constrict.

'Of course you remember it. You were on duty that night. You were the driver of the Land Rover that followed the Mercedes. You were the first at the scene. So you saw what happened, you saw everything, isn't that right?'

Lam nodded. 'I saw, yes. But not everything.'

'Nearly everything?'

'Yes, nearly everything . . .'

'And of course,' said Wong, 'you'll have to testify in court.'

'I have no choice,' murmured Lam. 'It's my duty.'

'Of course it is,' said Wong with a broadening smile. 'Of course, of course. And duty is everything, Ah Lam. But duty to whom, my friend?'

Seasons in Hong Kong were measured by flight schedules. It was a city of arrivals and departures. Adam knew the routine well. Kai Tak was no different from a thousand other airports. You landed, you tolerated the queues, abided by the bureaucracy of Immigration, waited for ever for your luggage to be coughed out on to the carousels. Then you tackled the traffic outside. One full hour to cover two miles, crawling towards the Cross Harbour Tunnel like a stream of poisonous lava, the discharge of some immense slow-bubbling volcano.

It was 8 p.m. before eventually he parked the Volvo outside his apartment on the Peak. A stiff wind was blowing. There was no mist so he had a fine view down over the Lamma Channel. He took his one piece of hand luggage out of the boot – he had dumped the suitcase with the false bottom in New York – and wearily made his way into the building. As he put his key into the front door lock, however, he noticed that there were lights on inside the apartment. Music was playing, too, slow smoky jazz. And he could smell food cooking. A smile broke on his unshaven face. He swung the door open, stepping inside.

Like a kid playing hide-and-seek, Nicky du Bois stuck her head round the lounge door. 'There was Chablis in the fridge so I made myself at home,' she said with that bright grey-eyed smile that seemed to light up her whole face. She lifted her wine glass. 'Welcome home, my darling. You look shagged.'

'Everybody keeps telling me that,' said Adam, laughing. He dropped his hand luggage on the floor and embraced her. 'God, you don't know how good it is to see you.'

'Careful,' she squealed. 'I'm going to spill my wine.'

'Damn the wine. Cheap carpets anyway.' And he kissed her, luxuriating in the soft, wonderful closeness of her body.

Nicky broke away, laughing. 'Twenty hours in the air obviously has a different effect on you than most men. I thought you'd arrive back all limp and jet-lagged like any decent human being.'

He grinned. 'Try me.'

Nicky kissed him on the tip of his nose and ducked into the lounge. 'Not until after dinner, I don't.'

'There you go – food again!'

'You've got fifteen minutes to bath and get that trans-Pacific stubble off your chin before I serve,' she said. 'Otherwise the fish will be as dry as old rope.'

Adam shaved as he ran a bath, he preferred a razor and lather to an electric machine, then stretched out in the hot water. It was good to be home.

Nicky came through and sat on the laundry box, sipping her wine. 'Why didn't you tell me you were in New York?' she asked. 'I could have flown down and met you there. I only flew back from Montreal yesterday.'

'Because I couldn't get hold of you, that's why. You were either closeted in meetings until midnight or jetting across the Prairie Provinces.'

She gave a cheeky smile. 'I know, it's hell at the top.'

'Anyway, how did it go?' he asked.

'Brilliant,' she said. 'And you?'

'So so . . .'

'Another Trump Tower in Manhattan?'

'I wish.'

'What sort of business was it?'

'A building commission,' he said with a shrug. 'A factory out in the New Territories. But you know how long these things take to emerge from the chrysalis.'

'Who's behind it?' asked Nicky.

'A few local Chinese . . .'

'Anybody I know?'

'I doubt it,' he mumbled.

Nicky peered at him over the top of her wine glass, puzzled by his evasiveness. 'What about financing?'

'Sorry,' he said, 'but they want it kept confidential at the moment.' Adam hated lying to her and he knew how inane it all sounded. But he had to keep it vague. The more detail you built into a lie, the more easily it came crashing down.

Nicky didn't pursue it further. While she went through to serve the fish, Adam shrugged on a Japanese-style kimono then joined her at the table.

Nicky was a good cook. She loved preparing food, she loved eating it, too, although she didn't weigh more than a hundred pounds. The meal that night was elegantly simple, grilled Macau sole purchased that morning at the Wanchai Market, lettuce salad and new potatoes. The wine was from California, cold, crisp, very dry. Afterwards they drank coffee and shared a Camembert. Then, taking two glasses and a bottle of Calvados, they went through to the bedroom.

Nicky undressed in the coppery half-light of a single lamp while Adam lay on the bed watching her. Her petite dancer's body with the honeyed freckles across her shoulders, the high bobbing breasts and that long curve from the tiny waist into the rounded hips always entranced him. She left her clothes on the carpet – their future home was going to be a mess, he thought – and came naked to him.

They made love slowly at first, delighted to be back with each other, sipping the plum brandy and kissing in its sweet, wet fire. Adam wanted it to last all night. He had shed the fatigue and jet-lag. But he hadn't accounted for one thing, that swelling dam of pain inside him. And as much as he tried to check his emotions, as much as he tried to hold back, within minutes he was making love to her with fierce almost desperate passion. 'Sssh,' she whispered to him as he came above her. 'Slower, darling, slower . . .' But there was no way on earth he could stop himself. All the hours of pain and fear, the long, lonely longing for her, all of it had to be scorched from his soul. And there was only one way he could do it. The power of his lovemaking, the pure desperate passion, amazed her. But within moments she was caught up in the fever too. She threw back her head. 'Oh yes,' she hissed, 'please, yes.' Every part of her was open to him, they seemed fused together. She cried out and then, suddenly, in a dazzling starburst of emotion, they were both consumed.

Afterwards, satiated, wet with shared perspiration, they lay together in silence. Nicky curled her small body against him. Her auburn hair was flecked across his shoulder. She knew there was something deep inside him, a great trouble that he couldn't disclose. But she knew too that she would only make it worse by pressing him. When the time was right he would tell her. Until then all she could do was be there when he needed her.

Adam lay on the dark edge of sleep, his mind filled with confusion. All he wanted was to unburden himself to Nicky. But how? What did he tell her? How did he ever explain? From the very beginning he had been in this thing alone and he would end it alone. There was no other way. But if he couldn't unburden himself to her, at least let him reach out to touch her hand and say what he wanted so desperately to say, the simple words: 'Marry me. Be my wife. Stay with me the rest of my days.' But even that was denied him. His life, his future, hung in a limbo. Nothing could be done, nothing at all, not until he was finished with that poison they called *pak fan*.

* * *

A dream came later, full of rushing images. Even as it was happening, he knew it was a dream. It was too grotesque to be real. That was the bizarre aspect of it. But the terror he felt was real enough.

There was a suitcase in his hand, a bulbous mushroom thing. He was fleeing along dark caverns, fleeing for his life, running and stumbling, staggering up again, his lungs raw, his body wracked. And all the time Harry was jogging next to him in his prison uniform, grinning facetiously. 'Get rid of the case, Adam. Haven't you learnt anything about this business? Look behind, you're trailing the stuff everywhere. Get rid of it!' Adam swung his head and saw it pouring out of a hole in the case, an endless swirling snake of crystal heroin. 'Get rid of it, Adam. What's the matter with you?' But, as desperately as he tried, Adam couldn't throw the case away. It was seared to his hand, welded to bone. And he kept shrieking at Harry, 'Help me! Help me!' But Harry just grinned, turning his head so that a gaping hole appeared at the side of his skull. 'I can't hear you, Adam, not on this side.'

Adam kept running and falling and staggering up again. All the time the police were closing on him. And disembodied voices were booming, 'We've got you cold, asshole! Twenty years! Do you know what's gonna happen to you in the pen, hey, bum boy? Do you know what you're gonna be like in twenty years, Mr Archi-tect? Screwed up, fucked out, jabbering to some canary in a cage!' Adam fell then, all his strength gone, rolling on his back. He saw a huge pair of handcuffs come down, clamp round his body and yank him into the air. He looked up into the black, shapeless maw of justice and screamed helplessly, 'Please, please, dear God, I never wanted to do it!'

With a gasp, Adam sat up in bed. His heart was pounding, he was bathed in sweat. He blinked, trying to focus.

Nicky woke up too, reaching out to touch his arm. 'Are you all right?' she asked. 'What's wrong, Adam?'

He was breathing hard. 'It's okay, I'm fine. Just a dream, that's all.'

She looked at him and knew that it was much more than that. 'What is it, darling? You've got something locked up inside you, I know it.'

But all he could do was shake his head. 'It's nothing,' he said gruffly. 'A bad dream, that's all. I need some water.'

He went through to the bathroom and Nicky followed him. 'If you're having problems, Adam, why don't you let me try and help you? It's not like you to stay so distant. What's happened? Normally we share everything. Why don't you trust me?'

'I told you, it's nothing,' he snapped. He saw the look of hurt in her face and instantly regretted it. 'Maybe it's too much travelling,' he said more meekly. 'Pressures at work. Don't worry. I promise you, nothing's wrong. I'll be fine.'

She knew he was lying.

They returned to bed. It was 3 a.m. He pretended to fall asleep but the echoes of the dream lingered, as surrealistic as a Dali canvas: warped images painted in terror. And, lying there, he knew that something had to be done. Drug trafficking was destroying his life, tearing him apart. He couldn't go on indefinitely trying to clear a debt that grew bigger the more he fed it.

One more run, he thought, his resilience would hold out for just one more, but that had to be an end to it. If it continued any longer he knew it would kill him.

Adam awoke with sunlight streaming through the window. Bleary-eyed, he looked at his watch. It was 10 a.m. Damn, he thought, by now he should have put in at least two hours' work at the office. He saw that Nicky had left a note on her pillow: 'Sorry, I didn't have the heart to wake you. You looked far too cute lying there snoring through your mouth! See you tonight, lover boy.'

He crawled out of bed, took a couple of aspirin to clear his head, shaved, showered and then dressed in one of the few suits still left to him after the acid attack. Nicky, bless her, had left coffee brewing in the kitchen. A Danish pastry stood on a plate with a note propped up against it saying: 'Eat me.' Adam did just that, sorting through the pile of letters that had arrived at the apartment during his absence. He had his second mandatory cup of coffee and at 10.30 stepped out into a brisk blue day.

'Are you Mr Blake?'

Adam turned to the sound of his name and saw a young Chinese man leaning on the wall by the gate. He was dressed in a T-shirt, denims and old running shoes. His hair was greasy, falling down over his eyes, and Adam saw that there were tattoos of dragons on both forearms. 'What do you want?' he asked.

'My boss wants to speak to you.'

'And who is your boss?'

'Cheng Tak-shing.'

'I thought as much. All right, where is he?' asked Adam, emphasising his irritation.

The man pointed across the road to where a blue Honda Accord was parked. Adam could see the short, heavy-shouldered figure of Cheng in the back. The avaricious bastard can't even give me twenty-four hours back in Hong Kong before he's pressing for payment, he thought. He walked over to the car, his face hard-set, and opened the rear door.

Cheng's pockmarked pan of a face grinned up at him. 'I hope you had a good trip, Mr Blake.'

'I don't have long,' said Adam curtly. 'I have to get down to the office. It's about money, I suppose.'

'Why don't you sit in the car. This won't take a minute.'

Adam climbed in next to Cheng. The car smelt of citrus air freshener and tobacco. 'All right,' he said, 'what's this about?'

'Money of course,' said Cheng, still smiling. 'My investor is an anxious man, Mr Blake. And the object is to clear your brother's debt, isn't that so? So tell me, how much do you intend to pay?'

'We need to clarify a few matters first,' said Adam.

The smile stiffened on Cheng's face. 'What sort of matters?'

'First, I need to know how much it's going to cost me to finance the second shipment.'

Cheng looked relieved. Finance was an uncontentious

matter. 'How much stuff do you need?' he asked.

'Five units.'

'When?'

'Within eight days, ten at the outside.'

Cheng gave him a surprised, quizzical look. Then he began to chuckle. 'Are you serious? You've read the newspapers, you know the situation. Eight days, you say. Fuck, it'll be a miracle if you can get five pieces in under a month! The cops seized over three hundred kilos. And there was a Thai trawler too, did you read about that? Another, two hundred kilos, all of it white powder meant for the States.'

'But you told me you hadn't been touched,' said Adam.

Cheng gave a smug grin. 'That's right. We had advance notice, if you know what I mean – a friendly cop.'

'Then what about your own stocks?'

'Gone. Sold. We took advantage of the market, Mr Blake. What do the financial men call it, windfall profits? Yes, that's it.' And he laughed. 'Windfall profits!'

'But what's five units? Christ, it's nothing for you people,' said Adam anxiously. 'Surely you can get hold of five.'

Cheng gave an exaggerated shrug. 'Maybe, if I hunt around. But I can make no promises. I'll have to ask a few favours.'

'What sort of price will I have to pay?'

'If I can get the stuff . . .' Cheng sucked loudly at his teeth, 'who knows, but it's going to be high. Thirty-five thousand a piece – minimum.'

Adam made no attempt to conceal his astonishment. 'One hundred and seventy-five thousand US dollars for five units, that's pure bloody madness!'

Cheng scowled at him, offended. 'Do you think I'm trying to cheat you? Is that it? Other buyers are paying forty thousand, forty-five – and they're agreeing to wait three weeks!'

Adam said nothing, just sat there with disappointment etched into every line of his face. His hopes of clearing Harry's debt with just one further run were now in tatters. 'What's the total amount of my brother's debt, calculated up to today?' he asked in a flat tone.

'Close of business tomorrow, one million.'

Adam gave a small grunt of disgust. 'What's the use . . .' he muttered.

'I spoke to my investor as you asked,' said Cheng. 'And he has agreed a lower interest rate. His normal rate is seven hundred and fifty per cent. But for you – to help you out, in a spirit of compromise – he's agreed to reduce it to just four hundred.'

'And you think that's generous?' said Adam, his voice filled with icy rage. 'The man is a fucking bloodsucker! And what happens over these next three weeks while I wait for you to find me some more stuff? What happens to the interest? It just keeps building and building, is that it?'

'Your brother's debt has nothing to do with the present problems,' said Cheng, his jaw muscles working as he grew angry himself. 'The debt has to be paid, the capital and interest. That was our agreement. We honour it, Mr Blake, we expect you to do the same. You've been paid for the two units but I don't hear any offer to reduce your brother's debt. You're making me lose face, Mr Blake, big face.'

Adam had an overwhelming urge to end it there and then, to turn his back on Cheng and never have to kow-tow to the bastard again. But, as tempted as he was, he knew that any precipitous action would place more than his own life in danger. A time would come, he hoped, somewhere, somehow. But for now he had to bite his lip and play the acquiescent victim.

'So,' said Cheng, 'how much can you pay?'

'With what I have to keep back to purchase the five units, all I can afford is one hundred thousand.'

'One hundred thousand?' Cheng looked disgusted. 'You might as well piss in the sea.'

Adam reacted angrily. 'The first run was a sample run, you know that. What more did you expect?'

Cheng held up his hand. 'All right, all right, just tell me when you can deliver it.'

Adam climbed out of the car. 'Send somebody to the office at five tonight. I'll have it for him then.'

Cheng looked up at Adam, as if trying to read his thoughts. Then, with a thin, callous smile, he said, 'I know you hate me, Mr Blake. I know you dream of ways to put a knife through my heart. That I don't mind – as long as it remains just a dream. But if you try going to the police, if you try to doublecross us in any way, then things will be very bad. We watched your girl friend come out of your apartment this morning. She's a very pretty woman, she has a very pretty face. Do you have any idea what sulphuric acid can do to a face like that? Think about it, Mr Blake.'

Fists clenched, boiling with impotent fury, Adam stood on the road and watched the Honda skid away in a blue cough of exhaust. I've got to end this, he thought. I'm getting close to breaking point. This just can't go on. But how? Things looked worse now than they had last night.

The most obvious way, the way his conscience kept directing him, was to go to the police. If he made a clean breast of it and agreed to work with them, there was no reason why Cheng couldn't be destroyed. The police would protect them against any retaliation. That was part of their job, they did it every day. Yes, he thought with bitter sarcasm, just as Harry had been protected.

Adam may have been educated in England but he was half Chinese, he spoke the language, he had been brought up in Hong Kong. As a boy he had explored its back streets with Harry. He knew how the city worked. And he knew about men like Cheng, men who worked through the Triads, secret criminal societies like the Sun Yee On and the Wo Shing Wo, societies in their own way just as powerful as the Mafia. If he went to the police, Adam knew that his mother and Nicky – and he, too – would be fugitives the rest of their lives. Harry would never make it out of jail alive, that was a certainty.

Even if Cheng was caught and imprisoned, what difference would it make? Men like Cheng could direct their affairs from behind bars as easily as from some apartment in Mongkok. From what Cheng had said earlier, it was clear that his network of informers stretched as far as the police. In any event, Cheng was not the fountainhead, he was muscle, that's all, a tool. The real power lay in the hands of the anonymous investor, the man demanding repayment of the debt. No doubt he was a Triad, too, no doubt even more powerful, perhaps a Dragon Head. So eliminating Cheng meant nothing, not unless the investor was eliminated with him.

Standing there on the road, Adam had a momentary vision of Nicky, her smiling face scoured with acid, her soft flesh melting. Could he live with that for the rest of his life? Could he live with Harry's death on his conscience? There was simply no way.

That left only one alternative, to continue in the heroin trade. But to do that indefinitely would break him – he was already on the edge of it – and with each run the risks grew greater. Somehow he had to find a way of clearing the debt with just one more delivery. That was the only way out.

But to do that, he had to achieve two things. First, he had to be able to deliver the five units to New York within the eighteen-day 'bonus' period. Second, he had to be able to obtain the units cheaper – far cheaper – than at the present inflated prices. If he could achieve these two things, he calculated he could scrape up enough to clear the full capital and interest due. But again the same question arose, how?

No matter which angle he came at it from there was only one way. He would have to find another supplier, somebody outside Hong Kong who was not affected by the local seizures, somebody who could supply heroin on the turn. But again the same question: how? Where did he find such a man and how did he get to him?

Ironically, there was only one person Adam could turn to now. Harry had got him into this mess, he thought. Hopefully Harry could help get him out of it.

The two brothers sat as they had in the beginning, separated by a sheet of bulletproof glass, communicating through a telephone.

Harry understood the problem. The quicker the debt was cleared, the better it suited him, too. He wanted the whole thing settled. Sitting in prison, waiting day after day, not knowing what was happening, was playing havoc with his nerves.

He glanced over his shoulder to make sure that the prison warder was not within earshot, then he whispered into the telephone, 'Thailand, that's the only place to buy stuff, close to the Triangle. But the risks are high, Adam, you've got to realise that. Every narcotics agency in the world has people there. You're stepping into a war zone.'

'But surely if it's just one run and I'm a stranger, no record, no known connections, just an architect on business?'

'Sure, sure, the risks will be lower that way.'

'So what sort of prices am I looking at?' asked Adam.

'In Bangkok it'll cost you half of what it'll cost you in Hong Kong, probably less.'

'What about further north, up near the Triangle, along the border?'

Harry glanced over his shoulder again, keeping the warder under surveillance. 'If you can get up there it's as cheap as dirt. You won't pay more than three thousand US a unit. You'll get the lot for fifteen grand. But remember, you've still got to get it out of Thailand.'

'What about delays?'

'A day or two, that's all. That's where they grow the damn stuff.'

Adam gave a grim nod. 'Then that's what I've got to do,' he said.

Harry shook his head, smiling at Adam's naivety. 'I wish it was that simple, Adam. People don't step out of the jungle and just hand the stuff to you. You don't buy it at the side of the road like watermelon.'

'I didn't expect to,' Adam replied, angry at the sarcasm.

'What I'm trying to tell you is that you've got to have contacts,' said Harry. 'And they're not easy to get. Believe me, Adam, I know what I'm talking about. I've tried. I spent six weeks up in Chiang Mai once and came away with nothing more than a hotel bill. It can take you six or seven months of patient negotiating to set up a supplier. And how long have you got? Two weeks! You'll never do it.'

Adam considered the matter a moment. Then he asked in a quiet voice, 'But doesn't Cheng deal up along the border? Doesn't he import from there?'

Harry checked that the warder was still out of hearing. 'Yeah, sure, but Cheng doesn't operate on his own. He's got investors behind him, old-time money. Some of those men have been financing drug deals since the sixties. They've got suppliers up there who they've been dealing with for over twenty years. Why should Cheng bring you into a relationship like that? Why should he cut himself out of the action?'

'Maybe he can be persuaded.'

'You've got to have leverage, Adam. And what sort of pressure can you hope to put on him? You're nothing in his book, just a debtor, that's all.'

Adam looked at his brother through the glass. 'Then I'll have to find a way,' he said.

He met Cheng that night on the roof of the Ocean Terminal where delivery of the first two units had been made. It was an overcast night with rain in the air.

Cheng was irritated at having to be there. He had had to leave a mahjong game with his cronies. 'What do you want?' he asked. 'What's so important that you had to drag me here?'

'I want to make one thing clear to you,' said Adam in a voice of quiet assurance. 'I'm prepared to make one more delivery to the States, just one more. I'll deliver the five units in order to meet my brother's debt but that's it – no more.'

Cheng's eyes narrowed. 'What are you getting at? Why only one more delivery?'

'There are a lot of reasons, too complex, too subtle to explain here. So let's just say I can't stick it any more.'

'But you can't clear the debt, not with just five units.'

'There is a way it can be done,' said Adam. 'I've calculated the figures. But I need to move fast, and I need your help.'

Cheng blinked. 'Help?' he asked suspiciously. 'What kind of help?'

'I need to get those five units and I need them within ten days.'

'I can get you three.'

'That's no good. I must have all five.'

'I've tried, it's impossible, not within ten days.'

'In Hong Kong maybe but not elsewhere.'

'Huh?' Cheng sniffed as if somehow he could smell a deception. 'What are you trying to tell me?'

'I can obtain the units in Thailand without any delay,' said Adam. 'I can also get them at the right price, especially if I go up to the border. And that's where I need your help.' He paused a moment, then he said, 'I want you to introduce me to your supplier. I want you to arrange for me to purchase five units from him.'

Conflicting emotions of outrage, anger and pure astonishment crossed the pitted yellow pan of Cheng's face. He gave a small grunt, shook his head, and then burst into a scornful laugh. 'You want to be introduced to my supplier so you can buy five units? You want to go all the way up to the Triangle for that? You must be crazy! Who do you think you are? You're nobody, nothing, just a shrimp pretending to be a shark.' And he laughed still more.

Adam's face remained expressionless. 'If I wait until you can sell me the five units, I'll lose a favourable price in New York,' he said. 'I'll also have to buy from you at an inflated price. Your investor will be at least two hundred thousand short, maybe quarter of a million.' He fell silent a moment, letting the facts sink home. Then he continued. 'But if he's prepared to accept that in full and final settlement then I'm happy.'

'Fuck your mother!' Cheng exploded with the everyday Cantonese crudity that he used more than most. 'My investor wants full payment, you know that! Don't get funny with me, Mr Architect!'

'Then introduce me to your supplier in Thailand. If I can buy the stuff cheap and make the delivery in time, I'll be able to clear the debt.'

'What would my supplier want with you?'

'It's your choice,' said Adam in a soft, rational voice. 'But I'm only making one more run, I don't want any misunderstanding about that. These five units are the last. Whatever money I earn, I'll pay to you. But it's going to be in full and final settlement. And if I'm quarter of a million short, it'll be up to you to explain it to your investor.'

Cheng swung away, angrily lighting a cigarette. He was muttering to himself beneath his breath. Then he swung back to face Adam. 'If there's money still outstanding and you won't pay, we have other ways of collecting.'

Adam looked at Cheng, shook his head very slowly and then answered in a manner that was icy calm. 'If you try to harm any member of my family, and that includes Nicky du Bois, I promise you one thing, you'll regret it. That's not a threat, that's a statement. Because I'll fight you, Cheng, I'll fight every one of you bastards until you're all dead or behind bars.'

Cheng laughed but it was a poor disguise for his surprise. 'Then your brother will be dead meat. And that girl friend of yours, how will she look with acid in her face?'

'You still don't seem to understand,' said Adam. 'So let me spell it out for you. First, I'll go to the police. I'll tell them everything. And you'll be the first man I point the finger at. I'll give evidence in court, I'll do whatever is necessary. And so will my brother. Because, you see, he'll have nothing to lose. It'll be your life or his.'

'We'll still get to you,' blustered Cheng.

'Perhaps, perhaps not. I'll take that risk,' said Adam. 'You know as well as I do that violence, like white powder, has to be carefully measured. Too much only destroys the effect it's intended to create. Push me too hard and I promise I'll turn on you so fast that all you'll see is the blur.'

For once Cheng said nothing, lost for words. He sucked deep on his cigarette and blew the smoke out of his nostrils in a long acrid stream.

'As I said, the choice is yours,' said Adam quietly. 'If you introduce me to your supplier in the Triangle, I'll be able to pay minimum prices, I'll be able to deliver within the specified time. Your investor will be paid in full. We'll all be happy men. The alternative is a blood bath. And who does that serve? Tell me, who benefits then?'

The taper was lit, flickering a bright orange under the crinkled foil. Cheng swayed from side to side like a cobra watching the charmer play his pipe. The granules of heroin began slowly to melt before his eyes, and vapour, eggshell blue, meandered above the foil. With a small moan, he leant forward and began to inhale. Bright colours burst in his eyes. The smoke of the poppy filled his lungs. He let out a couple of short gasps and then, as his brain clouded, he lay back, floating on a dream tide down a long dark river of yearning.

What should he do with Blake, he wondered, kill him or help him? What should he do with the half-caste, the shrimp who wanted to be a shark?

If he consulted Ah Leung, he knew what his instructions would be. Despite all his wealth and power – probably because of it – Ah Leung never compromised, never lost face. But Ah Leung was invulnerable, Cheng knew that he was not.

Blake was right, violence was like *pak fan*. It had to be carefully measured. If you pushed a man like Blake too far then, just as he said, he would turn on you like a snake. Even if you crushed him, he'd still have his fangs in your ankle. There was something about Blake, too, that had always worried him, a streak of madness deep inside.

Why risk it? Why invite all the trouble? Repayment of the debt, that was all that mattered, and the quicker it was done the better. Adrift in that void between dream and substance, Cheng could see the logic in Blake's proposals. Sometimes, he thought, you had to bend a little to be successful.

They met in the afternoon at the entrance to the Star Ferry and boarded one of the venerable green-painted vessels for its short journey across the harbour to Tsim Sha Tsui.

'You must go to northern Thailand, to Chiang Mai,' said Cheng. 'Here is a letter of introduction to a man called Yu, a trader. The envelope isn't sealed, you can read it if you like. It says you are interested in buying tribal crafts. Yu will understand. It also says you can be trusted.'

'So Yu is the go-between?'

Cheng nodded. 'You will have to be patient. It may take two days, it may take a week before the supplier reveals himself. There's nothing I can do about that. Who knows, he may agree to deal, he may not. It's in the hands of the gods.'

'Who is the supplier?' asked Adam.

'He's from Laos.'

'And his name?'

'His name,' said Cheng, 'is Tinko Chaisiwan.'

Chapter Six
THAILAND – NEW YORK

It was a sweltering night, thick and still, pungent with the smell of decaying vegetation. Bone-jarred, Adam climbed down from the jeep. Sweat sluiced down his temples, his shirt clung to his skin. Every part of him – clothes, skin, hair – seemed ingrained with dust. The journey from Chiang Mai had taken three hours, a slow grinding ascent into the eastern hills. But this was where the track ended. Ahead of them lay the clearing and, on the far side, the deserted lumber mill. Far to the north, high above the jungle-clad hills, an electric storm lit up the night sky. It was too early for the monsoons so there was no rain, not yet, just the halo of turbulence and the salvos of thunder rolling down from Burma.

Adam checked his watch. It was 2 a.m. The air was filled with the drone of cicadas. Somewhere close by he could hear the resonant croaking of bullfrogs. As he stepped towards the clearing, he had to brush cobwebs from his face.

Yu Wen-huan, dressed in his inevitable white,

short-sleeved shirt and black slacks, walked next to him. 'Laos is just a mile to our east,' he said. 'Burma is less than ten miles north. This is the hub of the Golden Triangle, the land, they say, that nobody owns.'

Yu Wen-huan was in his mid-thirties, about Adam's age. He was Chinese, tracing his ancestry to Yunnan Province, and Yunnanese was his native dialect. He was a slender, softly spoken man. 'Four Eyes' was the name they gave him in the border villages because of the thick, gold-rimmed spectacles he wore. The spectacles and the build, together with a certain vagueness of manner, endowed Yu with a bookish air. He could so easily have been some college history professor. He ran a modest business on the Loy Kroh Road in Chiang Mai, an establishment called Golden Elephant Tribal Crafts. But the business, of course, was no more than a convenient front.

For decades now the Yunnanese merchants in northern Thailand had monopolised the business of buying opium from drug-army commanders like Kuhn Sa and the scores of other freelance suppliers who operated out of the Triangle. Yu didn't buy, not direct. He found it more profitable, and safer, to act as a broker. He was both that and a supplier of chemicals to the jungle laboratories in the Triangle – the acids, ether, chloroform, activated charcoal and alcohol necessary to convert raw opium into morphine base and the base into the fine white powder they called China White.

Yu, they said, like his father and his grandfather before him, was in tight with half a dozen drug-army leaders and miscellaneous growers of opium. He was in tight with the Yunnanese merchants, in tight with the Thai police. Yu, they said, despite his absent-minded, bookish ways, had the business sewn up.

The two of them reached the edge of the clearing. Distant lightning flickered, lighting the sky with a bloodless white neon. Adam could make out the deserted lumber mill on the far side of the clearing, a ramshackle wooden structure slowly being devoured by white ants. 'How long do you think we'll have to wait?' he asked.

'It is impossible to say,' Yu replied. 'Chaiwisan could be out there now, watching us. He might show himself immediately or he might wait an hour or more, just waiting and watching. He is a cautious man, very cautious. Who knows, he might smell something in the air, a scent of danger, and not show himself at all.'

'And if that happens,' asked Adam, alarmed, 'if he doesn't show himself, what then?'

'Then we will have to make other arrangements. What else can we do? Another place, another night . . .'

Adam had already spent six days kicking his heels in Chiang Mai waiting for Yu to set up this meeting. Time was running critically short. 'But you know him well,' he said. 'He trusts you. Why should he smell danger? We haven't been followed. We've checked a dozen times.'

'Why?' Yu gave a small, good-humoured laugh. 'This is the Golden Triangle, Adam. These hills are alive with smugglers, spies, mercenaries of all kinds, men paid by the CIA and DEA.' He laughed again. 'Across the border, when he is in Laos, Chaiwisan may be safe, protected by the Pathet Lao. But when he crosses that border, it is a different matter. I have known

Chaiwisan – Uncle Chicken – since I was a young boy. He is Yunnanese, too. We speak the same language. He knew my father. So it is not a question of trust or mistrust. He will tell you that himself. It is simply a question of survival.'

Adam stepped out into the clearing. A soft breeze dried the sweat on his cheeks. He gazed north to where the electric storm, like some far-off battle, still filled the night sky. That strange, unnerving sensation possessed him again, the feeling that, although his body was here in this desolate jungle clearing, it was inhabited by another man's personality, another will entirely. How could he be doing this? How could this be him waiting to deal with some tribal opium king?

Earlier that evening, as he had done every evening, Adam had telephoned Nicky in Hong Kong. And it seemed that even she was beginning to sense it.

'What is it, Adam?' she had asked. 'What's wrong? Every time I speak to you these days, you seem so tense, so far away all the time. Sometimes I feel I'm talking to somebody else entirely, a stranger.'

'It's nothing,' he had answered defensively. 'Pressure of work, that's all.'

But Nicky wouldn't be fobbed off. 'Please, Adam, don't feed me with platitudes. Something is happening to you, I can sense the change.'

'Nothing is happening,' he had retaliated. 'You get pretty tense yourself sometimes. We both live under a lot of pressure. It's the nature of our jobs, you know that. And sometimes things get to you.'

'But we used to talk everything out. Now I get the

feeling you're holding all the important things back from me.'

'I'm not holding anything back! I'm here on business, Nicky, that's all, dull, routine business. What do you want me to talk to you about, bulk factors, square footages? I didn't know you were interested!'

It had been a stupid outburst and he knew it. All it did was prove her point. But Nicky had refused to rise to the bait. 'Trust me, Adam, please,' she had said in a soft, low voice that cut to his heart. 'It might sound crazy, but sometimes I feel as if I'm losing you, as if the tie between us has been broken and you're just drifting away. I'd prefer it if there had been some argument, some huge screaming session. At least then I'd understand. But this slow, silent drifting away . . . don't you realise what it's doing to me? Confide in me, Adam, please, just confide in me . . .'

Confide in me – dear God, if only he could. But what could he tell her? That he was dealing in drugs, that he was up here buying heroin in order to smuggle it into the States? How could he tell her anything without totally destroying what was left between them? The only chance they had was for him somehow to live out this lie, to brazen it through until he was free again.

Behind him, Adam heard the swish of Yu's legs as he walked through the knee-high grass. 'If Chaiwisan doesn't show,' he asked, 'how long will it take to set up another meeting?'

'I wouldn't worry about that now.'

'Easy to say, but I'm getting dangerously close to my deadline. What happens if Chaiwisan falls though, what about other suppliers?' Adam waited for the response. But there was none. Through the enveloping mesh of jungle noises, he could sense something, a presence. He turned.

Six men stood facing him.

The breath caught in his throat. The shock was complete. He stood rooted, speechless. But, ironically, it worked to his benefit. For, in the darkness, the lack of movement and the silence hid his surprise. And confidence at that moment, he knew, was vital.

The six men who faced him were dressed in an assortment of sweat-drenched camouflage, faces blackened like commandos. They were small men, short and lean. But there was an air about them of unspoken menace that mercenaries, men who kill for a living, exude. A couple of the men had bandoliers of ammunition draped over their chests, three at least carried grenades. Their weapons were an assortment of US and Soviet automatics, black market stuff: M16s and Kalashnikovs mainly.

The man in the centre of the group looked to be the oldest; a little shorter, round-shouldered with bow legs. He wore an olive-green bush hat that shaded his eyes. He stepped forward, cradling an AKS-74 assault rifle in his arms. He regarded Adam in the flickering quarter-light of the distant lightning. Then he said in heavily accented Cantonese, 'So you're Adam Blake, brother of Harry Lee. You're the man Cheng Tak-shing tells me I must trust. But tell me first, Mr Blake, how far can I trust Cheng?'

Adam had to react on instinct. He smiled. 'Not too far.'

Chaiwisan smiled too, his teeth showing white beneath

the rim of his bush hat. 'Good, that proves one thing.'

'What is that?'

'That at least we're talking about the same man.'

And they both laughed.

The tension was broken. Adam glimpsed Yu, standing off to one side, grinning with relief. Even Chaiwisan's henchmen, who had formed a threatening semicircle, appeared visibly to relax.

Chaiwisan reached out to shake Adam's hand. 'Come,' he said in his distinctive gravelly voice, 'we must talk. I have to be back across the border before light. Walk with me a little.'

Adam was aware of the firmness of his handshake; the grip of a man who, despite his years, was still very much in his prime. There was a slight stoop, a small favouring of one shoulder when he walked, arthritis probably, but there wasn't an ounce of fat on his frame. He was leathery and brown, all sinew and veins.

'You will forgive the manner of our meeting,' said Chaiwisan as they walked together. 'You see, there's word that the Yankees have a contract on me. No doubt they're just rumours. People here live on rice and rumours. But sometimes rumours make the best intelligence so I cannot afford to ignore them. If it was just a question of my arrest, it would be no problem. In Chiang Mai, even Bangkok, it is simple enough to bribe witnesses and jailers, judges too. But a contract, and that's what the rumours say it is . . .' And he chuckled, as if it was all some macabre joke. '. . . a bullet from the darkness, now that is a different thing.'

Adam wondered what made a man like Chaiwisan

persist with a life like this. After so many years in the drug trade, he had to be worth millions. He could be one of the richest men in Asia for all he knew. They said the drug-army commanders were some of the richest men in the world. But what good was it to him? The cash collected interest, the gold bullion collected dust. And what did he do? He lived here with the leeches, worse off than the average hill tribesman who at least could sleep at night without fear of assassination. But Chaiwisan looked content enough with his lot. Who knows, thought Adam, maybe in some strange way this is the only life he wants, the only one he feels happy with.

And, as if he agreed with Adam's silent thoughts, Chaiwisan smiled broadly. 'So,' he said, 'you got into this business to help your brother, the Fat Boy. From the stories told about him, I could imagine Harry Lee being generous with other people's money. It's just a pity that you have to pay for that generosity. But tell me, once the debt is cleared, what then?' He gave a quizzical smile. 'Is this a distasteful episode or something more permanent?'

It was the standard question and Adam answered with the standard lie. 'I've decided to stay in the business, for the time being at least.'

'Why?'

'Money. Why else?'

Chaiwisan laughed. 'So you have decided that dope is more lucrative than building great buildings, is that it?'

Adam grinned. 'You could put it that way.'

'Don't worry, you're not the first to discover that,' said Chaiwisan jauntily. 'In my forty years in this trade,

Mr Blake, I've dealt with professional men of every kind: engineers, doctors, lawyers – oh yes, a great many lawyers. But it's a dangerous business, you must appreciate that, especially for a beginner.'

'I understand the risks,' said Adam dryly.

Chaiwisan stopped, seating himself on one of the hundreds of teak logs that lay scattered around the mill. He took out chewing gum from his pocket, offering a piece to Adam.

'I grew up in the poppy fields, Mr Blake. When I was a boy, there was no dishonour to it, not like they suggest today. Hong Kong was founded on the opium trade. All those great imperialist trading companies with their great buildings, all the pomp and glory, all of it was purchased with opium. About a hundred years ago an English chemist boiled morphine and acid over a stove, that's how it all began. The German company, Bayer, marketed the white powder that the chemist had discovered. Bayer sold it openly over the counter for more than twenty years under its own special brand name. And do you know what the brand name was? "Heroin", that's what they called it. At the turn of the century, when my father was alive, opium was legal tender. But today? Pah!' And he spat into the dust at his feet.

Adam said nothing. He had expected hard, sharp bargaining with a narcotics mercenary but instead this dignified, ageing warrior sat reminiscing about the past.

'If I had been born in Brazil, Mr Blake, I might now be selling coffee. If I had been born in Virginia, I might now be selling tobacco. As it is, I trade in opium. That is fate. But fate demands only one thing, that you make the best of it. Look at me, I am sixty-five years old. But I have not spent one day in jail. Why? Because I know how this business works, that's why.' He chewed loudly on his gum. 'Westerners have a liking for spy novels. I see so many of the paperback books in the airport bookshops, always the CIA and KGB buying off each other's agents, turning lies into an art form. But how many such books are placed here? Let me spell out the true reality for you, Mr Blake. In a single month in this world of white powder there are more spies created, more double agents, more bribes paid, more treacherous deals done and betrayals executed than you will find in the records of the CIA and the KGB spanning ten whole years. The inhabitants of this earth spend more money on drugs – China White, cocaine, marijuana – than they do on food. Did you know that? The facts are fascinating. The annual revenue of the world's narcotics industry exceeds half a trillion dollars, three times the value of all US currency in circulation. People don't have any idea of the staggering size of this business. It dwarfs countries, it dwarfs empires. I was born into it as a boy and hopefully –' he looked up at Adam with a humorous twinkle in his eyes '– hopefully, I will die in it as an old man.'

Chaiwisan climbed to his feet, his jaws working as he chewed his gum. They walked on again, down a small slope towards a stream where the chorus of the bullfrogs was loudest.

'There is an old Sanskrit saying, Mr Blake, that power makes tigers of us all. And in this business we do have power, immense power. I can buy a police chief, I can have laws changed, I can kill a man and never pay the penalty. But we have to protect ourselves. And how best do we do that, men like you and I? There is only one way. We can't stand out in the open and proclaim ourselves. Your brother was too flash, too fast, that's what finished him. No, that's not the way. The price we pay is that we must live in the shadows, pretend to be always what we are not. Power makes tigers of us all, Mr Blake. And we are the tigers of deceit. Why? Because that is how best we survive.'

They came down to the stream. The water was stagnant. Chaiwisan looked towards the north where the sheet lightning created its own aurora and the thunder came towards them in rumbling bass echoes. He was silent for a time. But then, with an abrupt energy, he broke away from his thoughts. 'So,' he said. 'I trust now you understand what kind of man I am a little better. And that's important because in this business everything is founded on trust.' He smiled. 'And, as time goes on, I will come to understand you too. But time runs short, business is business. So, if I agree to sell, what quantities do you require?'

'To start, just five units,' said Adam. 'But I have buyers in New York who will shortly be requiring ten units a month, maybe more.'

Chaiwisan nodded. 'My price is four thousand US a unit.'

Adam was surprised. Harry had told him the price would be in the region of two thousand. 'That's higher than I had expected,' he said.

'Ah, but expenses grow,' said Chaiwisan with an exaggerated shrug. 'I might be protected across the border,

Mr Blake, I might grow my opium there, but it costs. I have to get permission from the government, the Pathet Lao, to plant and to sell. To ensure I don't cheat them, the Pathet Lao insist that the opium is processed at one of their places. And always, always there are bribes for senior government men and police officials, bribes here in Thailand, too. So you see, inflation is not just a problem in the business of motor cars and cabbages, Mr Blake. I regret that it plagues us all.'

Adam had to laugh. Chaiwisan had a genial, avuncular way about him; part teacher, part philosopher, part old hillbilly on the stoop talking about the good ol' days.

As they turned back towards the group, Chaiwisan said, 'I trust Four Eyes advised you that I require half the purchase price in advance?'

'I have the money here,' said Adam. 'But one matter that's critical is the speed of delivery.'

'Ah yes, your deadline. Yu told me of it. Well, if it is that important to you, and if it is only five units, I can deliver within twenty-four hours. No problem.'

Adam breathed a sigh of relief. 'How will you get it to me?'

'I have a sergeant major in the Chiang Mai police who acts as a courier for me. He will deliver it to Yu's store.'

'And the balance of the money?'

'Pay that to Yu.'

Adam was content. The five units would cost him twenty thousand US plus ten per cent commission to Yu. That was thirteen thousand dollars less than one single unit would have cost him in Hong Kong. Returning to the jeep, he removed ten thousand US dollars in dog-eared cash from a leather bag and handed it to Chaiwisan.

As the Yunnanese opium seller counted it, Adam was able, for the first time, to get some view of his features beneath the bush hat: a surprisingly beaked nose, high cheekbones and tapering chin, sun-leathered skin dissected with wrinkles. It was a dignified face, reminding Adam of those old sepia photographs of Sioux or Apache Indians, doomed men facing the camera with a doomed kind of pride.

Satisfied with his money, Chaiwisan wrapped it in a clear plastic bag and shoved it into one of the pockets of his camouflage trousers. He hissed orders in a Laotian dialect that Adam didn't understand and his men came out of their defensive circle, ready for the march back across the border.

Chaiwisan first bade Yu Wen-huan farewell, then turned to Adam. 'I look forward to many years of successful partnership, Mr Blake. What is it the English say, from an acorn great oak trees grow?'

'Something like that,' said Adam with a grin. There was no way he could dislike the man. Chaiwisan was an amiable rogue.

Adam and Yu stood together watching the small group fade into the night. Then they climbed into the jeep for the gruelling journey back down through the hills to Chiang Mai. The deal had been struck. And there was still time to get the stuff into the States.

To the north, amid the granite peaks of Burma, lightning still lit up the crystal sky.

* * *

As they bounced and rattled along the rutted jungle tracks, Adam spoke to Yu about one further matter, the crucial problem of hiring a courier to carry the five units.

'From Thailand it's always risky,' said Yu. 'US Customs search everybody who flies in from Bangkok. The best thing is not to fly direct. Fly to another destination first, say Manila or Jakarta, and from there on to the US.'

'But I'm still going to need a courier here,' said Adam, 'somebody who can physically carry the stuff right through to the States.'

'I can find you a mule if you want. It's not a difficult matter.'

'But somebody good,' said Adam, remembering the coolness of Polianna Kim. 'Somebody very good.'

'I think I might have just the man for you. Give me a day, I need to make some phone calls,' said Yu.

The following afternoon, in the shimmering heat of a Thai siesta, a vehicle of the Provincial Police drew up outside Yu's wood-framed shop at 75 Loy Kroh Road. A burly police sergeant major got out. He was carrying a canvas satchel. He walked inside, went straight through to the back office where Yu worked and placed the satchel on the desk. He waited for Yu to pay his extra 'commission', a payment of 500 baht, and, without a word, departed.

'The only difference between the criminals and the police in Chiang Mai,' said Yu, 'is that the police wear uniforms.'

Adam examined each of the units, studying again the

logos of the tigers leaping through circles made of Chinese characters: the tigers of deceit, he remembered.

The resident agent of the DEA in Chiang Mai had a map on the wall behind his desk marked with coloured pins which showed the main opium-growing areas of the Triangle; all very proper, all very professional. Beneath the map, however, he had taped a handwritten slogan which read: 'Despairing? Discouraged? Depressed? Who cares a shit?' After twenty years in the business, the resident agent had discovered that a healthy dose of cynicism was the only way to stay sane.

Chiang Mai, to the outsider, was a dozy tourist town but in the battle against the purveyors of China White, Chiang Mai was to heroin what Berlin had been to the Cold War. It was a town full of spies, mercenaries, deals done, deals betrayed. Intelligence poured in on a daily basis, most of it rumour, ninety per cent of it useless. But from time to time something a little more solid landed on the resident agent's desk. And that afternoon, just an hour after the police sergeant major had made his delivery, the agent sent a coded report to the DEA officers at the US Embassy in Bangkok:

RE: TINKO CHAIWISAN

1. CONTINUED SURVEILLANCE OF SUBJECT BY MEO FREELANCE AGENTS REVEALS HE CROSSED INTO THAI TERRITORY ON THE NIGHT OF 15th.
2. A MEETING WAS HELD AT THE SUANDOK MILL WITH TWO MEN, ONE IDENTIFIED AS

YU (WEN-HUAN), A KNOWN ASSOCIATE OF YUNNANESE TRAFFICKERS OPERATING OUT OF LAOS.

3. IDENTITY OF THE SECOND MAN IS UNKNOWN. HOWEVER, INFORMATION RECEIVED AND SURVEILLANCE TODAY INDICATES THAT YU HAS MET SEVERAL TIMES OVER THE PAST WEEK WITH A HONG KONG RESIDENT, A EURASIAN MALE NAMED ADAM BLAKE, APPARENTLY AN ARCHITECT.
4. CAN HK OFFICE ASSIST WITH BLAKE'S BACKGROUND?

When Benny Barack in Bangkok received the report, he did exactly as suggested and within twenty-four hours had received a reply from the DEA representative at the US Consulate General in Hong Kong which read:

RE: TINKO CHAIWISAN

1. CONFIRM BLAKE IS AN ARCHITECT WITH HIS OWN HK PRACTICE.
2. BLAKE IS ALSO BROTHER TO LEE WAI-HONG (aka HARRY LEE, THE FAT BOY) WHO IS PRESENTLY IN CUSTODY HERE FACING CHARGES OF TRAFFICKING.
3. NEW YORK OP 'TINDERBOX' REFERS.

Benny Barack amalgamated both intelligence reports into one and transmitted it to the Asia Task Force in New York marked for the immediate and personal attention of Carl Drexel. He added only one sentence at the very end: 'Maybe this will ease the pain of the gout.'

When Drexel read Benny Barack's message, sheer delight shone on his heavily wedged features. Yes, it had eased the pain of his gout – and most of his other ailments, too.

Carl Drexel remembered Op Tinderbox well. It had been the operation which resulted in the death of the courier, the Chinese kid who had dropped from the balcony. He also remembered Harry Lee, the Fat Boy, the Hong Kong trafficker too terrified to co-operate with the police, the one who had had his ear sliced off in a prison debt-collecting exercise.

Drexel read the message a second time then tossed the message across to Sue Martin, his newest Task Force member. She picked it up and read it. It meant next to nothing to her. She was far too new to the Force.

Sue Martin, a one-time tennis professional, was tall and blonde. Far too damn sexy to be in a thankless job like this, thought Drexel. She was a good operator, though, no doubt about it.

Drexel took off his bifocals and began vigorously to clean them. 'Do you know what that report proves, Sue?' he asked.

Sue Martin smiled, showing perfect white teeth. Carl Drexel's delight was infectious. 'No, Carl, what does it prove?'

'It proves that all you need in this business is one thing – the patience of Job!'

* * *

Yu Wen-huan found the mule in Bangkok. The man's name, he reported to Adam, was Prasert Prakorp, a boat builder who lived with his wife in a humble dwelling along one of Bangkok's *klongs*, the thousands of tidal canals that acted as the city's roads, sewers and front-door laundries. Prakorp was sixty-two years old, said Yu, a hard-working artisan with no criminal convictions and no previous connection with the narcotics trade. Prakorp had obtained his US visa because his eldest son lived in California where he worked as a gardener – another hard-working honest individual with no criminal convictions.

Yu was delighted with the find. But Adam was puzzled. What made an otherwise honest man agree to undertake such a hazardous course of action? 'If he has never carried drugs before, why now?' he asked. 'At the age of sixty-two?'

'Circumstances,' said Yu. 'Circumstances that add to the picture of innocence.'

'What sort of circumstances?'

Yu answered as if it was a matter of no concern. 'He has a tumour on the brain.'

Adam closed his eyes. Oh God, he thought, feeling sick inside.

Yu continued, 'He is also suffering from kidney complications. He can only walk short distances, five or six yards at a time. Otherwise he is restricted to a wheelchair. He is travelling to America under doctor's orders. What more could you ask for?'

'How bad is his condition?' asked Adam, still appalled.

Yu laughed. 'Don't look so grief-stricken, Adam. His condition is not necessarily terminal. He has already seen doctors in California and they say the tumour is operable. But, as with everything in America, it will cost a great deal of money. Prakorp and his family have saved as much as they can but they are not wealthy people. He is just a boat builder, his son a gardener, his wife runs a small candy store.'

'So he's carrying the stuff to help pay for his operation, is that it?'

Yu gave a whimsical smile, amused at Adam's sudden display of conscience. 'I can see you still have a lot to learn, my friend. Mules carry merchandise for many reasons – to pay off gambling debts, to find a dowry for a wife, to buy a house or a car. I know an orthopaedic surgeon in Bangkok, a most reputable man, who put himself through medical school carrying white powder. What does it matter? Each man has his own motives. Believe me, Prakorp is grateful for the opportunity.'

'How will he carry the stuff?' asked Adam in a dry voice.

'He has so much medicine, so many bottles and packages, that he carries a medical bag. We have built a false bottom into it. On the airport X-rays, the stuff will just show up as powder of some kind, dietary fibre perhaps.' Yu chuckled to himself. 'Maybe he has haemorrhoids to add to his woes.'

But Adam was still too shocked to see any humour in the situation. 'Do I get to see him?' he asked.

Yu didn't think it was a good idea. 'He's new to the game, Adam. If anything goes wrong, he's liable to panic. If he knows who you are, he'll point the finger. A mule is not just paid to carry the stuff, he's paid to take the punishment if the drugs are intercepted, remember that.'

Adam appreciated the logic of it. He remembered his own panic at San Francisco Airport, terrified that Polianna Kim had been caught and was shoving all the blame on to him. 'But how will I recognise Prakorp?' he asked. 'Presumably I'll be travelling on the same aircraft.'

'Yes, I've booked you on United Airlines out of Tokyo. There are seats available for the flight which leaves the day after tomorrow. As for any problems of recognition, here.' He handed Adam a small passport-sized colour photograph, the kind that are taken in automatic booths. It showed a thin, earnest individual, cheeks sunken and with large, searching eyes. He was bald and his skin was blotched a deep mahogany brown from a lifetime working under the sun.

'Once Prakorp has passed through Customs,' said Yu, 'he will be met by his son and his family. He will wait in the concourse for you. All you have to do is go up to him and ask if he slept well on the flight. He speaks a little English, enough anyway. That is how he will recognise you. He will then wheel himself to the public toilets. As I said, he can walk four or five yards unaided so he will be able to get into the cubicle on his own. He'll carry his medical bag with him. He'll remove the five units and place them in a bag. You must make sure that you are waiting outside the cubicle to go in directly after him. Knock on the door and ask if he is all right. Then he will know that you are there. He will come out and you will go in. As simple as that.'

'How much will he charge for his services?' asked Adam.

'His return air fare plus two thousand US dollars a unit, a total of ten thousand dollars. I know it's expensive, especially for a Thai courier,' said Yu almost apologetically, 'but you wanted the best.'

The night before he flew out of Bangkok, Adam telephoned Nicky. 'I'm sorry, darling, but I've got to go on to New York. There's no way I can get out of it. But I'll only be there a few days, I promise.'

She tried to make a joke of it. 'How do I get to see you, become an air hostess?'

'It's just that we've got a project gelling and there are Wall Street interests . . .'

'What sort of project?' she asked.

'A hotel,' he replied, off the top of his head, not thinking.

'A hotel?' There was a moment's pause. Then Nicky said with a surprising edge to her voice, 'I thought the only people who went to Chiang Mai were tourists and drug traffickers. What are you going to call the place, Adam, the Holiday Inn Poppy View?'

Stunned by the remark, Adam struggled for an answer.

Before he could find the words, Nicky retracted what she had said. 'I'm sorry, that was tactless and bitchy of me, I don't know why I said it, especially with Harry in jail. Just stupid. I'm sorry, darling, I'm missing you, that's all.'

'I like the name, I'll recommend it,' said Adam, trying to ease out her remark by turning it into a lame joke. But the shock of her remark still remained. Had it been no more than she had said, a moment's frustrated bitchiness, or something more deeply seated, some intuition of what he was really doing?

'Where are you staying in New York?' Nicky asked in a subdued voice.

'The Madison Towers,' he answered. 'It's in Manhattan.'

'How long will you be there?'

'Three days, maximum. Then I'm home.'

'And after that?'

'After that,' he said with too much emphasis, 'absolutely bloody nothing!'

'Famous last words . . .'

'Not this time. If necessary, I'll burn my damn passport.'

Nicky gave a tepid laugh. She appeared to be at least half persuaded. 'Forgive me,' she said. 'I'm getting a little twitchy, I suppose. I don't know what it is, I've got no right to hang onto your shirt tails. The way things are going with us at the moment, I'll probably be on a plane to Ottawa the day you get back.'

'That's the Hong Kong syndrome,' he said, trying to make light of it. 'There's no way you can fight it. On planes, off planes – like ships in the night.'

'Yes,' she said with a certain sadness, 'like ships in the night . . .'

The following morning, Adam boarded a Thai Airways

flight to Tokyo. For extra security, Yu Wen-huan had arranged that he and Prakorp should travel to Japan separately and it was only when the United Airlines flight boarded at Narita that Adam saw his courier for the first time; a small, brown-skinned individual, passive and humble, being helped out of his wheelchair by the cabin crew.

The perfect mule, Yu would have said. All Adam could think of were the crushing circumstances that had reduced the man to this extreme.

Prakorp's medical bag, the container for the five units, had been carried on to the plane by a steward and was placed carefully at the sick man's feet. It was made of black leather, shaped like an old-fashioned Gladstone bag, the kind country doctors carried at the turn of the century. It was scuffed and worn, pretty much an antique itself. A good choice, thought Adam.

He had hoped that this second delivery would be easier than the first. But all the way across the Pacific, for fourteen endless, droning, claustrophobic hours, he sat, unable to eat or sleep, his neck and back muscles knotted with tension. It was only an hour or so out of Los Angeles that eventually he managed to drift off into an exhausted, fitful doze and had to be nudged awake by an air hostess as they came in to land. Thick-headed and puffy-eyed, his feet swollen from the long flight, he sat staring blankly ahead as the wide-bodied Boeing touched down and taxied to the terminal.

When the aircraft doors were opened, Prakorp was helped to his wheelchair and then pushed off the aircraft ahead of the other passengers. Adam followed with the crowd.

He didn't see Prakorp pass through Immigration but when he reached the baggage carousel he saw him sitting in his wheelchair next to the conveyor belt waiting for his suitcase with a member of the airline ground staff. His case was one of the first to come trundling along; as old and scuffed as his medical bag, a cheap cardboard container tied up with string. Adam had to smile at the look of distaste on the face of the ground staff employee, a paunchy, middle-aged man, as he hauled the case off the carousel and then, half dragging it, pushed Prakorp in the direction of Customs Control.

Adam's own suitcase followed a few seconds later. He scooped it off the carousel and made his own way towards Customs, shadowing the wheelchair. Prakorp appeared to be displaying no signs of outward emotion, no fear, no worry. That's it, thought Adam, stay that way. So far, so good.

The ground staff employee stopped the wheelchair close to a burly officer dressed in blue police-style uniform. 'He speaks hardly any English,' said the employee. 'He's come to the US for medical treatment. We had advance notice. He's got doctor's papers and all.'

The Customs officer pointed to the black bag on Prakorp's lap. 'What's in the bag?'

'Medicines, I guess.' The employee leant over Prakorp's shoulder and opened it. 'Yeah, just a lot of bottles and pills and stuff.'

'Okay, then.'

In that instant Adam heard a moan. It was low, animal-like, filled with pain, and it stopped him in his tracks. For a moment he hesitated, uncertain of its source. Then it came again, louder this time.

The burly Customs officer was gawking at Prakorp. 'Jesus, what's happening to him? What's wrong with the guy?'

Adam witnessed it all. He saw Prakorp jerk forward and back in a series of violent spasms, sending the medical bag crashing to the floor. He saw him clutching first at his belly and then at his head, writhing in his wheelchair. My God, he thought, it must be his tumour, he's having a stroke!

With a series of short, gasping shrieks, kicking his legs, Prakorp rose from his wheelchair, staggered a couple of feet and collapsed. In between the terrible sounds of pain, he was crying out in Thai, a meaningless jumble of words.

Everybody around was stunned; Customs officers, passengers, air crew. Nobody moved. All they could do was stare. It was Adam who was first there, falling to his knees next to the writhing body. 'Somebody call a doctor!' he shouted. 'Get a doctor! Hurry!'

Prakorp had curled himself into a foetal position. He was whimpering now. Saliva, a sulphurous yellow, dribbled down his chin. His eyes rolled back in their sockets. Kneeling by him, Adam could do nothing other than murmur in English, 'Help will be here any minute. Just hang on, hang on . . .' He had never felt more totally helpless.

Onlookers had started to gather now. Adam surveyed

the crowd, silently pleading for help. A few edged nervously away but most remained there gawking at the stricken figure. Only one man, a youngster in his early twenties, dressed in jeans and a shiny black windcheater, came forward. 'I'm a navy medic,' he said in a strong Midwest accent. 'Have you got any idea what's wrong with the poor guy?'

All Adam could do was shake his head. 'I don't know . . . a stroke, a heart attack . . .'

'There's an ambulance on its way,' said the young man. 'Best just make him comfortable. There's nothing more we can do.'

Adam saw the medical bag lying on the floor a few yards away. He picked it up and opened it. 'Maybe there's something in here that could help him,' he said, forgetting all about the heroin. He picked up the first packet of pills but everything written on it was in Thai, unintelligible to him. Shaking his head, he dropped it back in and closed the bag.

Prakorp lay still now, barely moaning, no more than a spittle-strung mumble. His gnarled artisan's fingers quivered on the floor.

'He's got to have family waiting for him,' said Adam in a hollow voice. 'Somebody should tell them . . .'

'Yeah, good idea. Why don't you go through? Don't worry, I'll wait with him here.' The navy medic had taken off his shiny black windcheater, rolling it into a small bundle which he now placed under Prakorp's head. 'Get back, folks, please. Give him room to breathe.'

Adam edged back into the crowd, hardly aware that he

still held Prakorp's medical bag in his right hand. From somewhere behind him he heard a male voice shout that the paramedics were on the way. He walked without looking to either side, staring straight ahead. He had his suitcase in his left hand, Prakorp's bag in his right. As if on the outer perimeter of some dream, he was aware of the blue of uniforms. But nobody challenged him, nobody spoke his name. The doors opened into the concourse, and he walked through.

The shock of it remained with him the rest of that day. During the flight across the continent from Los Angeles to New York, he couldn't get Prakorp out of his mind, the clammy feel of his skin, those animal moans. He was consumed with guilt for leaving him lying there and walking away. But what more could he have done? How could he have helped? Prakorp had been a desperately sick man. The risk of an attack like that, sudden and overwhelming, must always have been there. There was no purpose, he thought, in blaming himself. But it made no difference. The guilt remained.

He landed at J.F. Kennedy at 10.30 that night, and caught a yellow cab into Manhattan. By the time he reached the hotel, he was so tired he could barely keep his eyes open. He made it to his room, tipped the bellhop, managed to kick off his shoes and then fell fully clothed onto the bed in a poleaxed, dreamless sleep.

The rumble of the rush-hour traffic down Madison Avenue woke him in the morning. He checked his watch but it was still operating on Thai time, thirteen or fourteen hours out of synchronisation with New York. He shaved and had a steaming hot shower, scrubbing himself clean. Then, dressed in fresh clothes and feeling stronger, he telephoned Slug Delaney.

'Forty-eight hours to spare. That's pretty shit hot.' Delaney was impressed.

'When do you want to collect the stuff?'

'Are you booked into the same hotel?'

'The same one.'

'I'll be there in sixty minutes. What's your room number?'

Adam had to check his key. 'Seven six three.'

With time to kill, Adam left the hotel and went across to Reubens, the deli on the opposite corner. He carried Prakorp's medical bag with him. For some reason he felt ravenously hungry and devoured a breakfast of fruit juice, hash browns, fried eggs and toasted buttered bagels. He read the morning paper, drinking coffee, and watched the world go by – the well-dressed secretaries, the pasty-faced businessmen, the orthodox Jews in their black coats and beards.

Slug Delaney arrived at the hotel as scheduled. If anything, he seemed to have grown bigger in the past couple of weeks. He wore an Hawaiian cotton shirt, as big as a tent, emblazoned with palm trees and leaping blue dolphins. The weather was mild enough but Delaney had great sweat stains under each armpit. There was grease on his trousers. He dropped himself whale-like on the edge of the bed. Adam noticed that he carried the same emerald green sports bag but this time it was bulging.

'Where's the merchandise?' asked Delaney.

Adam removed the five units from the false bottom of the medical bag.

Delaney took each one, weighing it in the pale, pudgy palm of his hand. 'Tiger's Claw again. So we're showing a little consumer loyalty, are we?' He opened the sports bag, removed a small cream-coloured cloth bag from it and placed the five units inside. 'I've got to tell you, Casement is impressed. He never thought you'd get the stuff here on schedule. None of us did.'

'What about the cash?' asked Adam who wanted to complete the handover with the minimum of delay.

Delaney grinned, his jowls trembling. 'All here, buddy, all in used one hundred dollar bills – a total of nine hundred and fifty thousand. I think this time you'd best take the whole bag. Just feel the weight of the thing. Now that's money!' He handed Adam the sports bag. 'So when can you make your next delivery?'

'We agreed every thirty days,' said Adam in a clipped, businesslike fashion. 'The question is, how many units do I supply?'

'Casement says we're ready to move into top gear.'

Delaney struggled to his feet, the bed groaning beneath him. 'Next delivery is ten units.'

Adam smiled, playing the part.

With the cloth bag in his hand, Delaney lumbered to the door, leaving the sour odour of sweat in the air. 'See you in a month,' he said. 'Keep well.' And he was gone.

Adam sat on the bed in the stillness of the room. He hardly dared believe it. It was done. Finished. The whole obscene episode was behind him. He looked down at the sports bag bulging with the money that would clear Harry's debt. Thank God, was all he could think, thank God, thank God . . . he would never have to traffic in drugs again.

Flopping back on the bed, he reached for the telephone. First, he had to confirm his flight out of this damn place. New York would never be the same for him again. Second, he had to telephone Nicky to tell her he was coming home.

There was no problem with the airline. He was confirmed for the Hong Kong flight that evening via Seattle. The hotel telephonist reminded him that it was midnight in Hong Kong but he said that didn't matter and she put him through to Nicky's apartment.

Adam half expected her to be asleep but, when she came on the line, she was clearly wide awake and brimming with excitement. 'Adam, is that you? I tried to phone you an hour ago but there was no reply.'

'I was out having breakfast,' he answered. 'Why, what is it?'

'Your office had a call from Helmut Gasser earlier this evening.'

'Oh, God, the commission. Has the decision been made?'

'Signed, sealed and delivered. You've done it, Adam, you've won!'

It was too good to be true. 'Are you sure?'

'Of course I'm sure! I phoned Gasser myself to say you were out of town. It was a clean sweep, Adam. The whole goddamn board voted for your design!' She was laughing, bubbling with excitement for him. 'So when are you coming back? You've got work to do!'

'Tonight,' he said and he was laughing too.' I'm finished here, finished for good.'

'So, Mr Genius, how does it feel? Are you happy at last?'

'Ecstatic! And I love you. The problems, the moods are over, I promise.'

'So you're all mine again?'

'Any way you want me!'

'Just one of you – the old you – will be fine.'

'Then that's the way you've got it. No more schizoid behaviour. As predictable as rain in an English summer.'

'Sounds wonderful,' said Nicky.

And that's when Adam heard the knock on the door.

He froze, not daring to breathe. Who could it be? Perhaps it was Delaney . . . but why?

There was a moment's silence. Then the knock came again: three sharp raps. Adam's heart began to thud against his rib cage. Don't be stupid, he said to himself, it's just the hotel staff. The cleaners want to get into the room. But even so, his chest was so tight he could hardly breathe.

'Look, darling, I'm sorry, can I phone you back in a couple of minutes?' he said to Nicky. 'There's somebody at the door.'

'Okay. But don't be long.'

'I love you,' he whispered.

'I love you, too.'

His mouth suddenly dry as ash, Adam put down the phone. He stepped over to the door, paused a moment, took a deep breath, and then opened it.

A woman stood in the doorway, strikingly good-looking, tall and blonde. 'Mr Blake?' she asked.

Adam nodded, perplexed. 'Yes, can I help you?'

In a blur of movement, he saw her wrench a gun from her handbag. Simultaneously, from either side of the door, men rushed him. Adam was slammed back into the wall with such ferocity that his head cracked against it. Unable to resist, he was spun round and his arms pinioned. His head was bursting. He tasted blood in his mouth. 'Who are you?' he gasped. 'What do you want?'

And the answer was spat back at him. 'DEA, shitball, you're under arrest!'

Chapter Seven

NEW YORK – HONG KONG

She read from a yellow dog-eared card in a brisk monotone as if she had read the same words a thousand times before: 'You have the right to remain silent. Anything you say can be used against you in court. You have the right to talk to a lawyer for advice before we ask you any questions. You have the right to have a lawyer with you during questioning. If you cannot afford a lawyer, one will be appointed for you before questioning. Do you understand? If so, say yes.'

Adam swayed dizzily on his feet, blood dribbling from his nose.

'Do you understand?'

'Yes,' he mumbled, 'yes . . .'

Then the man spoke, one of the two who had rammed him back against the wall and cuffed his hands behind his back. He was black-eyed and swarthy with a torso on him like a bull. Black hair sprouted from his nostrils. 'Okay, Mr hotshot fuckin' architect, we're gonna get you down the back stairs now, away from all those prying paparazzi with their Nikons and zoom lenses. Because we don't want a lot of embarrassing publicity, you get me? We don't want word spreading. Later, we'll hang you out to dry. But right now you're our little secret. So I don't want to hear a squeak from you, get me? One squeak and I'll crush your fuckin' larynx.'

Adam allowed himself to be hauled along the corridor and down the back stairs. He didn't resist. What was the purpose? He felt no despair, no terror, just a torpid, passive stoicism as if all this had been preordained.

The swarthy one was pulling him from the front, the woman was at his shoulder. He could smell her perfume, a light lemonish fragrance. She was tall, almost as tall as he was, very athletic, very blonde with startling blue eyes.

There was a car waiting on the street and they bustled him into the back, sitting on either side of him. Adam felt strangely in control of himself, almost calm. The car set off, moving into the traffic down Madison.

'We shadowed you all the way from Chiang Mai,' said the swarthy one, 'all the way from Thailand.' He was clearly in a state of agitation, hyped up after the arrest, his adrenaline pumping. 'We even had the room in the hotel rigged up waiting for you. We've got the lot on video – you meeting with the fat harp, Delaney, the handing over of the stuff, the whole fuckin' works. What do you think of that, huh?'

Adam kept his silence.

But the swarthy agent couldn't keep his. 'Do you know what you're looking at, Blake? Twenty years. Yeah, that's right – twenty. With luck, you and that slime of a brother back in Hong Kong might just get out at the same time. Now there's something to look forward to – a family fuckin' reunion!'

Adam let the abuse wash over him. What did it matter? What did anything matter now? The future was prescribed for him in letters of iron.

Nicky waited two hours for Adam's return call, pacing her apartment, angry at first and then very worried. It wasn't like him, not like him at all. Eventually, at 2 a.m. Hong Kong time, unable to sleep, she made the call herself. She expected to be put straight through to Adam's room but was connected instead with reception.

'I'm sorry,' said the desk clerk, 'but Mr Blake had to check out urgently. No, ma'am, I don't know where he went.'

For three hours they had tagged him, all the way to this isolated cottage in the Connecticut woods. They had seen him meet with his two accomplices and now those men were under surveillance too. It had been a good, clean, professional operation. So far Delaney hadn't suspected a thing. Carl Drexel removed his .38 Special from its holster. Now was the time to move in.

It was an idyllic spring afternoon. A good day for fishing, he thought. A breeze rustled the fresh green leaves of the spruce and the cedars. Sunlight dappled the soft green undergrowth. The air smelt of fungus and ferns. He could hear birds singing.

Drexel had two agents with him: Pete Turnbull, six foot three, lean and gung ho, and Dick Ridgeway, more his own vintage, a little out of condition and happier with a computer than a .38 Special. The three of them together would effect Delaney's arrest.

Fifty yards along the track, Drexel caught his first glimpse of the cottage: unpainted clapboard and russet roof tiles. He crept closer, and knelt by a moss-covered log. A green lawn, like a moat, ran round it. A kid's bike lay out in the sunshine. There was an air about the place of middle-class innocence, silent and serene, an unpretentious weekend retreat for some accountant and his family.

Drawing closer, Drexel could see a car parked at the back of the garage. It was a metallic grey BMW with New York number plates, NZG 895, the car that Delaney had driven from Manhattan.

There was music coming from inside the cottage, a hangover from the sixties, a medley of the Mamas and the Papas' greatest hits, 'California Dreamin', 'Monday Monday', Drexel's kind of music. But there was no sign of Delaney.

Emerging from the fern and bracken of the woods, bent so low that his belt cut into his belly, Drexel sprinted across the lawn and flattened himself against the garage wall. Turnbull followed, running with graceful ease. Ridgeway, red-faced, brought up the rear.

'The main entrance must be round the back,' whispered Turnbull. 'The porch is meshed in with a fly screen. No way in that way.'

Carl Drexel gestured to Ridgeway. 'Stay here,' he hissed. 'Keep the front of the cottage covered. Pete and I will make our way round the back.'

Ridgeway gave a grateful nod, hunching himself down in the cool shadows under the eaves.

Drexel edged his way along the garage wall until he reached the corner. He glanced around, seeing the front door. As he did so, the music from inside the cottage abruptly stopped.

Drexel ducked back. He heard the front door open and click shut again. Then Delaney's ponderous footfalls could be heard, first on the wooden steps and then on the loose granite chips spread out around the garage. A second later Delaney himself lumbered into view, moving with the pendulous gravity of an elephant. He carried a set of car keys in one hand and the cream-coloured cloth bag taken from Blake's hotel room in the other.

Drexel held his breath, waiting for the perfect moment. Delaney reached the car, inserting the keys into the door. His head was down, he was standing flat-footed. 'DEA!' Drexel shouted. 'You're under arrest!'

Delaney swivelled his huge body, dropping the cloth bag onto the granite chips. His eyes were lost in pouches of flesh but his small purse of a mouth fell open as he gawked at the three armed detectives.

'Turn slowly towards the car,' said Turnbull in a cold, very controlled voice. 'Put your hands on the car roof where we can see them.'

Recovering from his shock, Delaney glanced to his left and his right, then back towards the three DEA agents. 'Yeah, okay,' he muttered, slowly raising his arms.

That's it, thought Drexel, nice and easy, nice and—

With a speed that was amazing in a man so vast,

Delaney suddenly dropped to his knees. Drexel saw him hauling an automatic from under the voluminous folds of his Hawaiian shirt.

'Oh, shit, Delaney, don't be a fool!' he shouted.

But the only response was a savage burst of automatic fire that chewed into the clapboard inches above his head. Drexel staggered back, half tripping, dropping down by the garage wall. On pure reflex he fired a shot, puncturing a hole in the BMW's windshield.

Delaney had thrown open the driver's door of the BMW and was standing behind it, raking them with fire and bellowing all the time like some mad animal. 'I'll kill you! I'll kill you!' Bullets threw up the granite chips and whined through the trees.

Drexel hugged the wall. Then, behind him, he heard Dick Ridgeway grunt. 'Carl . . . oh God, I'm hit!' He swung his head and saw Ridgeway down on the grass, clutching a shattered knee. Blood, bright crimson, was spurting from an artery. The whole thing was turning into a disaster. 'Dick is down!' he shouted to Turnbull.

But Turnbull was in a world of his own. Scorning cover, feet apart, perfectly poised, he was methodically pumping .38 slugs into the driver's door of the BMW.

Delaney screamed from behind that door. 'Bastards!' He tried to return fire, shrieking with pain and rage. But he was out of ammunition and had to waste precious seconds while he reloaded. Drexel heard him muttering as he fumbled frantically with a new magazine.

Turnbull moved. Loping, like a wolf on the hunt, he covered the twenty paces to the bonnet of the BMW, crouched a moment, checking his weapon, then reared up and blasted two shots in a downwards trajectory through the window of the driver's door.

An instant later Delaney toppled backwards away from the car. He was so fat that he couldn't roll and lay there like some beached seal, his body shuddering.

'Drop your weapon,' Turnbull ordered. 'Drop it, I say.'

But Delaney, in a kind of mad, blood-soaked hysteria, was still trying to reload. 'Fuck you!' he screamed. 'I'll kill you, kill you—'

Turnbull fired.

The slug hit Delaney in the left cheek below the eye, tearing through his brain and out the back of his skull. Death was instantaneous. Drexel saw the head jerk back, he heard the loud sigh and then witnessed the gargantuan body fall slack. The cloth bag taken from Blake's hotel room lay a few inches from Delaney's head. But now it was stained with a fine spray of brain and bone.

Climbing wearily to his feet, Drexel holstered his weapon. 'What in the hell did he open fire for?' he asked out loud, shaking his head in dismay. 'Where was the percentage in it? Jesus, sometimes I think the whole world has gone mad.'

After the formalities of booking him – taking his fingerprints and personal details, getting a mug shot, front and profile – after the humiliating bureaucracy of it all, Adam was taken to a holding cell and dumped there, left on his own to sit and stew. Day crept laboriously into evening, evening into night. Food was provided, a hamburger, french fries and coffee in a paper cup from some diner downstairs. But he had no appetite for it.

With each passing hour the shock and disbelief diminished and he came quickly enough to understand the stark reality of his predicament. He could appreciate how men in situations like this, suddenly sucked dry of hope, contemplated suicide. But, as he had been from the moment of his arrest, Adam remained in the grip of a dull, unquestioning fatalism. Somehow, deep down in the darkest labyrinths of his subconscious, he had always known it would come to this – the arrest, the trial, the sentence. The irony was that all his life he had believed in the sanctity of the law.

He wondered how his mother would react to the news: two sons now, both condemned by the courts, both criminals of the worst kind. She was a resilient woman but resilience only went so far. Everybody had their breaking point. How would she react to the pain and the humiliation? Both her husbands lost to her and now both her sons. It was more than any one person should have to bear.

Alone with his thoughts, Adam even had time to wonder, with a little bitter humour, how Helmut Gasser would react to the news. He could imagine the consternation in that stolid Zurich boardroom, the chaotic pantomime as they scrambled to suppress the news that the commission to design the bank's Hong Kong headquarters had just been given to a drug trafficker. Dear God, the scandal!

As for Nicky, any hopes for their future were shattered beyond redemption. In time he knew he would fade into nothing more than a bad, bitter memory. Some other man would love her, marry her, have children with her, accomplish all the things he had dreamt of for so many months. Some other man would know her body now, sleep next to her at night, hear her soft, rhythmical breathing and kiss those warm, freckled shoulders.

Yes, thought Adam, he *could* understand how men in his position contemplated suicide.

At long last, around ten that night, he was taken from the holding cell to an interview room.

Three agents were waiting for him; the two who had arrested him at the hotel and one whom Adam hadn't seen before, a much older individual in a crumpled suit, heavyset and weary looking. The stranger pointed to a chair, indicating that Adam should sit. He had a slow, phlegmatic way about him. 'My name is Drexel,' he said. 'I've been looking forward to meeting you, Adam.'

Adam gave a cautious nod and sat. The use of his first name, the easy amiability of the introduction, surprised him.

Drexel removed his glasses, cleaning them with a checkered handkerchief. With a tilt of his head, he indicated the woman on his right. 'You've already met Special Agent Martin – Sue Martin. And on my left-hand side here, Nico Divaris.'

Adam again gave the barest nod. The blonde woman, he noticed, kept her head down, reading a file. Divaris, the short, foul-mouthed one, lounged back with an expectant, aggressive look on his swarthy face.

Drexel pointed to a thermos on the table. 'Do you want coffee?'

Adam shook his head. 'No, thank you.'

'If you want anything, just ask.'

'Is it necessary to wear these handcuffs?'

'Regulations, I'm afraid.'

'I'm not going to try and make a run for it.'

'Okay, if you feel more comfortable.' Drexel nodded to Divaris who got up irritably from his seat, muttering to himself, 'Fuck, everybody gets privileges in this place,' and came round the table to unlock the cuffs.

'Before we discuss matters,' said Drexel. 'I want you to watch a short video.'

'Taken in the hotel room?' asked Adam.

'That's right.'

'There's no need.'

'Bear with us, Mr Blake. It won't take long.'

There was a television monitor set up in the corner of the room. When the video came on, it was in black and white, grainy in texture and poorly focused. But Adam had no difficulty identifying himself and Delaney. When the blocks of heroin were removed from the medical bag, they were clearly visible. The sound recording, made through a hidden microphone, was poor too. But the voices were distinct enough: *'Tiger's Claw again. So we're showing a little consumer loyalty, are we? I've got to tell you, Casement is impressed. He never thought you'd get the stuff here on schedule. None of us did.'*

Drexel had made his point. Adam could see for himself just how overwhelming the evidence was.

'We have the physical exhibits, too,' said Drexel in a voice full of quiet reason. 'Your courier's bag, for example, Adam, the one you took off him at Los Angeles

Airport. Remember the young navy medic? He was a DEA man monitoring your progress.'

'What happened to Prakorp?' asked Adam in a dull voice. 'Did he pull through?'

'The courier, you mean? They got him to hospital and put him on the stomach pump. But no, I'm afraid it was too late.'

Adam was bewildered. 'Why a stomach pump?'

'Obviously the shekels you paid him as a mule weren't enough,' Divaris interjected. 'He was trying a little business on his own.'

'You see, it wasn't the brain tumour that killed him,' said Drexel.

'What was it then?'

'Before he left Japan, he had swallowed two condoms, each of them stuffed with heroin,' said Drexel. 'It's an old trick, Adam. Except on this occasion one of the condoms burst inside him – that's what did the job. And I'm afraid that your friend, Delaney, didn't fare any better either. We tailed him to a small place up in Connecticut—'

'But the schmuck tried to shoot it out,' interrupted Divaris with crude relish. 'So now he's in the morgue, too.'

Adam blinked. Inside he felt hollow as if everything had been ripped out, heart, bowels, everything. For Slug Delaney he felt very little. But for Prakorp he was filled with an immense sadness. Dear God, why was fate so cruel? Why did such a fundamentally good man deserve such a wretched, terrifying, agonising end?

Drexel looked at him, seeming to see right through

him. 'It hurts, Adam, doesn't it? The stupid waste of a decent life always hurts.' He removed his spectacles again, polishing them with the same handkerchief. Then he poured himself coffee from the thermos. 'Is this decaffeinated?' he asked.

'Afraid not,' answered Divaris. 'Sugar, caffeine, cholesterol, the works.'

Drexel grimaced but drank it anyway. He studied Adam for a time, the two men's eyes meeting. Then he said in a slow conciliatory voice, 'Two men dead, Adam, but you might just be the lucky one. You see, we know a good deal about you. And where we are short on information, we've been able to put two and two together. For example, we know how you got into this mess. Your brother owed money to his suppliers, am I right? That's how it began.'

Adam hesitated. 'Say nothing' – that was the cure-all advice. But what was the point? He looked at Drexel, trying to assess the man. Then he nodded. 'Yes, that's how it began.'

'But Harry couldn't pay, right? Harry was like the rest of us here, Harry was a borrower not a lender. So they put the screws on you, the successful half-brother. We know how it works. A little old-fashioned Triad terrorism – a decapitated chicken in your mother's kitchen, the ritual of slashing off your brother's ear. Textbook stuff. Your brother's genitals would have followed next. And, of course, there was only *one* way to raise the amount of cash they demanded. A young architect starting out, piled high with overheads, couldn't raise that kind of money legitimately, not all of it plus interest. Am I right?'

Adam nodded.

'Tell me, Adam, who were your brother's suppliers, the ones who pushed you into dealing? Triads obviously. Wo Shing Wo, 14K, Sun Yee On?'

Adam answered in a dull voice, 'Sun Yee On, I think. But I only dealt with the front man. I never met his backers or his financier.'

Drexel smiled to himself. 'Sun Yee On. And what was this front man's name?'

Adam paused, frightened that, in giving the name, he might be endangering Harry, endangering his mother and Nicky, too.

Nobody spoke. The only sound was from the pen of Sue Martin as she took down everything that was said in shorthand.

'Why are you hesitant?' asked Drexel. 'Are you frightened for your family? Don't be.' His wearied, hangdog features had undergone a hardening, especially around the eyes and mouth. 'Co-operation is a two-way street, Adam.'

Adam stared at him.

'What was the front man's name? It's important.'

Adam hesitated a second longer. Then, knowing that it would all have to come out sooner or later, he answered, 'His name was Cheng Tak-shing.'

Drexel smiled again. 'Yes, I thought as much. Dai Ngan, they call him. Am I right? Is he the one?'

Adam answered with a nod.

The smile remained on Drexel's heavy-wedged features. 'Cheng and his backers have had long-term dealings with Chaiwisan. Was it Cheng who put you onto Yu in Chiang Mai and then Chaiwisan himself?'

Adam nodded again.

Drexel looked surprised. 'It's an unusual move.'

'I wanted to get out of the business as soon as I could,'said Adam in a torpid monotone. 'If I could get the units cheap enough and make delivery within a specified time, I knew I could clear my brother's debt with one last run. I pushed Cheng until he agreed. That's how I got to Thailand.'

Sue Martin continued to scribble her notes.

Drexel considered matters for a moment, looking down at his fingernails. Then he asked, 'Did you have any dealings with a man called Leung?'

'No, nobody by that name.'

'A drug financier?'

'No.'

'Did Cheng ever mention his name?'

'Not that I recall.'

'What about Chaiwisan, did he ever mention it?'

'No, sorry.'

'So you don't recall the name at all?'

'If I did, I'd tell you.'

Drexel nodded, his glasses falling forward on his nose. 'We're pleased you're co-operating, Adam, not trying to play hardball, not trying to be clever. That's why I say, you might just be the lucky one. It's up to you. If you're prepared to start thinking of yourself for a change and not that asshole of a brother, you might just get out of this situation much easier than you thought.'

Adam felt a small flurry of hope. 'What do you want me to do?' he asked.

Drexel paused a moment. 'We want you to keep dealing in drugs.'

Adam blinked. 'I'm sorry, I don't understand.'

Drexel sat back in his chair, smiling. 'Then let me explain.'

Drexel didn't mince his words. Adam, he said, was small fry and he was interested in bigger fish, men like Cheng Tak-shing but, in particular, Chaiwisan himself. Chaiwisan couldn't be touched in Laos. He paid protection money to the government there and the government lived up to its side of the bargain. Even if the DEA managed to catch him in Thailand, it was doubtful they could ever extradite him back to the US. He had too many people in his pocket: police, judges, politicians. There was only one effective way of getting him back to the United States to stand trial, that was to entice him out of Laos to Hong Kong. Because Hong Kong had an extradition treaty with the US. Hong Kong had efficient police and an honest judiciary.

'And that's where you come in, Adam,' said Drexel. 'We want you to work for us, you see. We want you to get Chaiwisan out of the jungles of Laos and into Hong Kong.'

'So you want me to act in an undercover role, is that it?

'That's it exactly.'

'But how do I convince him to go to Hong Kong? As you say, I'm small fry, just ten units a month. Why should he leave his sanctuary and come to Hong Kong for me?'

'Because you're going to start dealing on a much bigger scale, that's why.'

'You're moving into the big league,' said Divaris.

'And who will fund me?' asked Adam. 'You?'

'The US Treasury,' said Drexel.

'Good ol' Uncle Sam,' snapped Divaris.

But Adam was dubious. 'I know Chaiwisan. He's been dealing in drugs for over forty years. He's got a sixth sense. It's going to take a hell of a lot to get him to Hong Kong.'

Drexel gave a cursory nod. 'I understand all of that. But he has made plenty of trips before when the need arose and there's no reason why he won't make them again. His business is selling drugs, and sometimes you can't sell, you simply can't set up a deal, without travelling.'

All Adam could see were a thousand problems dooming the idea from the start. 'This might be good in theory,' he said, 'but how's it going to work in practice? Look at the reality. I've been arrested, hauled out of my hotel. You say Delaney has been killed. The word has got to get out, rumours start spreading. Chaiwisan won't come within a thousand miles of me.'

'Nobody knows of your arrest,' said Drexel. 'I can promise you that. Nobody except a few people in this organisation.'

'That's why we hustled you down the back stairs,' said Divaris. 'That's why we put you into an unmarked car. That's why we paid your hotel bill, tips and all, and said you had checked out.'

'But what about my buyers here in the States? With Delaney dead and the drugs seized, how am I going to convince them?'

Drexel gave a knowing smile. 'It's all worked out. We knew you were coming, Adam. Believe me, we had the whole jigsaw puzzle put together before you even stepped off the plane. You'll be able to continue dealing with your buyers and with Chaiwisan, too. Delaney's death will make no difference. Agree to the deal and we'll have you back in a hotel by tomorrow lunchtime.'

There was one further matter that worried Adam – his family. How did he ensure they remained protected? 'I got into this in the first place to try and protect them,' he said, 'and I'm not going to see them put at risk now.'

Drexel understood the problem. 'They won't be at risk, I can assure you of that. Agree to this deal and they'll be even safer.'

'How? It's easy to make assurances,' said Adam, his voice suddenly sharp as acid. 'It's more difficult to live up to them.'

'If we're going to put you back on the streets,' Drexel explained, 'we've got to put you in a credible position. You were paid by Delaney—'

'But you've got that money now.'

'In escrow, Adam, just in escrow. Agree to the deal and we'll arrange for it to be sent by draft to Hong Kong, that and any extra you may need. That way you'll be able to clear your brother's debt, get Cheng off his back. And that puts your mother in the clear, too. Remember, Adam, we want you to look like a successful dealer, a man bitten by the bug. From now on you're not going to be dealing with Cheng on a debtor–creditor basis, from now on you're going to be dealing with him eyeball to eyeball. Whichever way you look at it, this deal has got to be your best way out.'

Adam was possessed by a sudden, desperate hope. 'But if I do help you, if I do what you ask, what's in it for me?'

'A huge reduction in your sentence.'

'But I'll be risking my life.'

'There is a risk, yes.'

'Then what about a full immunity?'

'No, I'm afraid not, Adam.'

'Why not?'

Drexel explained patiently. 'Let me spell out the deal for you because I don't want any confusion. The deal is that you plead guilty to importing and distributing heroin. Tomorrow morning we take you before a District Court judge here in Manhattan. The hearing will be in his chambers, in secret. The record of proceedings will be sealed. The judge will formally find you guilty but he will suspend sentence and place you in our custody. At the end of the day - if you co-operate, if you play this the way we tell you - you're likely to receive a sentence of about five years. With parole, you could be out in two.'

Adam tried to contain his disappointment. 'But you've just admitted it, you're asking me to put my life on the line.'

'I said there was a risk, yes.'

'A risk? Look what Cheng Tak-shing did to my brother, for God's sake! And that was just a warning!'

'I'm sorry, but that's the best deal I can offer,' said Drexel quietly but firmly.

Adam was playing for desperate stakes. He couldn't let it go at that. 'And if I say no?'

Drexel sighed quietly, pouring more coffee from the thermos. 'If you say no, then I'm afraid we'll have to forget any kind of deal, Adam. And that would be a pity because it wouldn't help you and it wouldn't help us. Nor would it help your family. But if that's the way you want it, we can have you before a magistrate first thing in the morning, we'll get an indictment and in a few months' time you'll go to trial. That way, if you're found guilty – and you've seen the kind of evidence we've got – you'll be looking at twenty years. Remember, too, that Cheng won't get paid his money. Your brother, Harry, will remain in debt. Back to square one.' He sipped his coffee, the heat from the drink fogging the bottom of his glasses.

Adam gritted his teeth. 'What about protection when I'm serving my sentence?' he asked, a sullen edge to his voice. 'Once I've finished doing what you want me to, I'm going to need it – assuming I'm still alive,' he added.

'You'll get all the protection necessary. You won't serve your time in a hard case penitentiary. We'll make sure you get into a place for first-time offenders, white-collar criminals.'

'The Watergate Country Club,' said Divaris sardonically.

'It's the best deal I can offer you,' said Drexel. 'Yes or no?'

Adam looked at the three of them, his eyes shifting from face to face. They all gazed back. Divaris was grinning, his olive-pip eyes alight. Sue Martin, much softer, looked almost sad.

Adam took a deep breath. 'All right,' he said with an air of resignation. 'I'll do what you want.'

For everybody it had been a long, hard, sapping day. For Carl Drexel, with so much now at stake, it was impossible just to go home, take the dog for a walk and flop into bed. He needed time to unwind, time to let the adrenaline seep away. So he percolated some decaffeinated coffee, took out one of his rare cigars and got Sue Martin to join him in his office.

Flopping down in his swivel chair, he put his feet up on the desk and gave a long groan of satisfaction as he lit the cigar. 'I knew we'd turn him, I just knew it. And he'll be good, Sue, wait and see, damn good. I'm not normally happy with basically honest men, too often they don't have the guts for it. But beneath that soft exterior, the dreamer in him, Blake has a hard, calculating streak. He's no coward. A fool maybe, but not a coward. He'll do fine.'

Sue Martin gave a tired shrug. 'I hope so.' She looked across at Drexel and said, 'There's blood on your shirt.'

Drexel looked down. Dried black blotches spread diagonally across his chest. But he couldn't remember whose blood it was, Delaney's or Ridgeway's, friend or foe. Christ, it had been a day.

He looked across the desk to where Sue Martin sat, her eyes shadowed with tiredness. She was a beautiful woman, no doubt about it, the kind of classy, lanky blonde they put in advertising films for expensive European cars. Even now, at the end of a long day, gritty-eyed, her sexuality shone through. Drexel often wondered what had pulled her into this business. She was a good detective, a first-rate operator, but he worried about her. Too big a heart, he thought and not enough callouses.

'You're going to be working with this guy for maybe two or three months, you know that,' he said. 'I mean, living in each other's pockets. You're going to get close to him, real close.'

Sue Martin regarded him with a quizzical half-smile. 'What are you trying to say, Carl?'

'You feel sorry for the guy, don't you?'

'Are you worried my heart is going to rule my head?'

'I just don't want any foul-ups.'

'Sure, I feel sorry for him. Don't you? What would you have done if you had faced the same predicament?'

'The guy brought five units into the country, Sue, over six pounds of heroin. In the circumstances he's getting a good deal.'

'Provided he doesn't end up dead.'

'He made the choice.'

'Yeah? I thought *it* made him.'

Drexel gave a weary smile. 'It's too late for semantics. Just so long as you realise how important this operation is going to be. There's more hanging on this than you may realise. A lot, lot more.'

She gave him a swift, hard glance. 'Why are you so edgy about it?'

'Because I worry, that's why.'

'Do you think I'm going to mess up, is that it?'

He looked her straight in the eyes. 'If I did, Sue, you wouldn't be sitting here. You know me better than that.'

She finished her coffee. 'You've been telling Blake that Chaiwisan is the man you're after in this operation. But Chaiwisan isn't the ultimate target, is he?'

The humour left Drexel's face.

'It's Leung Chi-ming, isn't it, the Hong Kong financier, he's the one you really want.'

Drexel stared back at her. 'Bet your ass it is.'

In the morning, in a cold drizzle, Adam was taken down to the basement of the DEA offices to a waiting car. Divaris, stinking of garlic – Adam wondered what on earth he had for breakfast – drove the car while Drexel sat in the back seat next to him.

They drove to Foley Square, to the old courthouse with its Grecian columns and crowds of people bustling in and out; witnesses and jury persons, relatives and defendants, all of them looking equally harassed. This was it, said Drexel, the US District Court for the Southern District of New York.

They went up some stairs to an office to meet the Assistant US Attorney, a bumptious moustached little man with dandruff on his shoulders. His name, he said, was Latvik. 'We shouldn't have any problems, we've got Judge Lazarus,' he said to Drexel with a cocky smile. 'It should all be over in two minutes, like a Moscow wedding.'

'Or a California divorce,' grunted Divaris.

Latvik showed Adam the charges on the indictment. There were two, both, he said, contrary to Title 21 of the US Criminal Code: importing heroin, and possession with intent to distribute. 'Sound fair to you?' he asked.

Adam didn't argue the matter. The charges meant nothing, only the length of the prison sentence counted. That was to be decided later.

They climbed another couple of floors, passed through a door and made their way down a dark corridor to Judge Lazarus's chambers. Latvik knocked and then entered at the head of the small party. 'Good morning, Your Honour.'

Judge Lazarus sat in a red leather-backed chair, a silent witness as they trooped in. His desk was a war zone of files, papers, old pipes, tins of tobacco and family photographs.

The stenographer and the law clerk were already present. Adam sat on a straight-backed wicker chair while the law clerk, who had a bad head cold, read the indictment. When he had finished, he asked Adam if he pleaded guilty.

'Yes, I do,' said Adam.

Latvik, lolling in a deep leather armchair, spoke. 'The accused has agreed to assist the DEA, Your Honour. He is required for certain active, on-the-street investigations, both here and abroad.'

The judge gave an irritable nod. 'I've done these things before, Mr Latvik. You want the sentencing suspended, is that it?'

'Yes, Your Honour.'

'You want him released into the custody of the DEA?'

'Yes, Your Honour.'

'Very well.' He scribbled a few lines into a file that the law clerk had given him, looked up and said peremptorily, 'Thank you, gentlemen.'

They were dismissed.

Somehow Adam had expected more; the high

seriousness of the law, some words of admonishment. But the end result was the same. He was now a convicted felon.

Driving away from court, with the drizzle still falling, Carl Drexel laid out the game plan. 'Purely for internal purposes, each operation has a name,' he said and he gave a bashful grin. 'This one, heaven help us, has been called "Snow White". Snow, get it? Drugs.'

Even Adam had to laugh.

'Don't blame us,' said Divaris from behind the wheel. 'Some schmuck in Washington dreams them up. We just get the next off the list. Think yourself lucky you didn't get "Bambi"!'

Drexel let the smiles fade before continuing. 'From now on, Adam, you're going to be pretty much of a free agent. There's no way we can keep tabs on you, not twenty-four hours a day. So there's a high degree of trust involved.' His voice dropped a tone. 'But try and make a run for it, now or at any time, and you'll be looking at twenty years again.'

Adam looked him straight in the eyes. 'Where am I going to run to, tell me that?'

'Just so long as we understand each other.'

'What I want to know,' said Adam bluntly, 'is how long this operation is going to last. For just how long am I expected to play a double game at your beck and call?'

Drexel ignored the sourness in Adam's question. 'Thailand shouldn't take you longer than a week, ten days. Hong Kong, no more than two weeks. With luck we'll have it wrapped up within a month.'

'And if it runs longer, stretches into two months or three, what then? Do I still serve the same time in jail at the end of it?'

'It all gets weighed in the balance.'

'And what does that mean?'

'It means that the longer you spend working for us, the less time you'll spend behind bars.'

'Which don't mean that you string the fuckin' thing out until we're all old men,' said Divaris with a hard laugh.

'There's one other thing,' said Drexel. 'You can laugh at the name but remember that this operation is just that, an operation. It's not a one-man escapade. You're not going to reduce your sentence with a lot of individual stunts. John Wayne stuff might be great in the movies, in the real world it's a positive hazard.'

'I can promise you,' said Adam with a faint, bitter smile, 'gung ho is not my style.'

'Remember that if deals are set up, they have to be set up in consultation. Strategies have got to be planned. We don't want you zinging around out there like some ricocheting bullet.'

Adam nodded. 'I understand what you're saying. But I've got to be allowed some initiative, some leeway to make on-the-spot decisions. Otherwise we'll just get bogged down, hopeless.'

'We appreciate that.'

'Nor can I have a whole team dragging along behind me.'

'Nobody expects you to.'

'That's why you'll be dealing through one agent,' said

Divaris. 'Your own little guardian angel: blue eyes, blonde hair.'

Adam sat back, expecting the worst. 'And who is that going to be?'

'I've assigned Sue Martin,' said Drexel.

Sue Martin! Adam hadn't expected it to be a woman.

'Every deal you make, where possible, you discuss with her first,' said Drexel. 'Everything that's done, every relevant detail, you report back to her. And debriefings are vital, remember that. The records have to be full and they have to be accurate.'

A woman, that complicated matters. 'Do I take it she'll be travelling with me?' asked Adam.

'That's the idea,' said Drexel in a dry voice.

'Lovers usually stick together.' Divaris gave a swarthy grin. 'As they say, like shit to a blanket.'

'Lovers?' Adam was amazed.

'It's the easiest and the most feasible cover,' said Drexel without a trace of humour, indicating in no uncertain terms that it was pure business. 'You're a bachelor, you're reasonably presentable. It all fits.'

But for Adam, a further layer of emotional pretence, more lies to live with, was the one thing he didn't need. He turned to Drexel, shaking his head. 'You don't make it too easy, do you?'

'I'm not interested in what's easy Adam, I'm interested in what works.'

Twenty-four hours earlier, Sue Martin had arrested him, read him his rights and then bundled him into a waiting car. Now their relationship had been spun on its head. If it wasn't easy for Adam, it wasn't easy for her either. And it showed.

She was waiting for him in a suite at Adam's new hotel, the Milford Plaza on West 45th, and when Adam entered with Drexel and Divaris, she gave him a tight, uncertain smile. 'Has everything been explained?'

Adam gave a curt nod. 'I understand we're lovers – for outside consumption, at least.'

'One step over the line,' said Divaris with a leer, 'and she has permission to blow your nuts off.'

Sue Martin gave him a withering look. 'Do me a favour, Nico, go shoot yourself in the foot.'

Divaris, as always, was unfazed. 'Just spelling out the rules, Sue, just spelling out the rules.'

But Drexel, too, gave him a hard stare over the top of his bifocals and Divaris backed off, muttering to himself, 'Jeez, suddenly we've got a major sense of humour failure.' To console himself, he flopped down into a chair and telephoned room service for coffee and croissants.

Sue Martin, dressed in a tracksuit top, denims and white gym shoes, sat on the end of one of the two twin beds looking uncomfortably self-conscious. If this was the first time for Adam, this was very definitely the first time for her, too.

Drexel went to say something to her, thought better of it, gave a resigned shrug and turned his attention to Adam. 'Okay,' he said, 'first things first. Let's re-establish links with your Irish buyer, your theatrical leprechaun from Connecticut. The phone is monitored for all incoming and outgoing calls. Now, here's the scenario . . .'

When Toby Casement answered the call and recognised Adam's voice, his reaction was one of pure panic. 'Are you mad?' he spluttered, half hysterical. 'Why are you contacting me? You must be out of your mind. Dear God, haven't you heard?'

'Of course I've heard,' Adam replied, surprised at how relaxed and confident he sounded. 'That's why I'm phoning you. There's no need for concern, Toby. It was a freak incident, that's all.'

'An *incident*, is that what you call it? My God, he's dead. Delaney's dead. I can't believe it!'

'He's dead,' said Adam in a tone of harsh indifference, 'because he was stupid, because he panicked.'

'How can you say that? How do you know?'

'Haven't you read today's paper?'

'Paper? No, which paper?'

'The *Daily News*. Here, I've got it in front of me.' Adam picked up the tabloid which lay next to him on the bed and opened it at page three. 'Let me read you the headline: "Traffic violation leads to drug shoot-out".'

Casement gave a small, astonished gasp. 'What are they talking about, traffic violation?'

'Just listen, I'll read you the article. "Three police officers, following up a speeding violation, went to a weekend cottage near Twin Lakes, Connecticut, yesterday and ran into a hail of automatic fire. The man to be served the speeding ticket, Brooklyn resident Seamus

Delaney, opened fire with an Israeli-made Ouzi automatic before the police could explain the purpose of their visit, hitting one officer in the leg. In the ensuing shoot-out, Delaney himself was killed. Only afterwards did police discover the reason for the apparently motiveless attack. In a bag by the slain body was over seven pounds of heroin." '

Adam waited for Casement's response but all he could hear was the man's thin panting at the other end of the line.

'So you see what I mean, Toby, Delaney brought it upon himself. He drove too fast in the first place, got a ticket and then panicked when three cops – on their way off duty – came by to serve it.'

'Off duty? Does it say they were going off duty?'

'That's why there were three of them. They were going bowling.'

'But the story could be planted,' murmured Casement, suspicion compounding his fear. 'It's happened before, Adam, this wouldn't be the first time.'

'Of course it could be planted,' said Adam, the relaxed, rational tone of his voice indicating that he had considered the possibility himself. 'But how likely is it? Delaney went straight from my hotel. If they were tailing him, hoping to get to you, and it all went wrong, why didn't they at least pick me up?'

'But I telephoned your hotel last night, Adam, that's what got me so worried. I was told you had checked out and I didn't know what to think.'

Adam gave a small, self-deprecatory laugh. 'I checked out because, when I heard the news, I got worried too – until I sat down, that is, and used a little cold logic. If I had been part of a police dragnet, I knew they would have picked me up at the hotel before I had a chance to leave. They would have tailed me at least. If they had known about you, you'd be in custody too now. No, Toby, what happened was exactly as the paper reports. Delaney saw three cops and jumped to one conclusion – the wrong one.'

'Yes, well, that may be,' muttered Casement, the fear in his voice still apparent. 'But I'm not taking any chances. There's obviously going to be investigations. We're leaving tonight, the two of us, Patrick Ryan and myself.'

'Where to?'

'There's a safe place in Eire, County Cork.'

'How long are you going to be there?'

'Until we can be sure there are no *personal* ramifications. I'm sure you understand.'

'I understand entirely,' said Adam in a voice of smooth sympathy. 'But when you return, I sincerely hope we can continue our business relationship.'

'That depends.'

'But in principle at least, once you've been able to restructure?'

'Of course, yes, in principle.'

'So I can make contingency plans?'

'Yes, yes, by all means.'

'Good,' said Adam, 'then I'll be in contact again. Have a safe journey, Toby. My best regards to Patrick Ryan.' And he replaced the receiver.

Carl Drexel smiled at him across the room. 'Done like a true professional,' he said.

Adam nodded, smiling too. But for him it was a pure release of tension.

Drexel hadn't expected Adam to put on a performance as smooth or confident, not the first time. It augured well. 'You did everything that was necessary,' he said. 'You re-established your credibility and, in principle at least, agreed to continue trading. That's all we needed.'

Adam remained concerned, however, with the mechanics of what lay ahead. Even assuming that Casement and Ryan recovered their nerves and agreed to continue buying heroin, the amounts involved were not sufficient to entice Chaiwisan out of Laos. To tempt the little Yunnanese opium trader to Hong Kong, much bigger, fresher bait was needed.

Drexel had already anticipated the problem. 'That's why we've got you a new group of buyers,' he said. 'Major league players, too, guys on the move. Here,' and he tossed a buff-coloured envelope onto Adam's lap. 'It contains background information I want you to learn.'

Adam looked dubious. 'You think Chaiwisan is going to fall for a bunch of fictional characters?'

Drexel gave a slow, phlegmatic smile. 'Who said they were fictional? The information in that envelope concerns a ring we've had under surveillance in Newark, New Jersey, for over a year now. They're Vietnamese but ethnic Chinese mainly, recent immigrants, a hard bunch of bastards. We've had an undercover agent negotiating with them for the past couple of months and this morning he told them he'd found a new associate, a Hong Kong dealer who could import China White at twenty per cent less than the going rate.'

'Presumably I'm that associate?'

Drexel gave a wry smile. 'You're learning fast.'

Adam said nothing but he couldn't help being impressed. In just over twenty-four hours he'd been arrested, convicted, turned into an agent and supplied with a full cover story. Delaney was dead, he had been turned, and the men he'd dealt with in the Far East – Chaiwisan, Yu and Cheng Tak-shing – were the next targets. That only left Casement and Ryan unaccounted for. 'And what will happen to them?' he asked.

For the first time, Drexel paused. He cast Sue Martin a knowing glance and then turned back to Adam. 'If you want answers on Casement and Ryan, you'll have to look elsewhere.'

'Where?'

'The CIA.'

All of Adam's suspicions were confirmed. 'So there was a political connection? I always thought so. Who to, the IRA?'

Drexel shrugged. 'According to what little I know, they've been running guns to the hardliners, the Provisional wing. Casement is some kind of Irish independence nut, amazing for a guy so goddamn effete.'

'Drugs and then guns, is that it?'

Drexel walked over to the mini bar, removing a bottle of mineral water. 'Heroin, cocaine – they're both good cash crops, Adam, look how much you raised in a month. You sell the drugs, you buy weapons with the proceeds.'

'It's nothing new, half the terrorist organisations in the world do it,' grunted Divaris from the corner.

'The cocaine growers in Peru are backed by left-wing guerrillas,' said Drexel, shaking his head. 'The Karens and the Shans say they only grow opium to finance their war of independence against Burma. Go to the Beqa'a Valley in the Lebanon and all you see are poppy fields. Shit, every Muslim faction you can think of, or pronounce, fundamentalist or not, every Christian one, has its own acreage. What do you think they've been growing for the past ten years along the Afghan border? Drugs and politics, Adam, like peaches and cream, Ginger Rogers and Fred Astaire. You've got one, you've got the other.'

'How long has the CIA known about Casement and Ryan?' asked Adam.

Drexel sat himself down, sipping his mineral water. 'Difficult to say. Nine months maybe, a year.'

'And how long have you known?'

'Since yesterday,' said Divaris.

Adam looked amazed.

'It's a little thing called self-interest,' said Drexel in a tone of dry sarcasm.

'Again, nothing new,' grunted Divaris. 'Believe me, there have been more than a few occasions when we've cracked a drug cartel only to find out that they've been financed by the CIA – all in America's best interests of, course, saving the world from the commies.'

Adam shook his head. 'It's unbelievable.'

Drexel gave a mirthless smile. 'My sentiments entirely.'

* * *

By mid-afternoon they had received confirmation of their bookings: two seats, business class, to Bangkok and from there up to Chiang Mai. Adam and Sue Martin were scheduled to fly out of New York the following morning. No time was being wasted.

In the time left to him, said Drexel, it was essential that Adam continued, as far as possible, with the day-to-day routine of his ordinary life. Nobody – nobody at all, no matter how peripheral – should be put on their guard or left asking too many questions.

For Adam that meant, first, a telephone call – compliments of DEA – to his Hong Kong office to advise his secretary of his delay in returning and to deal, as best as he could long distance, with the problems that had arisen in his absence. It also meant a call to Helmut Gasser in Switzerland to thank him for the honour of the bank's commission. That second call was hard enough; the strained show of enthusiasm, the hypocrisy of discussing plans knowing all the time that he would never see so much of a sod of earth turned. But it was nothing in comparison to the final call he had to make that day, the one to Nicky du Bois.

When Nicky heard his voice on the line, her anger flared immediately. 'Where in the hell have you been?' she demanded. 'Why did you leave me in the lurch like that? For Chrissake, Adam, do you know what time it was here in Hong Kong? Two in the morning! And I was left pacing the apartment like a bloody idiot.'

Adam had anticipated the anger, trying to think of ways to explain. But how did he explain the inexplicable?

'In the end I tried phoning back myself,' said Nicky, 'and some clerk told me you had checked out. No forwarding address, no message, nothing! If this is how we're going to treat each other, Adam, then forget it!'

'Look, I'm sorry, Nicky,' he pleaded. 'I know how you must be feeling. I didn't want it to happen. But they just barged in—'

'Who barged in?'

'The developers, the ones pushing this development in Chiang Mai. You know what it's like. They were all excited, all up in the air.'

'No,' she said, her voice icy. 'Tell me.'

'They had found this new financier, they said, somebody willing to tie up the deal on the turn. It was a big thing for them.'

'All right. But why was it necessary to check out, all within less than an hour? No message, no return call.'

'The financier had a place up in Connecticut,' said Adam, playing it off the top of his head and knowing how thin it all sounded. 'He wanted us there for the night to hammer out the details.'

'So you checked out then and there, on the turn?'

'It was all happening so fast, Nicky.'

'Oh, bullshit! Please Adam, what sort of idiot do you think I am?'

'I know how it sounds, darling.' He sighed. 'All I can say is, I'm sorry. It won't happen again, I promise.'

'But it's happening all the time, Adam, don't you see that? What is it? Why are you shutting me out like this?' Her bewilderment and hurt were overwhelming. 'There's something wrong, I know there is.'

'There's nothing wrong,' Adam protested lamely.

'Is it something I've done?'

'Oh, God, no, of course not.'

'Then what is it? Tell me.'

But how could he tell her? What could he possibly say? The only answer he had was silence.

Late that night, with the calls finished and Adam looking as if it had been the most harrowing day of his life, he shared a half-bottle of Scotch with Drexel and Sue Martin in the hotel room. His brain was befuddled, he felt emotionally drained, but Drexel was obsessed with the details of the operation and there was one more aspect, he said, that had to be dealt with; a vital one, perhaps the most vital of all.

'The deal you're going to put to Chaiwisan will require investor finance. We're talking about millions of dollars. There's no way you, or any small operator, can find that sort of money.'

'Maybe Chaiwisan will invest himself.'

'No way, that's not his scene.'

'Then whom do I look to?' asked Adam.

'Hong Kong investors.'

'And how do I get to them?'

'Cheng Tak-shing has access to one.'

'His name?'

'Leung.'

'Is that it? No further names?'

'Mention Leung – Ah Leung – and Cheng will know who you mean. Chaiwisan has dealt with him too.'

'Is this man Leung capable of financing the deal on his own?'

'*Capable?* Oh yes, you can bet your life he is. Whether he wants the whole slice of the pie is another matter. He might want to bring in other investors, spread the risk around. Or he might just be greedy.'

Adam sipped his Scotch. 'And you want this man Leung pulled into the net, too, is that it?'

Drexel nodded, his heavy-set features waxen, his eyes drooping with fatigue. 'Yes, Adam, him more than any of them. He's the big fish, the monster one.'

Sue Martin gave a tired smile. 'Your Moby Dick.'

Drexel looked at her a moment, a sudden bitterness in his eyes. Then, with a barely perceptible exhalation of breath, the look softened and the shadow of a smile showed itself. 'You're right, Sue. It's a good analogy. Yes, I bear the bastard's scars and I want him hung out to dry.'

'So it's personal?' said Adam.

Drexel looked at him. 'Yes,' he answered, 'you could put it that way.'

'I thought the rule book said it was dangerous to get personal.'

Drexel refilled his glass, neat Scotch this time. 'Sometimes, Adam,' he said, 'the rule book sucks.'

Danny Abbott rolled over in bed and groaned. His head was pounding, his mouth – as he always described it – tasted like the inside of a Sumo wrestler's jock strap. He couldn't remember when he had felt so wretched.

He groaned again, full of self-pity, and the woman next to him awoke. She sat up, her large brown breasts hanging pendulously onto her stomach. Last night's extravagant make-up was still smeared across her face. Delilah was her name, her professional name. She was a Filipino whore. With a kind of purr that was meant to be tigerishly enticing but only sounded bilious, she ran a varnished fingernail down Danny's back, following the purple welt of a scar. 'You want to bang bang now, big boy? No extra charge.'

Danny's response was an agonised grunt. He sat for a time on the edge of the bed, listening to the drone of the air-conditioner. I've got to cut back, he thought to himself, the bloody booze is going to kill me. Then, tottering to his feet, he shrugged on a pair of shorts and went gingerly through to the kitchen.

Behind him he heard Delilah shout, 'Hey, big boy, I always get breakfast. It's part of the deal.'

'Yeah, yeah . . .' he muttered to himself. Then he shouted back. 'There's coffee, provided you make it, stale toast, yogurt or beer. Help yourself.' A couple of years back Danny Abbott would never have contemplated paying for a whore but now, hacked about as he was, he had no choice. But always, the morning after, the residual disgust remained.

Opening the fridge, he took out a can of beer. He cracked it open, drank some, burped and then, his head pounding, made his way to the front door to collect the paper.

The *South China Morning Post* lay on the mat, folded so that the top of page one could be seen. The headline glared up at him: PERJURY BLOW TO LEUNG PROSECUTION.

Suddenly sobering, Danny picked up the newspaper,

slammed the door shut and retreated to the lounge. 'I don't believe it,' he said between gritted teeth. 'I just don't bloody believe it.' And taking a long, angry swig from the can, he began to read.

> 'I do not wish to betray my colleagues but nor do I wish to see an innocent man condemned.' With these words, spoken at a surprise press conference called yesterday, Constable Lam Siu-ping added a dramatic new dimension to the impending manslaughter prosecution of Teddy Leung, son of business tycoon Leung Chi-ming.
>
> Flanked by his legal representatives, sweating heavily and looking nervous, Lam, one of the Crown's principal witnesses in the prosecution, said that shortly after the night of Teddy Leung's arrest he had been approached by fellow officers who suggested they invent evidence to 'ensure Leung's conviction'.
>
> 'They wanted to avenge the death of a colleague,' said Lam, often prompted by his lawyers. 'That was why they conspired to give perjured evidence.'
>
> Lam said that at first he went along with the scheme because he was frightened. He thought of reporting to CAPO (the Complaints Against Police Office) but had no trust in them. 'So in the end,' he said, 'I decided to take legal advice.'

Lam said that on the night when Teddy Leung was meant to have run down a police motor-cyclist, killing him, he was driving a pursuit Land Rover and saw exactly what happened. According to Lam, the police motorcyclist swerved in front of Leung's car, then without warning, fell from the bike.

'Maybe he skidded on an oil patch, I do not know,' said Lam, answering questions at the conference. 'But I can tell you that when he fell, it was impossible for the car to avoid him.'

Asked why he had decided to publish his allegations in this way, Lam said that he had only done so after taking legal advice. 'I accept I may be subject to disciplinary proceedings within the police force,' he said. 'But that is a small price to pay for a clear conscience.'

'A clear conscience, Christ! The lying prick doesn't need a clear conscience, he needs a new fucking script writer!' Danny Abbott read on for a couple of paragraphs more, then hurled the newspaper down in disgust and went to the fridge to get another beer.

He sat for a time, wallowing in his anger, listening to Delilah singing to herself in the shower. Every time, he thought, every time they manage it; all you need in this shithole of a place is money. The constable would be paid off, the law would be paid off. Nothing ever changed. Nobody cared. He finished the beer. His headache grew worse. He had to speak to the one person who he knew would share the same sense of outrage, even if it did mean a call to New York on his miserable pittance of a salary.

It was gone midnight in New York and he knew Drexel would be at home in bed. But he telephoned anyway. As it was, Carl Drexel had only just got back from the Milford Plaza, his own head thick with alcohol. But he listened patiently while Danny, in a thick, phlegm-filled voice, part rage, part hangover, read the article to him.

'What's the good of it, Carl, tell me? Money, that's all you need in this bloody world. His spoilt brat of a son is facing a jail sentence so what does Leung do? He buys off a bloody witness, a police officer, too! What's the bloody good of it? Do you think there's a just God? Forget it! If you can't beat 'em, then join the bastards. The rest of the world has.'

Carl Drexel wasn't that easily perturbed. 'The world is a venal place, Danny, I thought you would have accepted that by now. What's your Legal Department likely to do?'

'God knows. Spineless bunch will probably cave in.'

'I know it sticks in your gullet,' said Drexel, trying to defuse some of his outrage, the Scotch making him speak a little more freely than normal. 'But the wheel always turns, Danny. Don't worry, one of these days we'll get Leung.'

'Sure, when hell freezes over.'

'Maybe a lot sooner than you think.'

'Why?' Danny Abbott was beginning to show some grudging interest. 'Have you got something on the go?'

'It's in the embryonic stage at the moment.'

'Involving Leung?'

'We'll see how it develops.'

'We've had other operations involving Leung,' Danny scoffed. 'And look what happened to them – the garbage can of history.'

'Yeah, well this may just be different.'

But Danny Abbott wasn't convinced. 'When I see it, I'll believe it.'

Drexel gave a tired laugh. 'Come on, Danny, you've never been such a doubting Thomas before. Faith, that's what you need, faith.'

But Danny answered sourly, 'Faith, mate, is for people with no other solution.'

Teddy Leung stood on the deck of the *China Jewel*, a glass of orange and champagne in his hand, and gazed out over the boat-bedraggled slum of Aberdeen Harbour.

The *China Jewel* was his father's plaything, a sixty-foot cabin cruiser, a sleek white billionaire's status symbol outfitted with every gadget possible and manned by a permanent crew of four. Away from the rich jetties of the Aberdeen Marina Club, out among the rows of grimy green-hulled fishing junks, all ropes and tackle and grease and stench, Teddy Leung could see a small sampan chugging through the oily waters. A Hakka woman sat at the rudder in her black fringed hat and cheap black pyjamas. She looked as old and desiccated as the salted fish that made up her cargo. My shoes alone, he thought, cost more than she earns in two months. As for the white linen trousers, the sharkskin belt and the silk skirt, hand-made in Florence, she couldn't pay for those in a year of carrying fish.

Teddy Leung found boats like the *China Jewel* dull as death but he relished the wealth they displayed. Teddy basked in wealth, flourished in its golden rays. Wealth, he knew, was more than just a counting of money. Wealth was a potent alchemy that altered every aspect of life.

He was as different from those painters and masons out there working along the shoreline in the shadow of the housing tenements as a lion is different from a goat. They shared nothing. They were different beasts. Great wealth set a man apart. And that's what so terrified Teddy Leung, the prospect of being separated from it.

He knew that, if it came to the worst, his father would buy him protection in jail. Nobody would touch him. Everybody, from the governor down to the lowest inmate, would give him due face. Physically he would never be troubled. But the sheer grubbiness of it, the humiliation, that's what terrified him: the concrete beds, the inedible swill, the pathetic Anglo-Chinese discipline with warders barking orders, the endless days of mixing with gutter scum. The thought of it turned his belly to liquid. But it wouldn't happen, it *couldn't* happen. No, not now that Lam had given his press conference. Surely now he was safe. How could there ever be proof beyond reasonable doubt after what Lam had said? This wasn't China where they ignored the witnesses, took you out and shot you anyway. Hong Kong was still a British colony. Here they still had what they called the rule of law.

Teddy Leung gestured with a limp hand and one of the

uniformed boat boys came running with a crystal pitcher to refill his glass. As he sipped the drink he glimpsed his father coming from the club house accompanied by his lawyers and his heart began to race. He had to take a deep breath to control himself. They had been discussing matters all morning with the Attorney General's lawyers. Now he would know what had been decided.

He tried to glean something from his father's looks but, as always, the old man walked slowly, his head hung, lips pressed tightly together. Triumph or disaster, the expression never changed. It was infuriating.

The captain of the *China Jewel* went down to the jetty to greet his father and help him up the steps. Teddy Leung waited on deck, barely able to breathe.

His father came up on deck, cast him a baleful look and then said, 'Well, it's done. They will drop the manslaughter charge if you agree to plead guilty to a simple charge of drunken driving. Your licence will be suspended, you will have to pay a fine.'

'But no jail?'

'You will have to tolerate a chauffeur for six months, that is about the worst of it.'

A broad smile came to Teddy Leung's round, juvenile features, accentuating his soft double chin. The bravado, so much a part of everything he did, sprang back. 'Good, good,' he said. 'So your lawyers have earned their fees for once. But what about the drunken-driving charge? Can't we fight that somehow? There must be some technical grounds.'

Leung Chi-ming frowned. 'Fortune has smiled on you, Teddy. Don't press it for too many favours.'

His son gave a nonchalant shrug. 'Very well, if that's the advice, I suppose I had better plead.'

Leung was relieved. His son could be petulant. Sometimes, he thought ruefully, the gods played tricks. They had deprived his son of common sense but endowed him with arrogance.

One of the boat boys served Leung Chi-ming with his usual glass of distilled water. He didn't have the constitution for much else these days. The ropes were untethered and the *China Jewel* pulled away from the jetty. Slowly, its huge engines purring, it wound its way through the harbour, past the endless rows of fishing junks with laundry hanging from their rigging and piebald dogs barking from the bows. They cruised past the five huge chimneys of the Ap Lei Chau power station and out into the open water of the Lamma Channel.

Leung Chi-ming stood by his son's shoulder, clutching the rail. 'Hong Kong is a wonderful place, Teddy, we have everything here. But it is all worth nothing, just ash in the wind, without Western justice. Today has proved it, son. Consider yourself fortunate. There is no better system in the world.'

Teddy Leung smiled, all dimples and arrogance. 'Yes, Father,' he said, 'so it seems.'

Carl Drexel was even-tempered, most of the time, and considered his words before he put his tongue into gear. He disliked the kind of loud-mouthed vulgarity practised by Nico Divaris. But, when the need was there, he could be blunt enough in his own way.

'You've got to loosen up,' he said to Sue Martin that

morning when he had a moment alone with her before she joined Adam to drive out to J.F. Kennedy Airport. 'Hell, Sue, I've seen more romance in a wrestling ring.'

And when Adam joined them, packed and ready, he repeated the warning. 'Nobody expects you to be permanently pawing each other. I appreciate the problems. Just try and act natural. You don't know who is going to be on that flight to Thailand, you don't know who is going to be watching the two of you in Chiang Mai. For Pete's sake, you've got to at least *look* like you're attracted to each other.'

So, from the moment they stepped on board the aircraft, that's the way it had been, especially on Sue Martin's part – the occasional smile, the brushing of their fingers together, all the little intimacies lovers are meant to adopt. For Adam it was more difficult.

He didn't object to Sue Martin's company. She was sympathetic, bright, stunning to look at. But it didn't alter the one hard fact that she was the representative of the law and he was the convict. Nor did it alter the fact that his mind was filled with only one woman, Nicky – how much he longed for her, loved her, how much he missed her already.

For the first three hours or so of the flight, still unsure of herself, feeling the strain of it as much as Adam, Sue Martin didn't say a great deal. Mostly she read, first the in-flight magazine and then an old Le Carré novel about the Far East, *The Honourable Schoolboy*. But with the lunch finished and the wine consumed, mellower now and seeing Adam lost in his thoughts, she took the initiative and began to talk.

She knew that she couldn't encroach on Adam's life, not at this time with his future so bleak. So she took the only course open to her and talked about herself instead. And Adam, pleased to be distracted from his own morose contemplation, was content to listen.

She had been raised in Washington State, she said, she and a twin sister, up near the Canadian border in a small logging town. For her it had been a good childhood, all tennis and horses and mountains. She had always been, she said, an 'outdoors' girl. For her twin sister, Annie, however, it had been different. Annie had always been the poet, pale and melancholy, even as a little kid, always lost in herself, not the kind of person who fitted easily into small-town, backwoods America.

'What happened to her?' asked Adam, pleased just to be able to talk with no need of pretence.

Sue Martin shrugged and Adam thought he detected a little sadness in her eyes. 'She got a scholarship, did wonders, set the literati on fire, and dropped out.'

'Does she still write?'

'No, not now, not any more.'

'Where is she?'

'In New York. We share an apartment.'

'Not married?'

'No, not Annie.'

'And what about yourself?' he asked.

'Me?' She smiled. 'Yes, I was married once. I was nineteen, just started on the pro tennis circuit.'

Adam smiled. 'How old was he?'

She laughed, embarrassed. 'All of twenty. It lasted about eight months. He was a tennis brat, too. Six foot two, built like Adonis, twice as spoilt as I was and every bit as self-centred. It's not a time I look back on with fond memories. Married and divorced and not yet twenty. I've played it more cautiously since then.'

'Where's he now?' asked Adam.

'Brad? Oh, he's still coaching at some ritzy country club in California. Still getting laid by all the sun-wrinkled wives. That's Brad's idea of paradise.'

'And you? From tennis into the DEA, it doesn't sound like the most obvious progression. What made you make the move?'

'All the normal reasons,' she answered. 'A job with a difference, the excitement, doing something for the greater good. Everything you expect from the advertising posters. As for the tennis, well, you know what they say, those that can, do, those that can't, teach. And I was lousy at teaching.'

'So the DEA transferred you to New York?'

'No, I asked for it. They wanted me in Seattle.'

'You're a West Coast girl. Why New York?'

'Because Annie was there and, well, she needed me, I suppose that's the only way to put it.' She was silent for a time as if uncertain how best to explain. Then she continued in a slow, hesitant voice, 'Annie was always very emotionally fragile, always treading that fine edge between the real world and one she had created in her own mind. Maybe all artists are the same, I don't know. But with Annie, well, with the drugs and then the drink . . . I don't know, she kind of closed in on herself. "The pure profundity of all her pain" – that's what some crit said of her poetry. I remember it because it kind of sums her up. Most of the time she lives in her own world now, lost in herself. The doctors say she should be in an institution, somewhere she can be helped. But what do they know? She's my flesh and blood. I would do anything, I think, just about anything in the world to ensure she's not hurt.'

Adam turned to face her. There was no accusation in his voice, just the simple question. 'Why are you telling me this?'

She gave a small, pained smile, hesitated and then replied, 'I'm not saying I agree with what you did, Adam . . .'

'But?'

'But I know the kind of anguish you must have gone through, I know what a tough decision it must have been. I suppose I'm just trying to tell you that I understand.'

Chapter Eight
NORTHERN THAILAND

Chiang Mai lay supine in the burning haze of early summer. It was a deceptively drowsy town; the Thai people always so polite, so humble, old men sleeping in the shade, flies droning in the mango trees, every garden with its own Buddhist spirit house. It was difficult to imagine anything more criminal than petty theft in a town like this, impossible to imagine that it was one of the drug capitals of the world.

Adam contacted Yu Wen-huan at his tiny tribal artifacts shop on the Loy Kroh Road and they drank fruit juice together as they discussed Adam's 'new and much bigger business'. It sounded good, said Yu. Yes, he would agree to act as broker again. And yes, Tinko Chaiwisan did seem the best man to supply the heroin.

So word was sent across the border, deep into the jungle-clad mountains of Laos. The first, tentative steps had been taken. Sue Martin reported back to Carl Drexel in New York. There was nothing to do now but wait.

Adam and Sue Martin had booked into the Disuthani,

one of the better tourist hotels. They knew they could well be – and probably were – under surveillance. So it was imperative they played their allotted roles without any hesitancy: languid lovers lazing each sun-drenched day away in the sensual intimacy of each other's company; no care for time, no care for others, lost in themselves.

Sue Martin slipped into the role without any trouble. She spent most of each day by the hotel pool, her tall, bronzed, overpoweringly physical presence attracting wolfish stares from every man who came near. She read her Le Carré novel, drank Perrier and occasionally dived with barely a ripple into the blue water of the pool. She would swim a dozen lengths and then climb out, letting the water dry on her body. Nobody in his right mind would have dreamt she was a narcotics agent for the US government. When Adam joined her at the pool, she would oil his back or lie, sunbathing, with her head on his chest, her blonde hair spread out over his shoulders.

They ate every meal together, they went for long walks at dusk, hand in hand. They shared the same room at night. They were the beautiful couple, so obviously entranced by each other, so obviously exactly what they pretended to be. Carl Drexel had made the perfect choice.

But for Adam, each day with her was a private purgatory. Knowing how close he was to jail – to not having or even seeing a woman again for two years or more – her constant closeness, the smell of her perfume, the rise and fall of her breasts when she slept at night, all of it drove him to distraction. Even something so simple as watching her comb her hair after a shower and seeing the dewdrops of moisture roll down between her shoulder blades had his insides churning. Her physical aura was magnetic.

She liked to talk, too, in that fresh, revealing way so many Americans have, uncluttered with cynicism. She collected pottery and porcelain birds, she said. She loved cats and Mexican cooking. Her pet hate was men with pretensions, the kind who dangled gold medallions round their necks and drove sports cars with flames painted down the side. She was miserable at cocktail parties and had always wanted to paint.

There were so many things about her that Adam liked, so many things that she learnt to like in him. With every hour of the day, the more they understood each other, the closer they grew. A kind of bond developed, a mutual trust. But that, too, just made it worse. Because for her, in Adam's mind, the bottom line would never waver. She was the cop, he was the convict. And that, despite the bond of friendship, despite the physical compulsion, put a yawning, impossible chasm between them.

For five days they waited, playing their roles, alone in each other's company, five days without any news from Laos.

Do everything necessary to keep your ordinary life going, Carl Drexel had said; keep juggling those balls of deceit, just keep 'em in the air, that's all that counts. Don't put anybody, no matter how peripheral, on their guard. And Adam complied.

Every day he spoke to his office from Chiang Mai as his professional staff geared themselves for the Swiss bank project and wailed at the fact that he remained away. Helmut Gasser, they said, intended to visit Hong Kong in three weeks' time. Would he at least be there then or should they try and put Gasser off for another week or two? No, said Adam, let the visit go ahead. What difference? By then he would probably be in a US penitentiary and his professional career would be a smouldering ruin. It was all a charade.

He spoke to his mother who told him that Harry was appearing in the High Court the following week to be sentenced after his plea of guilty. She had hired a lawyer, she said, one of the best. A good lawyer could cut a couple of years off his sentence, even though Harry hadn't wanted one. No matter what Harry had done, it was essential they stand by him. She understood, she said, how busy Adam was at this time but it would mean so much to Harry if he could get back for the hearing. Without their joint support, how else would he live through the years ahead? My God, thought Adam, if only she appreciated the irony of what she was saying. But yes, he said, he would do his utmost to get back. He knew how important it was and he didn't want to let Harry down.

He spoke to Nicky, too, on three or four occasions. Those calls were the hardest of all. At first, he tried desperately to restore their relationship for what little, precious time they had left. But he couldn't say one thing without hiding half a dozen others. He still had to live the lie, even with her, and Nicky knew him too well.

Bewildered that he continued so obviously to hide so much from her, angry with herself, angry with him, not knowing what to do for the best, she swung wildly between icy distance and white-hot anger. As a result, the calls ended in disaster, she put the phone down in tears, he in muted, boiling frustration, his heart about to burst. He began to realise that he was tearing them both apart for no purpose. What did he hope to achieve by clinging to her? How much longer could it last, another two weeks, three at the outside? More pain, more heartache . . .

If he was honest with himself and her, if he had the guts, he knew he should end it and let her start her life again. If he loved her, truly loved her, what other choice was open? He could promise her nothing but lies, offer her no future. Nicky deserved more than that.

Each night, after Sue Martin had fallen asleep, Adam would lie awake, the silent hours seeming to drag on into eternity. In many ways those nights in Chiang Mai were the worst, the most inwardly traumatic, Adam had ever experienced: time to contemplate the dangers ahead in this Judas world he had been forced to enter, time to think of prison, time to grieve the loss of his career, the woman he loved, his friends, his place in society; time, in those dark empty hours, to contemplate the total, irredeemable ruin of his life.

On the morning of the sixth day, when it seemed that Chaiwisan would never respond, Yu Wen-huan arrived early at the hotel. He and Adam had breakfast in the gardens and Yu gave him the news that Chaiwisan had agreed to a meeting.

'Good, good,' said Adam, relieved that at last something was happening. 'When?'

'Tonight.'

'The same place?'

Yu smiled from behind his gold-rimmed bottle prism glasses. 'You should know him better than that. Uncle Chicken never meets in the same place twice. I'll pick you up at one o'clock.' And he added as he drained his coffee, 'Be prepared for a long drive.'

After he had departed, Sue Martin came across. 'So that was Yu, the broker? White short-sleeved shirt, grey slacks, glasses – looks more like a school teacher. Or a Mormon missionary.'

Adam smiled, surprised at the naivety of her remark. 'He's been in the trade all his life. His father was in it before him.'

'Is the meeting set?' she asked.

'For tonight.'

'Do I accompany you?'

'No, I go alone. This is Asia, not America. Your presence would raise too many questions.'

She smiled, her blue eyes wide. 'Don't worry, Adam, I trust you.'

He smiled back. 'At this stage of the game, you've got no other choice.'

Yu arrived at the hotel on schedule, driving an open Suzuki jeep. In the burning heat haze, they began the journey north, winding up into the hill country towards the distant mauve and brown peaks.

For the first hour or so they journeyed through thickly

vegetated farm country, the tall stands of bamboo and evergreens punctuated with tobacco fields. But slowly, as they climbed higher and the air grew thinner, the farms gave out and the landscape took on a savage, desolate air, all crags and jungled valleys, impenetrable ravines and slow-moving rivers the colour of jade.

They headed north-east, the tarred road replaced by an ochre-red track that wound its way through countless mountain hamlets, the thatched dwellings built high on bamboo stilts, the village pigs running squealing in front of their jeep while the hill folk, women and ragged urchins, eyed them with torpid suspicion.

'There are so few men,' said Adam. 'Why's that?'

'The men are off soldiering,' Yu replied. 'Guarding the opium.'

'Soldiering for whom?'

Yu laughed. 'It is impossible to say for whom. They are all in the thrall of one warlord or another. Who knows? There are remnants of the Shans here, they could be across in the west fighting for the Shan Independence Army against the Burmese. Some may have sold themselves as mercenaries to the Karens fighting the same war. Some may be with the Meo warlords, some just bandits, a few running with the remnants of the Chinese nationalists, the Kuomintang, who fled here from Yunnan Province back in forty-eight when the communists defeated them. There are still eight thousand or more Kuomintang here in the Triangle, settled with their families, still a potent army. They guard a great many of the opium convoys, the mule trains that come down from the most far-flung places. They have done that for over forty years – with CIA backing.'

'The CIA?'

'Oh yes, that used to be the way. The Kuomintang are anti-communist, you see,' said Yu, not bothering to disguise his sarcasm, 'fighting for democracy and Western values.'

'But surely the CIA doesn't support them, not since Vietnam?'

Yu shrugged. 'Maybe, maybe not. History in this part of Asia has spun a tangled web.'

On they drove, further north still until the motionless heat of day gave way to an evening breeze. They stopped to drink water from a stream and then continued. They had been on the road for over five hours.

'Where are we now?' asked Adam. 'We must be near the border with Laos.'

'We've already crossed it,' said Yu, 'back there at the stream. That was the border.'

'So we're in Laos now?'

'No passports, you'll notice,' said Yu merrily. 'No visas required.'

'And if we had been caught by Pathet Lao border guards?'

'Oh, there would have been no trouble. They would have demanded bribes, that's all, US currency or Thai baht.'

'And if we had none?'

'Then, of course, they would have shot us,' said Yu airily.

They followed the trail north along the high contour

ridges. Evening settled in a soft wash of pink and crimson that flooded the western sky. Yu stopped to refuel, using fuel drums loaded into the back of the jeep. Adams stood up, stretching his legs, and saw that, further north, the pewter-blue sky was smudged with pillars of smoke.

'What is it?' he asked.

'Fire from the poppy fields,' Yu explained. 'Most of the crop has been reaped, so now they're burning the stubble and brake to fertilise the fields. Phosphates are necessary for the next crop. This is Chaiwisan's country. This is where he was born and raised and has traded all his life.'

They rounded a bend in the track. Without warning, Yu applied the brakes, pulling their jeep off the track. He climbed down from the vehicle, wiping the dust from his glasses, and pointed to where a group of women were working in a stony field. 'There,' he said. 'See for yourself, Adam. This is where it all begins.'

The field was filled with the wispy white and crimson-edged blooms of the opium poppy, each plant waist high, each one crowned with a grey bulb, the size of a tangerine, where the precious resin rested. In the warm evening zephyrs, the plants swayed back and forth, thousands upon thousands of them, a sea of grey, white and red stretching up over the brow of the hill. And in the distance, more smoke, the colour of suede, where more poppy fields, reaped of their harvest, were set to the torch.

As they worked, the women showed no more than a passing interest in the two men watching them from the track. They wore broad-brimmed black hats as protection against the sun and most wore black blouses, too, with long skirts of cornflower yellow. They were tribal women dressed in the traditional way, bedecked with rough silver jewellery and beads; brown-skinned, sun-weathered women, small, slim, bare-footed, women whose faces showed their Chinese ancestry but Thai and Indian, too.

'The soil here is very good for the poppy,' said Yu. 'Porous limestone, very alkaline. The old women can taste good limestone soil by its sweetness. This is the best height, too. The crop can survive as low as three thousand feet but here, at over four thousand feet, it flourishes, grows as strong as a weed.' He gestured to Adam like a teacher with a nervous pupil. 'Go closer, don't worry, the women won't be alarmed. See for yourself how they reap the harvest.'

Drawing closer, Adam could see that as they moved in a broad swathe across the field the women carried small curved knives which they used to cut a series of shallow incisions into each poppy bulb so that the white sap inside slowly oozed out. A little like tapping rubber, he thought. As he watched, the raw, wet opium slowly darkened in the late rays of the sinking sun, changing into a fibrous, dirty brown. There was a smell in the air, too, the distinct, sweet, sickly smell of molasses and dung.

'The dried sap is scraped off the bulbs,' said Yu, 'then rolled into balls, each ball ten taels in weight, each one wrapped in leaves. That is the way it has been grown and harvested here for over a hundred and fifty years.' Yu turned back towards the jeep. 'The hill tribes grow it, the warlords protect it and we Chinese trade in it – that is the balance of nature in these mountains and it will never change.'

They walked back to the vehicle together and Yu climbed in behind the wheel, pausing one last time to watch the women at work in the field. He smiled faintly. 'Over a hundred years ago the Westerners, the *gweilos*, enslaved China to opium to buy the goods that previously they'd had to pay for in silver. Opium built commercial empires. Tell me, Adam, you live there, how many of the Hong Kong Westerners, the Scots and Welsh and Yankee traders, the high and mighty sitting in their church pews on a Sunday, can thank this brown, foul-smelling mud for the power they inherited? Great Britain fought wars to protect their opium trade. When they could make money out of it, there was nothing wrong with opium. Oh no, it was a plant that gave pleasure, that's all. Let the Han smoke themselves into oblivion. But now it is the *gweilos* who consume it, who seek their own oblivion, and now it is we who build the empires. Ironic, is it not?'

Adam nodded. Indeed it was.

Yu started the engine and they drove back onto the dusty track. 'You see that mountain directly ahead of us,' Yu said. 'That is Mae Kwong, Chaiwisan's fortress. The Southern Gateway, he calls it, his gateway to the world.'

It took them another twenty minutes to reach the village, climbing an eroded track past a sandbagged dugout into the untidy collection of bamboo dwellings. There was the smell of wood smoke in the air. A couple of emaciated village dogs barked at the jeep. Pigs snuffled in the refuse at the edge of the trees. So this was it, thought Adam, disappointed at the rural mundaneness of the place, this was Chaiwisan's Southern Gateway, the home of a man who must have made tens of millions in the drug trade.

As he climbed from the jeep, Yu said to him, 'Here he comes, the Pied Piper of Hamlin.' Adam looked up to see Chaiwisan striding towards them down the rutted dirt track that made up the village's main street, surrounded by a horde of dusty-faced children.

'They're all his, too,' said Yu with a broad grin. 'He has more – older ones, younger ones. He said he gave up counting at twenty.'

In his wildest dreams Adam had never envisaged Tinko Chaiwisan as a family man, certainly not like this with a child in his arms, a smile of pure contentment on his old, beaked face, and half a dozen laughing, arguing children trailing in his wake. But seeing him here in his home environment, still dressed in his camouflage, the master of his own small, rural domain, it seemed perfectly natural. Adam was able to see Chaiwisan as he truly was, a relic from a long-gone age when a man had his women, his children, his dogs, and his serfs and when the might of his arm was all the might he needed. Tinko Chaiwisan was not evil, any more than Yu Wen-huan was evil. They were simply men living out of their time.

Chaiwisan came up, smiling broadly, one of his children on his shoulders, and shook Adam's hand. 'So how was New York, my friend?'

Adam gave an exaggerated shrug. 'Some good, some bad. But mainly good I hope.'

'I believe you had some trouble.'

'News travels fast.'

'Bad news, yes. They tell me that a man was killed.'

'Who keeps you so well informed?' asked Adam with a smile. But his heart was thudding in his chest. He was amazed that Chaiwisan could have learnt so much so soon. Just how much more did he know?

'I am sorry I had to bring you on such a long, tiring journey,' said Chaiwisan as they marched along the village street still surrounded by children. 'But sometimes, as Yu has maybe told you, I can smell it in the air, a sense that perhaps everything is not right.'

Adam's smile froze on his face. If Chaiwisan knew he was working for the DEA, if he so much as *smelt* it, Adam knew he was a dead man. They would bind his hands and beat him to death with bamboo poles, then leave his body for the birds; that was the way of it for deserters and traitors in this part of the world. And Chaiwisan, for all his avuncular smiles, could be as ruthless as a cobra.

Just as Adam was starting to think desperately of some way of extricating himself, Chaiwisan burst out laughing. 'Don't worry about me,' he said. 'It's an old man's suspicions, that's all it is! All I can smell in the air is the pig dung!'

Adam laughed too. But icy tendrils of fear still clutched at his entrails. Chaiwisan was a man to be wary of, a man who demanded cautious respect.

'So,' said the old Yunnanese opium trader, 'did you at

least get away from New York with your money, Adam?'

'Yes, my money – and, I hope, another deal.'

'So Four Eyes Yu tells me.'

'When I was in New York,' Adam explained, 'I met certain men, ethnic Chinese, Vietnamese immigrants, men keen to do business.'

'What sort of quantities do these men require?'

'An initial delivery of a hundred units,' said Adam, struggling to keep his tone relaxed. 'That's just to set up a store. And then another hundred more within two months.'

'They must be ambitious men.'

Adam smiled but without humour. 'They and me . . .'

'Yes,' said Chaiwisan with a trace of cynicism in his voice. 'For a man so new to the game, you do move quickly.'

'Fate,' said Adam with a shrug. 'Sometimes it favours you, sometimes it does not. Just before my brother was arrested, he was dealing with a Vietnamese in New York, a man called Market Place Trung. Trung had associates in New Jersey, men Harry was beginning to foster.'

'So you inherited them from the Fat Boy?'

'My brother gave me the names,' said Adam dryly, 'I did the deal – with a lot more care than he tended to use. That's one thing I've learnt from you, Tinko, caution pays dividends.'

Chaiwisan seemed satisfied, 'Yes,' he said, 'I've heard of Trung, a small-time dealer, very much, as the Yankees say, "on the make". But he does have contacts, I remember that.'

'You seem to know a great deal about a great many people,' said Adam, not bothering to disguise the seriousness of his remark. 'I'm surprised – and impressed.'

Chaiwisan grinned up at him, his black eyes filled with a kind of mischief. 'You say you have learnt caution from me, Adam. Good. But remember that cautious men always carry insurance.'

'And in your case, insurance is information, is that it?'

Chaiwisan scooped one of his children up into his arms, a little girl of four or five, and tousled her raven black hair. 'They say that there is no better asset than information. With luck, I need never put it to the test. But insurance, of course, is not for when luck is with you, it is for when your luck runs out.' Then he laughed again. 'Come,' he said, 'what kind of host am I? First some beer and roast pork, time to rest – and then we'll talk.'

Later that night, after they had eaten, when the children were asleep, they drank beer and sat out under the stars around a log fire. Yu took no part in the conversation. His job as broker had been done by bringing the two men together. Now it was for Adam to take the initiative.

'I cannot finance shipments that big,' Adam explained, 'not two hundred units. So, if the deal is to go through, I must have investors. Where do I look?'

'To Hong Kong,' said Chaiwisan. 'For heroin, it is the financial capital of the world. Where else would you look? But even there, do you have access to such men?'

'My only access would be through Cheng Tak-shing,' said Adam.

Chaiwisan grunted before swilling back his beer. He obviously didn't think too much of the man.

Adam was silent for a time, gazing into the flames of the log fire. Then he said quietly, 'I have heard that Cheng has a wealthy backer, a man called Leung.'

Chaiwisan did not reply.

Adam looked into his face, searching for some reaction but, in the firelight, the opium trader's leathery face was a liquid chiaroscuro of flames and shadow, no expression discernible.

Adam pressed the matter more directly. 'If Cheng fails me, and that may be probable, I will need to look elsewhere. Perhaps there are people you can recommend.'

Chaiwisan considered the request. 'I don't think that will be necessary. Cheng is a crude animal of a man but he does have his sources.'

'This man Leung, they say, could finance a deal of two hundred units on his own, no problems. Do you know of him?'

Chaiwisan ordered more beer which was brought by the women. 'Leung? Yes, I know of him.' But he would say no more.

For a while Adam was content to drink his beer; Thai beer, Singha, he noticed. Nothing would be gained by pushing too hard. Then he came in from another angle. 'Assuming I can find investors,' he said, 'I cannot imagine them advancing the money until they are satisfied that the shipment will be delivered successfully. One hundred units is over a hundred and fifty pounds in weight. Care will have to be taken with how it is transported.'

Chaiwisan gave a brusque nod; the point was self-evident.

'A deal so complex, with so many responsibilities to be allocated, will take considerable management,' Adam continued in a slow, persuasive manner. 'The investors will have to be satisfied that every possible precaution has been taken. The risks are always great in these matters. If you agree to supply the merchandise, I take it you'll require payment of half in advance?'

'That is my practice, yes.'

'A great deal of money.'

'A great deal of merchandise.'

'The point I make, Tinko, is that I don't think my investors would be happy to pay out half in advance as you require unless they are satisfied that you can deliver. By that I mean get the merchandise out of the Triangle to the sea and on board a vessel.'

Chaiwisan gave a small chuckle. 'I have done trades like this before, Adam. I am old enough – literally – to be your father. If you want me to meet your investors, to satisfy them, then, subject to certain conditions, it may be possible.'

Adam held his breath. 'In Hong Kong?'

'Of course. I can't expect such men to come here. The DEA, the CIA, every police agency in Asia would have them marked within the week. It is easier for me to slip into Hong Kong.' And he smiled. 'Just another flea on the hide of the cow.'

Adam could hardly believe it had been so easy. No convincing had been required. Chaiwisan had volunteered to go. 'What are your conditions?' he asked.

Chaiwisan threw a couple of logs on to the fire, watching the sparks shower in the night like a million iridescent fireflies. 'First, I must be satisfied that your investors – the men you want me to meet – are trustworthy. Second, when I go to Hong Kong, I get there in my own way and in my own time.'

The opportunity had presented itself and instinctively Adam seized it. 'But how can I be assured that the investors will be trustworthy? Tell me who you've dealt with in the past, who you trust, and let me at least approach them first. Surely that way – no disrespect intended – we'll save a great deal of time and trouble.'

Chaiwisan looked into the fire as if trying to divine something in the flames. For a time he seemed uncertain. But then he said, 'Very well, Adam, go to Cheng Takshing. Tell him you are seeking investors. Mention my name.'

'And then?'

'And then tell him that I would be happy to do further business with Ah Leung.'

The following morning at daybreak, with a cockerel crowing, Adam and Yu drove out of Chaiwisan's mountain stronghold, down from the mountain ramparts of Mae Kwong, back towards the Thai border. Adam had achieved all of Drexel's aims. But he experienced no pleasure in it, no triumph, at best only a grudging sense of relief.

Within the month, if all went according to plan, Chaiwisan would travel to Hong Kong. He would be set up, just as Adam himself had been set up in New York, arrested and then extradited to the United States to face trial for breaking Federal narcotics laws. On the basis of Adam's evidence, he would be looking at twenty years to life – an old man brought up in the jungle, raised in an opium culture and condemned to die in some concrete cell on the other side of the world.

Adam harboured no regrets for what might happen to Cheng Tak-shing or the men behind him, the ones who gave the orders. Cheng was an animal. He had threatened Adam's family, hacked off his brother's ear and pushed Adam himself into this living nightmare. For Cheng he felt nothing. But what harm had Chaiwisan ever done to him?

It was all very well to say that he was an opium dealer, a threat to society, a criminal who deserved to be punished. But they were hollow words. Chaiwisan had been raised in the poppy fields. Opium was part of his culture, his livelihood, just as it was for every man and woman in these mountains. Adam bore him no grudge, he wished him no harm. And yet, to save himself, he had to betray him. Dear God, he thought, what more must I do?

Chapter Nine

HONG KONG

Sue Martin was buoyant. It could have taken months to secure Chaiwisan's agreement, instead it had taken just ten days. Nobody had expected it to run so smoothly. But in New York Carl Drexel received the news with no more than cautious, poker-faced contentment. He had been in the business too long to start counting chickens before they were hatched. 'So far so good,' was all Nico Divaris got out of him. 'Now let's see how they fare in Hong Kong. If the shit hits the fan, it's going to be there.'

Adam and Sue Martin flew into the colony in the late afternoon. It was a sultry day, grey and humid, with a haze of smog hanging over the harbour.

So often when Adam landed he was infected by the city's bustle. But this time, in the monochrome greyness of concrete and sky, in the endless nose-to-tail traffic, the building sites, the dust and mess, Hong Kong resembled nothing more than an overcrowded ghetto festering in its own pollution. Every city, he realised, was a state of mind.

They took a taxi from the airport through the Cross

Harbour Tunnel and along the waterfront into Central. Sue Martin had been booked into the Hilton just two minutes' walk from the DEA offices on Garden Road. She still had to play the role of Adam's lover, nothing had changed in that regard. His domestic entanglements would explain why she stayed in the hotel and not his apartment.

Adam continued in the taxi up the dizzying switchbacks of Magazine Gap to his apartment high on the Peak. The place smelt musty and unlived in, barely like home any more. He dumped his travel bag in the bedroom, found a can of beer in the fridge and then, slowly and deliberately, set about doing what had to be done, including the dismantling of his life.

First, he telephoned his mother to let her know he was back. He would collect her the following morning, he said, so they could be at the High Court when Harry was sentenced.

'I heard from Nicky about the Swiss commission,' his mother said. 'That's just wonderful, Adam. I'm delighted for you.' She laughed, her voice filled with pride. 'I always knew my son would be famous one day.'

Adam had no reply. What could he possibly say? He cut the conversation short with the excuse that he had been on the go for days and was exhausted. They would talk in the morning, he said. But once the phone was down, he dialled again, this time to try and contact Nicky.

Her secretary said she was out at a meeting and would be going directly home. 'If she phones in, tell her I'm back in Hong Kong, will you.'

'I'll make sure she gets the message.'

'Tell her I'll come up to her apartment tonight.'

'Certainly, Mr Blake.'

'Thank you.'

The phone went down. He finished his beer and sat for a time, brooding. Then he telephoned Cheng Tak-shing's paging centre, leaving a message that Cheng was to contact him urgently. He knew he wouldn't have to wait long for the return call. Cheng, like a pig snorting for truffles, could smell money buried in six foot of dirt.

Within twenty minutes Cheng was on the line. 'Where have you been?' he demanded, clearly agitated. 'I expected you back days ago.'

'Since when did you become my keeper?' asked Adam with undisguised sarcasm.

'Do you have it, the cash?'

'Yes, I have it.'

Cheng gave a sharp grunt of relief. 'When can you get it to me? What about tomorrow morning?'

'Tomorrow morning I have to go to the High Court.'

'Oh yeah, I'd forgotten, your brother goes before the judge. Wish the Fat Boy luck,' said Cheng with callous indifference.

Adam kept his silence.

'But the hearing won't take longer than an hour,' continued Cheng. 'What about after that?'

'Whatever you say.'

'The Shang City Restaurant, the same place we met before. You remember it?'

'What time?'

'Twelve thirty. I'll be at my table by the window.'

'Twelve thirty it is.' Under the passive tones of his voice, Adam nurtured a venomous hatred for the man. I'm going to get you, you bastard, he thought. By the time all this is ended, no matter what happens to me, I'm going to see you rotting in hell.

'Bring cash,' said Cheng. 'I don't want bank drafts or cheques, no bank papers.'

'You'll get the cash,' said Adam. 'But there are some matters I want to discuss with you.'

Cheng was instantly on his guard. 'What sort of matters?'

Adam paused a moment. Then he said. 'I have some new business you might find interesting.'

Initially, Cheng was startled. 'New business – you? What kind?'

'Our standard merchandise.'

As if it was some kind of joke, Cheng began to laugh. 'Fuck your mother, are you trying to tell me you still want to deal? I don't believe it. Why the change of heart?'

'Because I need to recoup losses,' said Adam in a matter-of-fact voice. 'You might be happy, your associate might be happy. But I'm bankrupt.'

'What about your business, all those fancy buildings you design?'

'Slow money, in comparison.'

'But you'll get out of debt in the end.'

'By then I'll be an old man. I can't afford to wait, it's as simple as that.'

Cheng was suspicious. It didn't fit, not Blake continuing to trade in white powder. He wasn't the sort.

It didn't fit at all. 'Who are your buyers?' he asked in a dubious tone. 'The same people?'

'No, a new syndicate.'

That surprised Cheng even more, compounding his suspicions. 'Fuck me, you move around.'

'When I have to.'

'I never expected it.'

'When the pressures are great enough, we all do the unexpected,' said Adam. 'You should know that.'

'Where are these buyers of yours, the States?'

'Yes, operating out of the New York area.'

'They must be Italians.'

'Why do you say that?'

'You haven't got strong Chinese connections.'

'They're strong enough.'

'Where are they from?'

'Ex Vietnam.'

Cheng was beginning to show some wary interest. He remembered that Harry Lee had been dealing with Vietnamese buyers at the time of his arrest. That might just explain the connection. 'What sort of quantity are they interested in, these diamond merchants of yours?'

Adam took up the impromptu code. 'The first delivery of diamonds?'

'Yeah.'

'One hundred carats.'

Cheng said nothing but his astonishment was almost audible.

Adam smiled to himself. 'They want a second shipment of the same quantity, within three months if possible.'

'Two hundred carats . . . fuck your mother, you don't joke around, do you.' Cheng gave a series of snorts. 'How did you get to these people?'

'My buyers are my concern,' said Adam sharply. 'You know that.'

'So what do you want me to do, supply the stuff?'

'No, this time I've organised my own source,' said Adam. 'I've seen our mutual friend in Laos. That's why I was delayed in getting back to Hong Kong.'

Cheng's astonishment grew. 'And he's agreed to supply?'

'Why do you sound so surprised? I've proved my good faith with him, just as I have with you.'

Cheng was silent for a moment, trying to come to terms with it all. Then he said sourly, 'If you've already got a source of supply, why talk to me?'

'Because with that sort of quantity,' said Adam, 'I'll need backing. I'm looking for investors, men who can supply the finance.'

'That's not my field,' grumbled Cheng. 'How much money do you think I have?'

'Our mutual friend in Laos asked me to pass a message on to you.'

'What sort of message?'

'I'm to tell you that he would be happy to continue his business relationship with one particular investor.'

'Who?'

'A man he both likes and trusts.'

'And who is that?'

'He gave me just one name, Ah Leung.'

Cheng lapsed again into a suspicious silence. He was

still stupefied that Blake, a half-*gweilo*, more English than Chinese, could come up with a deal so potentially lucrative in a business dominated by Cantonese and Chiu Chow. But if Tinko Chaiwisan had given it the okay, how bad could it be? Chaiwisan was notorious for his caution. Chaiwisan, they said, wouldn't get out of bed before checking that the floor was still there. Cheng hesitated a couple of seconds more. Then he committed himself. 'If I act as a go-between, I'll expect commission.'

At the other end of the line, Adam smiled. He had him. The avaricious bastard had taken the bait. 'Of course,' he said in a tone of benign acceptance. 'Nobody in this world does anything for nothing.'

Once the phone was down, knowing what still lay ahead that night, even the savouring of Cheng's demise was bleak comfort. Slowly and methodically, in a self-induced trance like a man preparing for his own suicide, Adam shaved and showered and changed into fresh clothes. For Nicky – especially this one last time – he should look his best.

It was dark when he went out to the Volvo and drove down to Mid-Levels. Nicky's apartment was on Bowen Road overlooking the harbour, a discreet, pink-painted block with an Art Deco lobby. Adam took the lift up to the twelfth floor and rang the bell.

When Nicky opened the door and saw him, those beautiful grey wintry eyes lit up, all flecked with gold. 'Hi, stranger.' She came into his arms. She kissed him, half laughing. 'My God, you've got to be the most elusive man on earth!'

Adam held her for a moment, his heart thudding. Then reluctantly he moved out of her embrace. 'It's good to see you,' he said in a hesitant voice.

Nicky stepped back. And the moment she saw the look on his face, the hard-set sadness, the grim determination, she knew instinctively why he had come. The smile froze on her face. 'When did you get back?' she asked.

'Late this afternoon.'

She felt tears sparkling in her eyes. So stupid, she thought. But she couldn't stop them. 'Would you like some wine? I was killing a bottle anyway.'

'That would be nice, thanks.'

Trying desperately to hold in her emotions, Nicky went through to the kitchen to pour the two glasses. She watched him through the open door as he walked out on to the balcony. He looked suntanned and fit, his tall frame as lean as ever. Superficially there was no change. But she knew him all too well and could see beneath the skin. There was a weariness about him that she had never seen before, lines of fatigue etched deep in his face. He looked haggard, greyer. In a few weeks he seemed to have aged five years.

Alone in the kitchen, Nicky took a couple of deep breaths. 'Please, God,' she whispered to herself, hoping against hope, 'don't let this be the end.' Then, carrying the two glasses, she joined him on the balcony.

They toasted each other with a simple touch of their glasses. Nicky gazed out over the city, not wanting to look too long into his eyes. 'It's a beautiful night, don't you think? At this time of night Hong Kong assumes a kind of grace.'

Adam nodded, a wistful smile on his face. One thing Hong Kong didn't aspire to – or deserve – was grace. And yet after a day's traffic-fouled mayhem, after the endless rattle of trams, the shouts and shoving and the pounding of jack hammers, when the sun set in a dusty haze over Lantau and the lights came on, something akin to grace, a sublime man-made beauty, did shine out over the water.

He tried to think of some way of gently easing into what he had to tell her but no way would come to mind. So he began with the first words that came to mind and tried to stumble through it. 'You've been telling me all these weeks, Nicky, that I've changed, that somehow I've been drifting away from you. I've denied it of course, got angry as hell, but you're right.' He paused a moment, not daring to look at her. 'I'm afraid I *have* changed, Nicky, things have happened to me, nothing good, nothing to be proud about, but things that have changed my life. I've tried to find some way of telling you but it's been impossible. I'm just sorry for all the lies and hurt I've caused you.'

'What are you trying to tell me?' she asked.

Adam looked at her and smiled, and it was full of pain. 'I love you, Nicky. You don't know how much. But there's no future for us, not now, not after what has happened.'

'Is it another woman?'

He shook his head. 'No, no, it's never been that, you must believe me.'

'Then what is it?' she asked in a bewildered voice. 'You say there's no future for us but you don't say why.'

Adam gave the barest shrug. There was a hopeless look on his face. 'You'll think I'm mad when I say this but I just can't give you the reason, not now. All I can tell you is that what has happened to me over the past few weeks has destroyed any hopes we ever had for a future. I wanted to marry you, I really did. I wanted you to be my wife and have my children. But now . . .' His voice trailed off into silence.

Nicky looked at him and suddenly she went a little paler, her eyes filled with dread. 'You're not sick, are you, it's not that?'

'No, it's nothing like that. I would tell you if it was.'

'Then what is it?' she asked. 'For God's sake, Adam, it makes no sense. Was it something I did wrong? What did I do? Why don't you just tell me?'

'It was nothing that you did, Nicky, nothing at all.'

'Then what is it? You tell me it's not another woman, it's not some illness. Momentous events have occurred in your life, that's all you're prepared to say. And you want me to accept it, swallow it all without a word.' Her voice was filled with exasperation and fresh tears sprang to her eyes. 'Dear God, Adam, why are you doing this to me?'

'Because I have no other choice,' he said, his hurt and frustration so obviously tearing him apart. 'Forget me, Nicky, I'm a lost cause. I'm not worth it. Just forget me.'

'But why, damn you?' she demanded with the tears beginning to roll down her cheeks. '*Why?*'

He let out a long sigh. 'Because I've let you down, I've destroyed my life, that's why. That's all I can tell you.' He leant forward and kissed her one final time, his lips wet with her tears. 'You'll find out why soon enough. In a few weeks you'll understand.'

He stepped back off the balcony into the darkness of the lounge. 'I'm just so sorry for the wasted months,' he said, 'I'm so very sorry, darling . . .' Then he turned his back on her – it was one of the hardest things he had ever had to do in his life – and walked to the door.

Cheng Tak-shing had spent the night pondering. Early in the evening he had played mahjong before going to a nightclub in Mongkok, a small tawdry place called the Jade Dragon where he had played the finger-guessing game with a few of his Sun Yee On cronies. He had taken a whore to an apartment house and then finally, alone, he had chased the dragon. But he still couldn't make up his mind. He didn't know why but Blake's proposal to do new business worried him. The man was too honest, too clean – he stank of it. On the other hand, if Chaiwisan was supplying the stuff, that was as good as a guarantee. And there was no doubt about it, both he and Leung could make a great deal of money. It was tempting, very tempting . . .

In the end he resolved that Ah Leung should know of the offer. Let him decide. A little after midnight, he dialled the number.

'It's settled at last, big brother,' he said when the call was answered. 'Blake tells me he has the cash, the full amount. I'm taking delivery tomorrow. No more fucking hassles. All finished.'

'Good, good,' came the reply. 'Blake seems a lot smarter than the Fat Boy.'

'Oh yes, he's smarter. So smart that he wants to do more business.'

'More?'

'He has new buyers, he says, guys in the New York area.'

'I never expected that, not from Blake.'

'I thought it was crazy too. Fucking suspicious.'

'You're right, it is suspicious.'

'We blackmailed him into this business. Do you think maybe he's gone to the cops?'

Leung gave a small acidic laugh. 'If he has, we'll know soon enough.'

Cheng laughed, too. 'You're right. If he's trying to play a double game, the bastard is dead before he starts.'

'What does he want from us?' asked Leung.

'He's looking for investors, big brother.'

'So he already has a source of supply?'

'So he says.'

'Who?'

'Our friend from Laos.'

Leung was surprised. 'How did Blake get to him?'

It had been Cheng himself who had put Blake on to Chaiwisan, a decision made on his own initiative to make sure Blake raised the balance of Harry Lee's debt. But he wasn't going to admit it. Leung's reactions in matters of that kind were unpredictable. So he simply evaded the question. 'Like you said, big brother, he's smart.'

'But our friend is prepared to deal with him?'

'More than that, according to Blake he was the one who recommended you as an investor.'

'In that case I might just back him.' It was clear that

Leung was flattered. It was always good to gain face.

Cheng's own suspicions were rapidly evaporating. 'Do you want to finance the whole deal, big brother, or just part?'

'Why complicate matters?'

'So you'll finance the lot?'

'Maybe, maybe.'

'What do I tell him?'

'Tell him, yes, I'm interested. Tell him we'll let him know. Play for time.'

'How much time, big brother?'

'Enough to check him out. We've got to be careful. As you said, there's something about Blake that is suspicious. Yes, we must be very careful indeed.'

Adam's mother was waiting for him in the morning, standing on the pavement in front of her apartment on Conduit Road. She was smartly dressed, the way women dress for a church service, and her face bore an air of strained courage. 'I'm so glad you could make it back,' she said as she climbed into the car. 'It's going to mean such a lot to Harry.'

They drove down into Central, parking the Volvo in the Murray Road car park, close to the site where the Swiss Federal Bank – Adam's bank – was to be built. Then they walked together to the High Court.

The courtroom was on the eighth floor of the building, a large room decorated in blond Scandinavian pine with grey carpeting and scarlet chairs. Their barrister was waiting, bedecked in his black gown and seventeenth-century wig. He was an amiable New Zealander, an ex-Crown counsel, quick-talking and articulate; good, they said, at this sort of thing.

Harry was brought up from below escorted by three warders. He was no longer in prison uniform but wore the same cream-coloured Italian suit and monogrammed pink shirt that he had worn on the night he was arrested. The manacles were removed from his wrists. He looked across at Adam and his mother, beckoning them over.

As Adam drew close, Harry reached through the bars to grasp his hand. 'One of the warders gave me a message from Dai Ngan,' he whispered before their mother drew near. 'He says you're clearing the debt in full, every last cent of it.'

Adam nodded. 'I'm handing it over today.'

Harry's dimpled chin began to tremble. 'You've saved my life, Adam. God, I don't know how to thank you. I'd be a dead man if it wasn't for you. What I can say?'

Adam shrugged, a sad smile on his face. But inside he was churning with emotions, and the dominant one was bitterness. Do you have any idea, he thought, any idea at all what it's cost me? I may have saved your life, but the price is the loss of my own. Adam shook his head. It was not the time for bitterness. It served no purpose. But deep in his heart he knew that, no matter how hard he tried, he could never forgive Harry for it, never forgive him for the impossible demands he had made.

'Everything is going to be fine now,' said Harry. 'You wait and see, just fine.' Then he grinned like a schoolboy, full of bravado. 'The lawyer says the judge is pretty lenient. Keep your fingers crossed. Let's hope he didn't argue with his wife last night or get heartburn at breakfast.

Could make the difference of a couple of years.'

Adam nodded, the smile fixed on his face. Poor damn Harry, so stupid, so crass.

There was a brief moment for their mother to take Harry's hands through the bars, tears in her eyes; no words said. Then, as a clerk called for the court to rise, the judge entered. Harry's plea of guilty was reconfirmed and the mitigation began.

The judge listened patiently to what their barrister had to say, taking notes. Drug trafficking, he commented at the end, was a heartless crime, preying on the weakness of others. These courts had extended no mercy in the past and did not intend to do so now. 'If it wasn't for your plea of guilty,' said the judge staring across the courtroom at Harry, 'I would have given you twenty years. As it is, taking your plea into account and also those things that counsel has urged on your behalf, I sentence you to fifteen.' Then he rose from his seat and, without a further look, strode out.

Harry remained standing in the dock, a foolish grin on his ashen face. 'Pretty well as I expected,' he said as Adam came over to him, maintaining his façade of bravado to the bitter end. 'With a third off for good behaviour, it will be ten years to the day. I'll be out before I'm fifty, Adam – still time enough for a good life.'

He thanked his barrister, kissed his mother one last time through the bars and then, with a jaunty thumbs-up sign, was led back down into the bowels of the building.

The barrister packed his books and papers. 'I was hoping for a little better,' he said and, with an apologetic grin, made his exit. Apart from a young Chinese clerk,

Adam and his mother were left alone in the courtroom.

It was only then that the tears spilled down her pale cheeks. 'Thank God I have you,' she said, gripping his hand tightly. 'If you weren't here, Adam, I don't know how I'd get through each day.'

Adam took the Star Ferry across the harbour to Tsim Sha Tsui. He carried the money in the same emerald-green sports bag that Delaney had handed him in New York, the same US currency: wad after wad of used one hundred dollar bills.

It was 12.45 by the time he reached the third floor of the restaurant. The place was crowded, the noise deafening. As the waitresses crowed their wares around him, Adam thought to himself that whoever had labelled the Chinese as inscrutable obviously hadn't taken the Cantonese into account. The Cantonese had to be some of the most voluble, hot-blooded people in the world. Even their dialect – full of long aahs, high-pitched vowels and convoluted tones – made everyday talk sound like the climax to a blood vendetta. But they were full of life, at least, a sharp, demanding, superstitious, excitable race; just being among them helped to raise his spirits.

Cheng Tak-shing was at his regular table by the window. The first thing Adam noticed was how much thinner he looked, the pockmarked cheeks sunken, the pallid skin tight-stretched: sure sign of an addict. Cheng was sinking in deeper every time he saw him.

Adam sat at the table. Cheng barely raised his head, concentrating on a plate of camphor and tea-smoked duck. Adam placed the green bag on the table. 'There it is, the final payment.'

Cheng slurped at a cup of jasmine tea. 'What happened to your brother?'

'Fifteen years.'

Cheng smiled, his glassy-green eyes popping. 'Your brother was smart. He didn't open his mouth. He stayed loyal. That counts for something. And now that the debt is paid, fuck your mother, wait and see – he'll be treated like a mandarin.' Cheng continued to chew at his duck, spitting out the bones. 'Order yourself something,' he said. 'You did well. And who knows, you could do a lot better.'

But Adam had no desire to eat. He poured himself a cup of jasmine tea. 'Have you spoken to Ah Leung?'

Cheng nodded. 'He's interested, very interested. If the deal looks good, he'll come in.'

'When do I get a chance to talk to him?'

'Soon, don't worry, it'll be soon.'

'You can tell him that Chaiwisan is prepared to come to Hong Kong to discuss matters.'

Cheng grinned, his mouth greasy with duck fat. 'I'll tell Ah Leung that. He'll be pleased. What are your plans for getting the stuff into the States?'

'I've got contacts with a toy factory here. Soft toys – teddy bears, pandas, that sort of thing.'

'So the stuff will be sewn inside?'

'That's it.'

'Shipped across in a container?'

'Ordinary, everyday business.'

'What about those sniffing dogs the US Customs have?'

'The toys are scented.'

'Huh?'

'To make them smell nice for kids.'

Cheng grinned, all yellow teeth and pink gums. 'It's good, I like it.'

'The goods will be shipped first to Canada.'

'And from there?'

'From Vancouver down over the border by rail.'

'What about your people in Canada?'

'I've got a company that will accept shipment, a trading company managed by a friend.'

'This friend of yours, any trouble with the cops?'

'He's an MBA from Harvard, clean as a whistle. He's got financial problems. That's the only reason he's agreed to help. He's got a father-in-law on the Vancouver City Council.'

Cheng was visibly impressed. 'I'll tell Ah Leung.'

Adam poured himself more tea. 'My buyers in the States are pushing me. I can't wait for ever.'

Cheng shrugged it off. 'Don't worry, we'll get back to you. These things take time, everybody knows that.'

'I can wait one week, that's all.'

Cheng frowned. 'Don't push too hard. You're new to this game. Ah Leung has influence.'

'There's nothing personal in this,' said Adam. 'Chaiwisan and I would both like to deal with Ah Leung. We know we can trust him. But I can't afford to lose this deal. I've got too much riding on it.' He finished his tea, rising from the table. 'One week, that's how much time I can afford.'

Cheng hunched his shoulders, his face clouding. 'And if we can't get back to you within that time, what then?'

Adam gave him a hard, combative look. 'Then I'll have to look elsewhere.'

Adam left the restaurant, milling with the crowds as he made his way to the Star Ferry pier. He caught the ferry back across the harbour, standing at the rail of the upper deck breathing the warm ocean air.

He had been under no instructions from Sue Martin to impose a deadline. That had been a spur of the moment decision, rash perhaps, but had he left it open-ended, he knew that the meetings would have dragged on for weeks, each meeting a drain on the fast diminishing resources of his courage.

In any event, Adam knew that the luxury of time allowed the luxury of doubt, while pressure might just push Ah Leung into the deal before the man had an opportunity to dig too deep. That's the way he would explain it to Sue Martin. But the truth, the deep, compelling reality of it all, was that Adam wanted this thing over with as soon as possible. If he had to serve a sentence in the US then let him get it done with and try to pick up the pieces of a shattered life again.

Lost in his thoughts, he disembarked from the ferry at Central. He walked out past the taxi ranks and the few remaining rickshaw boys, all emaciated, bare-chested octogenarians, who waited to take gullible tourists on a wheezing ride round the block. Staring absently at the pavement in front of him, Adam took the pedestrian subway under Connaught Road, coming up in front of the dramatic grey space station lines of the HongKong and Shanghai Bank, perhaps the territory's greatest building. The Hilton Hotel stood behind it and he quickened his pace, knowing that Sue Martin would be waiting to debrief him.

In the swirling, mid-afternoon crowds he had no idea he was being followed.

Sue Martin had a room on the eighth floor of the hotel and Adam went straight up. He had hardly knocked before she opened the door. 'How did it go?' she asked, unable to disguise her anxiety.

The shadow of a smile crossed Adam's harassed features. 'According to Cheng, your target is interested in investing.'

Sue Martin's sky-blue eyes lit up. 'So things are looking good.'

'Early days yet.' There was a note of caution in Adam's voice. 'But yes, at least the fish is nibbling.'

'Don't worry, I know the bastard, he'll take the bait.' The voice was a man's, coming from the far side of the hotel room.

Adam looked over Sue Martin's shoulder and saw Carl Drexel seated in the far corner. He was drinking tea, dressed in his shirt sleeves. A tie hung round his neck like a large noose. His crumpled jacket was thrown over the back of the chair.

Drexel grinned. 'Come on in, take a seat. Do you want some tea?'

'When did you get in?' asked Adam, surprised to see him. 'I thought you were in New York.'

Drexel's grin broadened. He removed his glasses and began to polish them. 'How else can I keep my finger on the pulse? New York is on the other side of the world. When it's last thing at night here, it's first thing in the morning there. When you're getting up, I'm going to bed. In New York I might as well be on the moon.'

'So you flew in today?'

'Touched down less than two hours ago. Situation normal – feet swollen, head like a grit bag and my body clock operating on the basis that I'm still somewhere over Hawaii.'

Drexel looked it, too. There was a day's stubble on his heavily wedged chin, deep bags under his eyes and a general air of dishevelled fatigue. He resembled an exhausted bloodhound. But beneath the slow, lugubrious attitude, the unflagging enthusiasm for the job could still be detected.

'So tell me,' said Drexel, chewing on a room service sandwich, 'what exactly did our friend Cheng have to say?'

Adam sat on the edge of the bed. 'Leung is interested, he made that clear enough. But he's stalling for time.'

'Of course he is,' said Drexel. 'He wants to check you out first. He'd have sawdust for brains if he didn't.'

Adam gave an accepting shrug. 'Even so, I thought it best to apply a little pressure.'

'What sort of pressure?' A wary note crept into Drexel's voice.

'I told Cheng that I couldn't wait for ever, that there was too much riding on the deal.'

'Okay, I see no harm in that. It depends how long you gave him.'

'A week.'

'Shit.' Drexel's eyes widened. 'What are you trying to do, get into the *Guinness Book of Records* for the world's quickest drug deal?'

'I can extend the time if I have to,' said Adam aggressively. 'But I wanted them to appreciate I meant business. These people can talk round a deal for months.'

'Okay,' said Drexel, conceding, 'you might just be right. Anyway, that's the way you've called it so that's the way we run the play. Just remember to be a little flexible. These are devious people and deviousness takes time.'

Adam smiled. 'Don't worry, I'll remember.'

Drexel was silent for a time. He took another sandwich, glancing at Sue Martin before he turned his attention back to Adam. 'Tell me, what's happened to your girl friend,' he asked, 'the Canadian woman, Nicky is it?'

Adam gave a small shrug, the hurt evident in his eyes. 'I decided it was best to finish it.'

'When was that?'

'Last night.'

Drexel nodded, his sympathy showing. He paused a moment. But he had to get on with the business at hand. 'So that means there would be nothing to prevent Sue moving in with you?'

Adam blinked in surprise. 'No, nothing . . .' He cast a quick glance at Sue, noticing that her cheeks had flushed. 'But I thought you were going to stay here in the hotel, close to the DEA offices.'

Sue Martin gave an uncertain smile. 'That was the

original plan. But things could happen quickly now, we just don't know.'

'You might find that Chaiwisan is in Hong Kong before the week is out,' said Drexel. 'You might find that he doesn't get here for ten days. But we've got to work on the "worst case" basis. As you know, while we're in Hong Kong, our role here is strictly liaison.' He grinned. 'Although of course we'd like it to be more. We operate under the wing of the Hong Kong Police, specifically Narcotics Bureau. Normally you'd have a Hong Kong police inspector working with you and Sue would just be an onlooker. But, because the timings are open-ended in this operation and because Sue's cover with you is already set, we've managed to get a papal dispensation this time. Sue will stay with you, she'll be your link to the local police. And, when the alarm bells go off, she'll be there to set things in motion.'

Drexel got up from his chair, chewing on his sandwich as he paced the room. 'Normally, once a meeting is set up, we'd get you to try and engineer it somewhere to our choosing, a hotel room like this, for example. That way we can wire the room for sound and put in a hidden video camera. But Chaiwisan won't fall for anything like that. Take my word for it, Adam, he'll come at you out of the blue like a goddamn missile. He'll pick his place and he'll pick his time – and you'll get about five minutes' notice.'

'That's the way he's operated with me in the past,' said Adam. 'What difference is it going to make?'

Drexel poured himself more tea. 'If Leung Chi-ming is at that meeting, then we've got to have it recorded – every last word. It's a legal imperative, a question of evidence, solid, credible evidence – something that Leung's scheister attorneys can't turn on its head. I don't want it to be a question of your word against his. Imagine how that will be twisted in front of a jury – the word of a convicted dope smuggler who would kill his mother for a lighter sentence against the word of one of Hong Kong's most respected men.'

Adam nodded, trying to hold in his emotions. But he was clearly stung by the words – *dope smuggler*. But there was no denying it, that's exactly what he was. That's what he had been reduced to. 'So how are you going to ensure I record it all?' he asked in a subdued voice.

'We fit you out with a recording device,' said Drexel. 'The equipment is the property of the Hong Kong Police because, in strict terms, this is their operation. But it's the best on the market, state of the art.'

'But it's still got to be fitted to me, presumably strapped on in some way?'

'Sure. But it's nothing bulky, nothing that will be detected.'

Adam shrugged. 'Bulky or not, if I'm found with it, I'm as good as dead.'

Drexel looked straight at him. It was time for blunt talking, no evasions and no excuses. 'We need that evidence, Adam. It's crucial. And a tape recording, properly proven in court, is the only way we're going to get it.' Drexel gestured towards Sue Martin. 'As I said, when the alarm bells go, Sue will be there to get everything into motion, that includes fitting the device on to you. She'll check that it's functioning properly, that it contains a new blank tape – all the legal gobbledegook necessary for court proceedings. She'll also make sure that you've got the necessary police back-up. You'll be under surveillance every inch of the way.'

'But when I'm in that meeting,' said Adam, 'I'm on my own. There's no way you can cover me there.'

Drexel nodded. 'That's right. There's going to be a time when you're on your own. But you and I have an agreement, remember that, an agreement that will enable you to reclaim your life. Nobody promised you an easy ride.'

Adam nodded. 'Yes, I accept that.'

Drexel looked at him. 'And nobody said it would be without risks either.'

Yu Wen-huan was working later than usual. It was already dark and he was seated alone in the small office at the back of his tribal crafts shop on the Loy Kroh Road when the call came through. He picked up the phone, speaking initially in his Yunnanese dialect. But when he heard the voice he switched to Cantonese. 'It's good to hear from you, Ah Leung. How can I be of service?'

'Our mutual friend has recommended some new business. I've had approaches made.'

Yu detected a hesitancy in his voice. 'Are there any problems?'

'There might be, I don't know. I'm uneasy.'

'In what way?'

'It's the man putting the deal together, he worries me.

Last month we had to threaten to chop him to pieces. This month suddenly he's taken control.'

'His links with the US buyers are genuine, if that's what is worrying you. We've checked it out. Their regular supplier has a new partner, they tell us, a Hong Kong man, an architect.'

'It's not that, it's more the nature of the man himself.'

'You think he's moving too fast?'

'Maybe.'

'In this business it happens.'

'Yes, maybe. So tell me, is our friend happy?'

'Apparently.'

'And what makes him happy?'

'He likes the man.'

'Liking is not enough.'

'But the liking springs from trust.'

There was a dubious sigh from the other end of the line. 'So he doesn't harbour any doubts?'

'He has no special qualms about the deal.'

'And he'll come to Hong Kong to discuss arrangements?'

'He has done so in the past.'

'Mmmm . . .'

'I would not recommend you to do anything, Ah Leung, not unless you feel secure.'

'Secure?' Leung gave a small, dry laugh. 'How can a man ever feel secure in this business? And now he's pushing me. A week, he says. Seven days! If he doesn't hear from me within that time he'll have to look elsewhere. The man is crazy, pushing too hard. Who does he think he is?'

'Then tell him you are not interested.'

'But the profits could be good.'

'That's true.'

'And our friend trusts him.'

'That is so, yes.'

'Then tell me,' said Leung, 'why do I still have this feeling that there is a vulture circling in the sky?'

That night, as arranged, Sue Martin moved into Adam's apartment. He collected her from the Hilton and they drove up the Peak together. As they climbed from the car, walking towards the entrance of the apartment, she whispered, 'Let's make it look good. You never know who may be watching.' And, slipping an arm round his waist, she leant her head on his shoulder. The wind caught the corn-yellow strands of her hair, blowing them across his cheek. Her skin was very soft and he could smell her perfume. Dear God, he thought, this is crazy. She's my jailer.

Inside the apartment, once she had unpacked, Sue Martin poured herself a glass of white wine from the box in the fridge – just as Nicky had always done – and walked out on to the balcony.

She had made herself mistress of the place in a couple of minutes, thought Adam. No sweat, no hassle, part of the job, that's all. But for him, still aching for Nicky, her presence was an intrusion and, deep down, he resented it. He poured himself a Scotch, draining the last dregs from a bottle. He put on some music, Billie Holiday singing the blues, one of Nicky's favourites. Stop thinking about her, he said to himself, get her out of your mind.

He slumped into a chair. It had been a hell of a day and

suddenly, alone there, just himself and Sue Martin in the apartment, he felt more frightened than he had ever felt before. His insides began to churn. He swallowed the Scotch, letting it burn down his throat. *Come on, you've held yourself together this far. Don't fall apart now. Get a grip on yourself.* But he couldn't shrug off the sense of foreboding. He felt as helpless as a child terrified of the dark.

Sue Martin could sense something was wrong. There was an indefinable melancholy in those dream-black eyes of his. 'What is it?' she asked.

But all Adam could do was shake his head.

'I'm happy to talk about it if you want.'

'It's nothing, don't worry. I'm tired, that's all.' He got up from his chair. 'If you don't mind, I think I'll have an early night. I've got a meeting in the morning with the structural engineers. It could go on all day.'

'Yes, I could do with an early night, too,' she said softly.

'Goodnight then.'

'Goodnight.'

Adam made his way towards the bedroom door, glancing at her one last time, and their eyes met. He gave a sad smile that said both so little and so much. Then he entered his room and the door closed behind him.

Sue Martin remained in the lounge for a time, listening to the music and sipping her wine. She walked across to the bookshelf, reading the titles of the books he collected. She liked his taste in music, she liked the books he read, she liked the paintings on the walls, even the furniture and carpets. The apartment reflected so much of his character. It felt good to be there. She smiled wistfully to herself. If only circumstances had been different, she thought, if only.

The ringing of the telephone clawed him out of a drugged sleep. It took all of Cheng's effort just to reach for the receiver. '*Wai*?' he mumbled, his throat thick with mucus.

'Cheng, is that you?'

'Ah Leung—' Cheng struggled to sit up, his muscles aching.

'What news have you got for me?'

'News . . .?' Cheng looked at his watch but he was too bleary-eyed to focus. The curtains of his window were pulled shut with just a little watery light filtering through. He had no idea of the time.

'You promised to keep a check on our man.'

'Yes, of course, big brother, that's been done.'

'Then what can you tell me?'

Cheng tried to gather his wits. His head ached and he felt nauseous. 'After my meeting with him, he went to the Hilton, big brother.'

'Why?'

'He had a woman there.'

'What woman, the Canadian one?'

'No, a new one, an American.'

'American?' Leung said the word as if it was a disease. 'Who is she? Where is she from? Does she live here?'

'I don't think so, no. They must have met in the States.'

'Then what do you know about her? She could be anybody, an FBI agent, DEA.'

Cheng was beginning to gather his senses and was surprised at how agitated Leung sounded. He was normally so composed, unruffled, a voice making pronouncements from some far-off, impregnable fortress. 'She's not a cop,' he mumbled. 'I'd bet my life on it, big brother. She's fucking him. She was fucking him in Thailand, too.'

'What does she look like, this woman?'

'Not like a cop, big brother. Very tall, yellow hair, blue eyes. More like something out of *Playboy*.'

'Still, see what you can find out about her.'

Cheng was puzzled. 'What's bothering you about this deal, big brother?'

'You were bothered too in the beginning.'

'Do you think Blake might have gone to the cops? Do you think he might have been turned? Is that it? Believe me, big brother, if that was the case I would have sensed it. Blake doesn't have the coolness for it. He's too straight, too dumb in these kinds of things.'

'So now you trust him, too?'

'For this deal, yes.' Cheng sat on the edge of his bed. He was beginning to suffer stomach cramps. He was chasing the dragon three or four times a day now. He knew he should pull back but it was hard. If he could just push this deal through and earn himself some commission, he would get out of Hong Kong for a while, go to Taiwan maybe, find a good woman and rest up.

'I want you to keep a tail on Blake.'

'Of course, big brother.'

'And I want you to speak to our new source.'

Cheng sniffed. 'The one I introduced?'

'He should know if there's any cause for concern. Contact him as soon as you can.'

Cheng had awakened sufficiently now to be able to focus on his watch. It was 11 a.m. 'I'll try and get to him today, big brother. But what happens if he wants more money?'

'Then offer it to him,' said Leung. 'It's one thing Chaiwisan taught me – good insurance never comes cheap.'

It had become part of the routine. Whenever Carl Drexel was in Hong Kong, he and Danny Abbott would spend time together, just lunch or a night in the Wanchai bars if Drexel was pushed, the whole day perhaps if he had time to spare. At this stage of his present visit, however, determined to stay close to a telephone, Drexel said that lunch was all he had time for. Maybe later, when the pressures had eased a little, they could get together again.

So they met at a pub called Mad Dogs, an expat watering hole up the hill from Central in the old part of town. Danny said that he liked the spit and sawdust atmosphere of the place, the European barmaids and squeaky floorboards, ceiling fans and Empire bric-à-brac. 'Notice something about the people in here?' he said. 'No yuppie Chinese with their Gucci shoes and portable telephones. I tell you, Carl, this town is getting to me, right where it hurts most.'

They ordered a ploughman's lunch – cheddar cheese, bread and pickles – served by a rosy-faced girl from Liverpool. Danny Abbott had English draught beer while Drexel, watching his waistline, suffered the purgatory of a soda water.

'How are you doing with that new yacht of yours?' asked Drexel.

'It would help if I could find the occasional woman to come on it – and I use the word "come" in both senses.'

Carl Drexel laughed, but Danny's answer had been predictable enough. One way or the other, every topic of conversation these days revolved around how badly life was treating him. There are quadriplegics out there having a better time than you, he thought irritably. So your face got chopped up and your ego took a beating – worse things could have happened.

'So what brings you to Hong Kong this time?' asked Danny as he drank his beer.

Drexel gave a nonchalant shrug. 'Nothing special, just liaison.'

'You said you were pushed for time. The way you spoke on the phone it sounded like you had some fancy operation on the go.'

'I've reached the unenviable stage of my career, Danny, when I spend more time trying to find revenue and resources than I do drugs. You're on the admin side yourself, you should know how time-consuming committees can be.'

'So you've got nothing on the go?'

'Afraid not, nothing that our local DEA man hasn't kept you advised of.' It wasn't that Drexel distrusted him, far from it. But with 'Snow White' at such a critical stage, one loose word could spell disaster.

Danny was in Narcotics Bureau, still holding down the post of Research and Admin Officer, and, while Narcotics was a professional outfit, leaks had been known to occur. Even back in New York, knowledge of 'Snow White' was on a strict need-to-know basis. Here in Hong Kong, in the killing ground itself, it had to be kept buttoned up tight. The only people who knew of Adam Blake's true role were the Chief Superintendent in charge of Narcotics Bureau and the officer he had allocated to work with Drexel, a Chinese detective named Xavier Tong. And until the operation blew, that, hopefully, was the way it would stay.

The barmaid from Liverpool came back to their table. As she approached, Drexel noticed the way she glanced first at Danny, saw the bloodless skin, the scars and split lip and instinctively turned her eyes away. 'Like a refill, luv?' she asked Drexel.

But it was Danny who said defiantly to her, 'Yes, I'll have another. What about you, Carl?'

Drexel shook his head. 'One soda is enough for any man.'

As the barmaid turned away, Danny gave an embittered sigh. 'You saw her reaction. Bloody typical. They treat me like Frankenstein's monster.'

'Sure, some maybe,' said Drexel. 'That's something you're going to have to live with, Danny.' And he couldn't help adding, 'The occasional smile might help a little.'

Danny scowled. 'What's there to smile about?'

The barmaid came back with his beer.

Danny paid her and made a show of not leaving a tip. 'If I got a smile from the likes of her first,' he grumbled, 'I might just smile back.'

Drexel said nothing. What was the use?

Danny gulped his beer and turned to him. 'Last time we spoke on the phone, you said you had an op on the go, one in which Leung Chi-ming was the target.'

Drexel smiled. 'In the embryonic stage, I think I said.'

'Any developments yet?'

'In a few months maybe, we'll see.'

Danny's face darkened. 'Translated, that means you're getting nowhere.'

Drexel shrugged. 'Let's just say we've had to put it on a back burner for a while.'

Danny gave a snort of anger. 'You really are becoming a bureaucrat, Carl, you've got all the euphemisms off pat – back burner, shit!' He gulped at his beer, lifting his chin so that his adam's apple bobbed. There were even scars on his neck. 'Fucking marvellous, isn't it, I can't even order a beer without being treated like a freak and he's up there in his mansion on the Peak smelling of roses. Have faith, that's what you told me on the telephone – what a bloody joke that is! When is somebody going to get out there and screw the bastard?'

'One day, Danny, one day.'

'One day, sure, when the moon turns to cheese.' Danny Abbott stared down into his beer, his face filled with bitterness. 'How do you get justice in this world, Carl, tell me that? How do you ever get it if you play by the rules?'

It was late that night, a few minutes before midnight, when Cheng Tak-shing eventually made contact with his source. The two men spoke over the telephone. The language they used was Cantonese, the sentences short and cryptic.

'Our friend requires your services,' said Cheng.

'So he wishes to trade again?'

'This month if possible.'

'That's okay, tell him to go ahead.'

'So you see no problems?'

'Not if he acts now.'

'But he worries about the opposition.'

'The opposition is asleep.'

Cheng chuckled.

'But the market could change.'

'That's why we pay you to monitor it.'

'It's delicate work, you appreciate that, difficult sometimes. There are certain overheads, too.'

'Money is no problem,' said Cheng, 'so long as we get value for what we pay. And value means certainty, no risks.'

'My services are guaranteed.'

'So I can tell our friend to proceed?'

'Tell him he can trade at his leisure.'

'And if there are any shifts in the wind?'

'I'll let you know in good time.'

'Good. He'll be grateful.'

'So long as he expresses his gratitude in cash, that's all that bothers me. Remember, business is business.'

'Of course, my friend.'

'I'm not your friend, that's something else to remember. We're in this for mutual benefit, no other reason.' And Danny Abbott put down the phone.

Chapter Ten

LAOS – HONG KONG

In the morning Cheng reported back. Abbott, the expat cop, their source, had given the all clear. 'Good,' said Leung. And the last of his doubts were dispelled. Abbott, after all, was an officer in Narcotics Bureau, working in liaison with FBI and DEA personnel. Abbott was close to the heart of things and he was a man desperate for cash. He knew that if Leung's operations were jeopardised, the cash flow would cease. To that extent at least he could be trusted not to play a double game.

Subject to satisfactory arrangements being reached concerning the shipment of the merchandise, Leung was now happy to finance the first one hundred units. So the word was sent to Chiang Mai and from there across the border into Laos: it was time for Allah to come to the mountain.

It was a bright blue morning and there was a lone eagle circling in the sky when Chaiwisan set forth. The bird was a good omen, he said, as he bade farewell to his family, to all twenty-three children from the eldest, a grown man of twenty-five, to the youngest, just a babe in arms. Then he boarded a Toyota truck, sandbagged against landmines, and with an armed guard of half a dozen men, drove down the winding track that led from Mae Kwong, his gateway to the world, into the endless rolling jungles.

It took a full twenty-four hours to reach the Laotian capital of Vientiane, a hard, cross-country haul. He left his men on the outskirts of the dishevelled old French colonial city and made his way alone to the airport. From Vientiane he flew first to Burma carrying the papers of a Laotian sapphire merchant named Trang. He spent just one night in Rangoon and the following day flew on to the world's most populous Islamic nation, Indonesia.

Chaiwisan had a great fondness for Indonesia. It was a country where a man, with just a little cash and a few friends, could obtain almost anything that his heart desired, from weapons to contraband to a legitimately issued passport in whatever name best suited his purposes. Chaiwisan spent three days in the capital of Jakarta visiting old friends and attending to private business.

Before sitting for his passport photograph, he dyed his hair a silver grey and purchased a pair of gold-rimmed spectacles, pleased that two such simple devices could so radically change his appearance. The passport took only a day to be prepared and he collected it from the Ministry itself. According to the document, he was now an Indonesian citizen, a Jakarta-based land developer by the name of Osman Cheung.

It was under that name that he boarded a flight for

Hong Kong. He landed in the British colony in the early evening, passing through Immigration without incident, and took a taxi to a small hotel on Nathan Road, a discreet middle-class establishment popular with Taiwanese tourists. He did not go out that night. He ordered a meal in his room, watched television and made one local telephone call.

Tinko Chaiwisan was hoping for a profitable and uneventful few days in Hong Kong. He had never experienced trouble before. But thoroughness, he knew, was the key to survival, and survival was always the bottom line. That was why the following morning, at around ten, he received a visitor in his room. It was the man he had telephoned the previous night, a man he had worked with before.

The man's name was Chiu, commonly called 'Onion Head' because of his bald, dome-like scalp. By profession he was a lawyer's clerk. He was about fifty years of age, short and portly. To the world at large he was not a person of any significance. But Chaiwisan knew differently; he knew the lawyer's clerk was the Hong Kong Dragon Head of the Wo Shing Wo.

Adam was working late that evening, checking through contract documents for the Swiss Federal building, still maintaining the façade. The staff had all gone home and only Sue Martin remained, his shadow for the past seven days. She was sitting in reception idly leafing through an old issue of *Time*. It had been a long hard day exacerbated by the strain of waiting, never knowing when the call setting the time and place of the meeting would come.

For seven days his belly had been liquid, the breath catching in his throat every time the telephone rang. Physically, mentally, emotionally, he was drained, doing little more now than going through the motions. He checked his watch: 8 p.m. Too late, he thought with a weary yawn, another day wasted – and the telephone rang. On pure reflex his hand jerked out, grabbing the receiver. He paused an instant, sucking for breath, then he lifted it to his ear. 'Hullo?'

'Good evening, Adam. How are you? You sound a little tired.'

He would have recognised the voice anywhere; the soft gravelly tones, like some fond uncle calling.

'I have arranged our meeting for this evening. I hope you're not otherwise engaged.'

Adam's mouth was dry as ash. 'No, no, that's okay, I can make it.'

'That's good,' said Chaiwisan.

'But where's it going to take place? What's the address? Hong Kong Island or Kowloon?' Adam was rushing his words. 'I'll also need to know the time. I've still got a few things to finish here at the office.'

Chaiwisan chuckled. 'Don't be so anxious, Adam. Everything is arranged. In fifteen minutes from now a red Honda Accord will draw up in front of your building. The registration number is easy to remember, DD 7878. The driver knows who you are. Just climb into the car and he will bring you to me.'

'Fifteen minutes,' echoed Adam. 'Okay.'

'I am sorry this has had to be so sudden but I'm sure you appreciate the reasons why.'

'Sure.'

'Till later, then.' And Chaiwisan rang off.

Adam sat for a moment, flushed with nerves. Christ, he thought, it's on. He half rose from his desk, shouting through to Sue Martin. 'That was Chaiwisan on the line. It's on! The meeting is set for tonight.'

She came rushing through to his office. 'Where? When?'

'I don't know where. A Honda is going to collect me downstairs in fifteen minutes. I just get in and go.'

'Damn,' she murmured, looking flustered. 'Drexel was right - straight out of the blue, like a goddamn missile.'

Adam was surprised. He hadn't seen her anything less than fully in control before. 'There's no problem, is there?' he asked. 'I mean, we weren't expecting much notice.'

'No, no,' she blurted, 'no problem at all. Narcotics Bureau have got two cars on standby. We'll have people shadowing you all the way.'

'Okay.'

'But just in case anything goes wrong - not that it will - you remember the hotline to Narcotics? It'll put you straight through to the Control Room.'

'Drilled into my head,' he said.

'Great.' Her mouth was as dry as his. 'Now where's my damn bag?' She saw it lying on a chair in the corner of his office and grabbed it, fumbling inside to pull out a bulky buff-brown envelope. 'First things first, let's get you rigged up with the recording device. Okay, off with your shirt.'

The tape machine was contained in a small lightweight harness which was strapped round Adam's waist, the machine itself lodged neatly into the small of his back. Sue Martin ran two wires up his back on either side of the spine, taping them to the skin. At the end of the wires were tiny microphones which she secured over his shoulders on either side of his neck, one into the left collarbone, the other into the right.

'Fine,' she said, 'You can put your shirt back on. Just before you go downstairs I'll activate it. It runs real slow so you've got plenty of recording time. How do you feel in it?'

Adam gave a nervous grin. 'Like I'm wearing a corset.'

'Under your shirt and jacket, nothing will show.'

'Just so long as it doesn't malfunction. We've got one crack at this and one crack only.'

Sue Martin smiled skittishly. 'Don't worry, it's guaranteed.'

'So was the *Titanic*,' said Adam.

Cheng Tak-shing was in a massage parlour on Tin Hau Temple Road when his pager, lost somewhere in the bundle of his clothes, began to bleep.

The masseuse, a Hakka woman with arms like a construction coolie, ignored the noise. She was asking if he wanted to 'go double', a slang invitation to pay extra for the pleasure of being masturbated with massage oils. That's why ninety per cent of the customers were there.

But all Cheng wanted was the relaxation of the massage. He was too heavily on heroin to care about the sexual side. As the saying went, he was married now to the drug. 'Where's the telephone?' he demanded, sitting up on one elbow.

The masseuse pointed through the curtains of the cubicle, disappointed that she was losing the extra cash. 'Down the passage there.'

Cheng wrapped a towel round his waist, his skin white, his ribs protruding, and made his way to the phone. His paging centre gave him the number. Cheng didn't recognise it. But as soon as the voice answered at the other end, he recognised the caller. 'Uncle Chicken,' he said, full of largesse, 'so you're here at last. We've been waiting. When are we going to talk?'

'Tonight,' answered Chaiwisan abruptly, not a trace of friendliness in his voice.

Cheng gave a surprised grunt. 'I don't know if Ah Leung can make it. He's a busy man. He has social engagements.'

'For such important business I am sure he can spare the time.'

'I'll contact him,' mumbled Cheng grudgingly.

'Yes, you do that. And do it now.'

'Where are we going to meet?'

'Drive to the Hopewell Centre in Wanchai, park your car and wait at the back on Kennedy Road. One of my men will pick you up. He'll be driving a beige Toyota Cressida.'

'When should we be there?'

'Within thirty minutes.'

Cheng spluttered. 'Thirty minutes!'

'Ah Leung knows how I operate. He'll understand.'

'What about me? I'm in the middle of a massage. All I've got on is a towel!'

But the only answer was the burr of the disconnected tone.

Carl Drexel and Danny Abbott were in the bar at the Royal Hong Kong Yacht Club when Sue Martin rang. 'It's all systems go,' she told Drexel breathlessly. 'Adam just had the call. Chaiwisan is in Hong Kong. The meeting is set for tonight. Like you said, no warning at all. Adam has got to be downstairs in ten minutes. A car will pick him up.'

'Where is it going to take place?'

'Chaiwisan didn't say.'

'Have you organised back-up?'

'Xavier Tong at Narcotics says he'll have two cars in position. Everything is set.'

'Good,' said Drexel. 'As soon as Adam is on his way, get a taxi up to police headquarters. I'll meet you in the Bureau's Control Room. Oh, and one final thing.'

'What's that?'

'Wish him good luck.'

Sitting at the bar, nursing a beer, Danny Abbott couldn't hear what Carl Drexel was saying on the phone but the sudden look of seriousness, the sharp nodding of his head and the urgency of his footsteps as he returned to the bar made it obvious that something big was on the go. 'What is it?' he asked. 'What's happening?'

Drexel drained his soda water. 'Hideous bloody drink,' he said with a grin, 'must have been invented by joggers. One thing I promise you, Danny, when tonight is over it's going to be twelve-year-old Scotch all the way. And we're going to get smashed out of our little brains! Come, the bugle is calling.'

Danny Abbott got off his stool. 'What in hell are you talking about?'

'We've got to get up to your offices. We're wanted in the Control Room.'

'Why, what's going on?'

'Everything is going on!' There was a look of fierce expectation on Drexel's heavy-set features. 'Tonight is the night, Danny, the night I've been promising you.'

'What are you talking about, for God's sake?'

'What have I been telling you all this time? Have faith, I said, have a little faith.'

Danny's eyes widened in disbelief. 'You've got to be kidding.'

'I'm not a kidding man, Danny, you know that.'

'Are you saying this is to do with Leung Chi-ming?'

Carl Drexel smiled triumphantly. 'Bet your ass it is!'

Danny Abbott said nothing, stunned by the news. As they walked out of the bar, blotches of pink showed on the stretched sheets of skin across his ravaged cheeks.

But nothing could dampen Drexel's elated anticipation. 'What's the matter, Danny? Normally when I mention Leung you rev straight into overdrive.'

Danny just grunted, pacing out, leaving Drexel in his wake, and it was only when they were outside the club house that he spoke. 'Why didn't you tell me about it before?' he asked bitterly. 'You haven't said a thing. Just the other day in Mad Dogs you said it was on the back burner. Nothing was happening, that's what you said.'

Drexel gave a perplexed smile. 'I'm sorry, okay. You know the way it is, we had to keep the lid screwed tight.'

'You didn't trust me, is that what you're saying?'

Drexel laughed, amazed at the anger in Danny's voice. 'Don't be so bloody sensitive, Danny. Of course I trust you. But all you need is one loose word, half a hint dropped out of turn. Up until now only two people in the whole of NB have known about it, your boss man and the case officer.'

They hurried across the Yacht Club car park, Danny Abbott, his lips tight pressed, lost in his own thoughts.

'What the hell is the matter with you?' asked Drexel when they reached his car. 'I thought you would have been delighted.'

'Maybe it's the fact that with Leung Chi-ming we share a common grievance, Carl. That's why I thought we were working together on this thing. Obviously I was wrong.'

Danny Abbott climbed in behind the wheel of his Mercedes Sports while Drexel climbed in next to him. They drove out of the Yacht Club grounds in silence.

Drexel was still smiling. 'Come on, Danny, loosen up. You should be used to categories of confidentiality by now. It's part of the business. Shit, if you start taking these things personally . . .'

Danny gave a grudging nod. 'Yeah, maybe you're right.' He gave a sullen shrug. 'So it's going down tonight, is that what you say?'

Carl Drexel grinned. 'By midnight we should have

Leung Chi-ming arrested and cautioned and in a cell with a view.'

'But how did you get it this far?'

'Do you remember back in February, just after Chinese New Year, we arrested a Vietnamese dealer in New York and simultaneously you picked up two men here? One of them was called Harry Lee, *Fai Chai* – the Fat Boy.'

Danny nodded. 'Yeah, Op Bamboo Dragon. Lee got fifteen years a week or so back.'

'That's where it started.'

'But how?'

'Because Lee was in debt up to his eyeballs to his investor. And who do you think that was?'

'Leung Chi-ming?'

'You've got it – Leung and his henchman, Cheng. It's always the case, wait long enough and the cards fall into place.'

'So they started putting on the screws, is that it?'

'Old-fashioned Triad style, the way they teach it in the squatter huts of Kwun Tong. Cheng's Sun Yee On associates got to Harry Lee in Lai Chi Kok. They hacked off his ear and threatened to take his balls as the next instalment unless the debt was paid. There was only one way Lee could raise the money, that was to organise more heroin deliveries.'

'Who did he manage to con into making them for him?'

'His half-brother,' said Drexel.

'But isn't he an architect?'

'That's the one. Adam Blake is his name.'

Danny Abbott shook his head. 'Christ, a bloody architect. Where did he get the stuff?'

Drexel smiled. 'The only source Harry Lee had was Cheng Tak-shing. Incestuous little game, isn't it? So Blake had to deal through Cheng. And Cheng, in turn, put him on to his Laotian supplier.'

Danny Abbott blinked. The surprises were tumbling on top of each other. 'You mean Chaiwisan?'

'That's exactly who I mean. We picked up Blake in New York, agreed a plea bargain and turned him. Standard game plan. Blake continued to trade – except it was now for us. It was an opportunity I couldn't miss, Danny, Chaiwisan supplying the stuff, Leung Chi-ming financing it and Cheng, like a pariah dog, picking up the scraps.'

'And it's all coming to a head here in Hong Kong?'

'Chaiwisan is in town. They've got executive decisions to make. The meeting is set for tonight. All three are going to be there: Leung, Cheng, Chaiwisan. And Blake will be the fourth one – wired for sound.'

Danny Abbott drove in through the main gates of police headquarters, parking the Mercedes Sports out on the forecourt. 'How can you be so sure Leung will attend?' he asked as he climbed from the car. 'He hasn't showed himself in the past. That one time out in the New Territories, the week before we were attacked, that's the only time I remember.'

'We're talking about a hundred units,' said Drexel, 'with a hundred more to come. He's putting a lot of money on the line.'

'But he's unpredictable. Most of the time he works

through front men, goons like Cheng. Why shouldn't he do the same tonight?'

Carl Drexel gave an easy shrug. 'Even if he shies off, wait and see, we'll still nail him. All we need is Chaiwisan. If we get him, we get Leung.'

'I don't understand,' said Danny as they walked together into the high block. 'How does one lead to the other?'

Drexel laughed. 'Come on, Danny, you know Chaiwisan. You've got a file six inches thick on the old bastard. How do you think he's stayed out of jail so long? In Thailand they say he's got enough information on the army, the police and half the politicians to bring the government down. That's why nobody there is too keen to have him arrested. They'd prefer it if he was just quietly shot, put six feet under in an unmarked grave. How old is he, sixty, sixty-five? For him, even ten years in a Hong Kong jail would be a life sentence. There's no way he's going to button up and do his time. He's far too smart. No, he'll do a deal, Danny. Survival, that's all he cares about. And if survival means sinking Leung Chi-ming, then he'll sink him for good.'

'But here in Hong Kong Chaiwisan will be our property,' said Danny. 'Are you sure we'll even want to trade?'

'Absolutely,' said Drexel as they stepped into the elevator. 'I've spoken to the men that count, Danny, legal and police.'

'And they're with you?'

'One hundred per cent. So you see, Danny, whether Leung attends tonight or not, all we need is the bird.'

And he began to laugh. 'Uncle Chicken is the key.'

Cheng Tak-shing had just climbed from a taxi and was waiting on Kennedy Road at the back of the Hopewell Centre when his pager bleeped a second time. It took two minutes to find a telephone inside the building, another two minutes to get through.

'What is it?' he asked. 'Why do you want me?'

Danny Abbott replied, 'Just listen. I'm phoning from my office in police headquarters. I'm taking a huge bloody risk. I've got information. But I want payment, you understand. Big money this time.'

'How much?'

'Twenty-five thousand US dollars.'

'Fuck your mother.'

'Take it or leave it. And live with the consequences.'

'You're trying to cheat us.'

'You fool, this would be cheap at double the price.'

Cheng could detect the strain in Abbott's voice. Something serious was happening. 'All right,' he said, 'it's agreed. What is it, what have you got to tell me?'

'The meeting is a set-up.'

'What are you talking about?'

'Blake is an undercover agent.'

'Blake? When did you find out?'

'A couple of minutes ago. You and Leung are walking into a trap.'

Adam saw the red Honda Accord the moment he stepped out of the building. The driver, a gaunt, anaemic individual, aged about thirty, with moles on his cheeks, looked towards him and lifted a bony hand.

It was a relatively cool night with a breeze coming in off the sea. But Adam was sweating badly. Under his shirt, the tape machine felt bulky and uncomfortable. He walked towards the car, checking the registration number. Then he opened the door and climbed into the back. Without a word, the driver set off, turning into Queensway past the High Court and Pacific Place and then into Wanchai along Queen's Road East. The traffic was thick, nose to tail. The pavements were filled with people. Adam checked his watch. It was 8.18 p.m.

Cheng Tak-shing was back on Kennedy Road behind the soaring circular tower of the Hopewell Centre when the metallic gold Mercedes 500 SEC drew up.

Fists clenched, arms shaking with rage, he walked over to the car. The driver's electric window hissed down. 'I must talk to you,' said Cheng, his sunken pan of a face suddenly as white as porcelain. 'I have just spoken to Abbott. It's bad news, Ah Leung. We have to act or we're both dead men.'

The Honda reached the top of Queen's Road East, moving towards the Happy Valley Racecourse. Stubbs Road was fifty yards ahead to the right. Adam still had no idea of his final destination and just prayed that in the dense clog of evening traffic, with so many vehicles feeding in from the side roads, the two police vehicles hadn't fallen back. The lights at the Stubbs Road junction turned red and the Honda came to a stop.

Then suddenly, without warning, the driver swung his head round. 'Get out,' he said. 'Get out here. Hurry, hurry!'

Adam looked at him, dumbfounded. The man was mad. There were two lanes for eastbound traffic, two for westbound, the four lanes divided down the centre by an iron railing. If he got out of the Honda, he would be jammed against the railing, stranded on a concrete island in the middle of the road.

But the driver persisted. 'Climb over the fence and get across to the far side of the road. Hurry, while the traffic is stopped. There's a car at the bus stop. Look, you can see it. There, the small Mazda, the white one.'

Adam still couldn't come to terms with it. 'Is this part of the arrangement?' he demanded. 'Did Chaiwisan organise this?'

'Yes, yes,' said the driver. 'Hurry, get out, go before the traffic starts.'

Reaching back, the driver swung the door open and Adam stumbled out, clutching the iron railing. He hesitated a moment then saw that, across on the far side of the road, the driver in the white Mazda was beckoning. Scrambling over the railing, he weaved his way through the jam of traffic. He reached the Mazda just as it was edging into the road, heading back in the direction he had just come.

As Adam clambered into the back seat he knew he could forget the two police cars that were tailing him. There was no way they could turn, not with the iron railing separating the east- and westbound traffic. The best they could hope to do was swing round at the Stubbs

Road junction. But by then Adam knew he would be long gone.

What worried him more, however, was the reason for the ploy. It could only have been designed for one reason, to shake off pursuit. But why? Why go to these kinds of lengths? Was Chaiwisan taking caution to a ridiculous degree or did he know he would have an escort, police protection?

My God, thought Adam, what the hell do I do now?

The Control Room at Narcotics Bureau consisted, in fact, of two rooms. The larger one contained maps, radios and banks of telephones where the permanent staff operated; in the smaller room operational personnel sat, viewing proceedings through a glass window. Sue Martin had seen other places like it – the crackling of radio static filling the air, tables littered with coffee cups, papers doodled into oblivion. And yet she couldn't remember one that possessed the same charged air of tension. Or maybe, she thought, it was just the way she felt inside, a manifestation of her own boiling anxiety.

As she walked in to join Carl Drexel and Danny Abbott, almost as she opened the door, the first radio message was received from the police pursuit vehicles.

Xavier Tong, the chief inspector running the case, a quiet, softly spoken man in his mid-thirties, translated the Cantonese. 'We may have a few problems,' he said.

'What kind of problems?' Carl Drexel frowned with worry.

'There's been moves to shake off any possible pursuit. The Honda was in the outer eastbound lane of Queen's

Road East when Blake was seen getting out.'

'What, in the middle of the road?'

'Blake climbed the centre railing, ran through the westbound traffic and climbed into a waiting car, a Mazda 323. The car then set off, driving back into Wanchai.'

'Chaiwisan,' grunted Drexel. 'This is his kind of stunt. It's got Chaiwisan tattooed all over it.'

'But the question is why,' said Xavier Tong. 'What reason would he have for doing it?'

Sue Martin went cold.

'Were your vehicles able to follow?' asked Drexel.

'They've lost contact, I'm afraid.'

'Did they get the Mazda's registration number?'

Xavier Tong gave a mournful look. 'Traffic, they say, was too thick.'

Adam had barely caught his breath when suddenly, a hundred yards back down Queen's Road East, opposite the Wanchai Municipal Market, the Mazda swung left into a side street. Half mounting the pavement, it squeezed past a row of goods vehicles, continued on another fifty yards and then swung right.

This was the old part of Wanchai. The buildings, mostly four or five storeys high, were dilapidated and unpainted; a mixture of garages, metal-work shops, printers and working-class eating houses. Upstairs were the residential apartments, laundry dangling from windows, water dripping from ancient air-conditioners.

The Mazda took a second turning to the right, continued for about twenty yards and came to a halt. The driver pointed to the dark entrance of a three-storey building. 'Take the stairs,' he said. 'There's an apartment on the top floor. Uncle Chicken is waiting for you.'

Adam climbed from the vehicle. A few feet away a blind fortune-teller sat on his fold-up stool with a mangy dog at his feet. Old signs, crudely painted with Chinese characters, dangled above the man's head – Moon Kee Tailors, Radiant Rattan. The air smelt fetid and sour.

Just above the entrance to the building, Adam could read the address etched into the lintel: 14 Stone Nullah Lane. On one side of the entrance a Taoist shrine had been placed in an alcove. It looked as if nobody had tended it for months; the red and gold paint had peeled away, a couple of mandarin oranges lay rotting, burnt-out joss sticks protruded from a gold-painted tin.

Adam hesitated, playing for time, nervous of the reception he would get. But the driver called to him gruffly, 'Go on up, he's waiting.' And he began to climb the rickety wooden stairs, forced to feel his way in the dark. My God, he thought, only Chaiwisan would choose a place like this. He reached the top floor and knocked on the door.

He could hear movement inside the apartment, footsteps approaching the door. The adrenaline was pumping, he felt as if he was balancing on the edge of a cliff: pure, raw fear. Any second and he knew that his fate could be decided. He took a deep breath, trying to steady himself.

'Adam, my friend, it's so good to see you!' Chaiwisan stood in the doorway, a bright smile on his face. 'Come in, please, come in.'

Adam blinked, taken aback by the warmth of the greeting and by the fact, too, that Chaiwisan had silver-blue hair. Adam had never seen him in anything other than jungle fatigues before but now he wore a flowing, open-necked silk shirt and cream-coloured trousers.

Chaiwisan smiled. 'Yes, it's me. The grey hair is a little theatrical precaution, that's all.'

After the subterfuge of getting him there, Adam had expected the worst. But Chaiwisan looked as relaxed as always, not a hint of antagonism in his attitude.

Adam smiled, the easiest disguise for his relief. 'Do you make all your visitors complete an obstacle course?'

Chaiwisan answered with a disarming smile. 'Ah yes, but you must see it from my side, Adam. Alas, your brother is now a convicted drug trafficker. You have been travelling a great deal, to New York and then Chiang Mai of all places. I don't know how the Hong Kong police work but if that intelligence is put together . . . well, I'm sure you understand.' And he laughed. 'But come in, come in.'

The apartment was small, no more than three or four hundred square feet. On the walls were faded black and white photographs of deceased ancestors, grandparents, uncles, aunts; solemn portraits that could have been taken fifty years ago. The furniture in the place appeared to be as old as the photographs, shabby now, the carpet threadbare. French windows led onto a small roof garden cluttered with potted shrubs and laundry.

'The place was offered to me by a friend,' said Chaiwisan. 'It is humble but discreet. Would you like a drink, cognac perhaps?'

'Thank you.' Adam took a seat, constantly aware of the tape recorder and its wires strapped to his body. 'I take it that Leung will be joining us?'

Chaiwisan poured the cognac. 'Both he and Cheng should be here soon.'

'Good, the sooner we can get down to business the better.'

Chaiwisan gave him an avuncular smile. 'Are you that anxious?'

'White powder is a business,' Adam replied, playing the role he had set for himself of the new man pushing hard. 'The quicker business is done, the quicker profits come in. Remember, I have buyers waiting in New Jersey.' He smiled. 'And when it comes to cash resources, I also have a lot of catching up to do.'

In the Control Room at Narcotics, tension was mounting by the minute. Xavier Tong listened to the reports coming in over the radio. 'I'm afraid there's still no sign of the white Mazda.'

'So we've lost him,' said Drexel.

'It looks that way.'

'But isn't there something we can do?' said Sue Martin, ignoring Drexel's look of admonishment. 'We promised him back-up, for Pete's sake!'

Xavier Tong, always the polite Oriental, tried to explain the reality of the situation. 'Mr Blake could be anywhere in Wanchai, Happy Valley or Mid-Levels by now. Do you know how many buildings that comprises, how many individual apartments? This is Hong Kong, Miss Martin, one of the most densely populated areas on earth. I'm sorry, I understand your concern, but for the time being I'm afraid Mr Blake is on his own.'

A clock hung on the lounge wall above the faded photographs of the anonymous ancestors. Draining the last of his cognac from the glass, Adam looked up at it for the hundredth time. He had been waiting in the apartment for nearly twenty-five minutes and there was still no sign of Leung or Cheng Tak-shing. He noticed that Chaiwisan, too, kept glancing up at the clock, nervously rubbing his hands. 'Where are they?' asked Adam, unable to disguise his mounting apprehension.

Chaiwisan removed his glasses, rubbing his eyes. 'They should have been here by now. I don't like it.'

Adam walked across to the sideboard, pouring himself more cognac; anything to steady his nerves. He could sense the sweat dribbling down his back, collecting in the harness that held the tape machine. 'How are they getting here?' he asked.

'I have a man meeting them at the Hopewell Centre. By car it should only be two or three minutes from here.'

A briefcase lay open on the sideboard next to the cognac. Adam glanced down and saw a passport lying among the papers – an Indonesian passport. So that's how he got in, he thought. A portable telephone also lay in the briefcase. 'Can't you phone your man?' he asked.

Chaiwisan shook his head. 'I didn't get telephones for any of the drivers. It was a mistake I won't make again.' Clearly agitated, he walked out onto the small roof garden.

Adam joined him.

Chaiwisan looked up at the night sky. It possessed a brownish pewter sheen, luminous on the low horizon from a million lights. 'I don't like this town, Adam. It's too big, too crowded, too full of strangers. I do not feel at ease here. You say you want to get your business done. Well, I do too – so that I can leave this place.'

They stood in silence for a minute or two, Adam drinking his cognac too fast. Then they walked back inside. Chaiwisan looked up at the wall clock again, staring at it like a man hypnotised.

'I am like the pilot of an aeroplane,' he said in a low voice. 'If a red light starts blinking, just one, that is enough. I take the aircraft back to the airport. That way at least I live to fly another day. And right at the moment a red light is blinking.'

'What do you intend to do?' asked Adam.

Chaiwisan went quickly to the sideboard, closing his briefcase. 'If there is some innocent reason for their delay, then we can meet another night. But we can't wait here any longer. It would be stupid to take the risk. Come, I have a car nearby.'

Adam nodded. Frankly, he was pleased to be out of there too. Like Chaiwisan, he was filled with foreboding.

They walked out of the apartment together. Adam waited while Chaiwisan locked the front door. Then he turned towards the stairs – and he was facing Cheng Tak-shing.

Their eyes met. Cheng curled back his lip, his teeth gritted, and Adam knew instantly that something was terribly wrong.

'Where's Ah Leung?' asked Chaiwisan.

But Cheng ignored him, focusing his attention on Adam. 'You thought you could fool us, huh, is that it? Fuck you, you half-*gweilo* ghost bastard. Fuck you!' And suddenly, lashing out, he punched Adam hard in the chest, throwing him back against the wall.

'Are you mad?' exclaimed Chaiwisan. 'What are you doing?'

It was only then that the two men with Cheng emerged from the darkness of the stairs.

'Who are these people?' protested Chaiwisan. 'Just you and Ah Leung, that's what I said.'

Cheng glared at him. 'Open the door. Do as I say. Get inside.'

Chaiwisan stood his ground for a moment, glaring back. But Cheng had support. The two men with him, both in their mid-twenties, long-haired and tough, their arms tattooed, began to edge up the stairs.

From where he stood, his back to the wall, Adam could glimpse the ominous curves of the meat cleavers held tight against their legs. Oh God, he thought, suddenly filled with horror, they're going to kill me.

'Open the door!' Cheng was panting like a dog. 'Open the door, I said! Or do we do it out here?'

Now Chaiwisan had seen the weapons too. Blanching, he fumbled to unlock the door.

Cheng kicked it open, shoving the Laotian hard in the shoulder. 'Get inside!' Then he swung back to Adam. 'I know all about you,' he snarled. 'I know about New York, I know how the DEA got to you.'

Adam stumbled back into the apartment, sick with shock. His mind was whirling, desperately trying to think of some way to escape. And every step he took, Cheng followed him, prodding at him with his finger. There was spittle on his chin. 'Fuck you, you stinking undercover pimp. I know all about you coming here with your DEA woman, pretending to be lovers. Tell me, huh, do women cops fuck good? They'd better because it's the last fuck you're ever going to have!'

Adam glanced towards the open french windows that led onto the roof garden. It was his only route of escape. But one of Cheng's henchmen, obviously a Sun Yee On fighter, a rank and file Red Pole, edged across to cut him off.

Chaiwisan, his beaked features bloodless, was staring at Adam. 'Is this correct?' he asked so shocked that his voice was little more than a mutter. 'Are you acting for the police?'

'Of course he is!' shouted Cheng. 'He's wired with a recording device – look!' And, hurling himself at Adam, he ripped at his shirt.

Adam resisted, trying to push him away. He stumbled back against the wall, bringing a photograph crashing down. Cheng tried to pursue him and stumbled too. But one hand had managed to seize the shirt and that was enough.

'There!' shouted Cheng in frenzied exultation. 'There, you can see the belt!'

Adam stood rooted, trapped like an animal. The front of the harness that held the tape recorder could clearly be seen. There was no way he could talk his way out of it now. He had no weapon on him, no way of fighting back. He was at their mercy.

Cheng could see the terror in his eyes and a cold-blooded smile, like the grin of death, settled on his face. He reached into his shirt, removing a knife. It was a back-alley weapon, crudely made, the blade as thick and squat as a bayonet.

Seeing the knife, Chaiwisan intervened. 'What are you going to do?' he demanded. 'You can't kill him here. If he is working for the police, it's suicidal. Does Ah Leung know anything about this? No, I won't allow it.'

'Won't allow it – you!' Cheng spun round, glaring at Chaiwisan with bloodshot eyes. 'You're no better than him. The cops know you're in Hong Kong. And what happens if they get you, huh, what happens then?'

Chaiwisan backed off, shaking his head. 'They'll never get me. I've made contingencies, you know that, I always do. I've got routes planned.'

Cheng stepped towards him. 'Fuck your escape routes, old man! They're going to get you. And what then, huh? I know all about you, I know about the information you keep stored in that brain of yours. What will you do when the cops catch you, huh? Fuck you, you'll trade, won't you, huh? You'll trade like you trade in everything – except this time the merchandise will be me!'

Amazed that Cheng should be turning on Chaiwisan, too, Adam watched as he bore down on the Laotian. 'You're a dangerous man,' said Cheng. 'You'll sell me, you'll sell Ah Leung.'

'No,' stuttered Chaiwisan, 'no, no, it wouldn't happen . . .'

'Trader bastard, always so clever. No, it won't happen, you're right. Because you're going to be a dead fish, that's why.'

Chaiwisan, mouth agape, staggered back until he hit the wall. He saw Cheng's knife poised and let out an involuntary moan. Suddenly, all the strength in him, all the sinew and muscle, seemed to give out. His shoulders sagged, he seemed totally crushed. Bent almost double, clutching at his belly, he murmured something incomprehensible, a pitiful plea for mercy.

With a look of utter contempt, Cheng reached out with his left arm, grabbing him by the scruff of the collar, like a man might grab a dog. Adam was watching, mesmerised, sick with doom, knowing that any second now he would share the same fate. He saw Cheng yank at Chaiwisan's shirt, trying to pull him upright so that, with his right arm, he could plunge the knife into his belly.

'Bastard!' In a blur of movement, Chaiwisan flung his arms up, throwing Cheng back. 'Bastard! Kill me, would you!' he screamed.

For an instant everybody in the room, even Cheng, was paralysed, stunned by the show of retaliation. Then Adam saw Chaiwisan thrust out his right arm and he glimpsed a small, squat black object in his hand.

The sound of the first shot filled the tiny room, as deafening as an explosion.

Cheng Tak-shing let out a shriek, lurching back, staring down at the jagged tear in his trousers where the bullet had entered his leg. He gave another cry, more incredulity than pain, and then, bellowing like a wounded bull, threw himself at Chaiwisan.

Adam saw Cheng's knife slash down in a huge arc, he saw Chaiwisan try to raise an arm to protect himself. But the arm went up too late. There was a sound of material ripping, a short, sudden gasp and Chaiwisan toppled backwards.

Cheng tried to get to him, to finish the job, but, as he threw himself forward, his leg gave under him and he fell to the threadbare carpet clutching his wounded leg. Seeing the first bright gush of blood, he gave a cry of pain. 'Kill them!' he shouted to his two Red Poles. 'Kill—' The explosion of the second shot drowned out his words.

The shot was high and wild, fired in panic. But it served its purpose. Both Cheng's men threw themselves down, colliding with each other.

Adam saw Chaiwisan scramble to his feet, grab his briefcase and stumble out on to the roof garden. Galvanised now, seeing a chance for life, Adam seized the nearest weapon, a brass ashtray, and charged after him.

As he reached the door, a hand grabbed him. He kicked out with all his strength, catching the man in the thigh. But the man still clung on, clambering to get a tighter grip. Adam flailed at him, using the ashtray as a club, desperate to break free. He felt the ashtray connect with bone and cartilage, heard the sickening squelch of flesh. And still the man clung to him.

Adam shouted incoherently, hammering in again with the ashtray, seeing everything suddenly through a fine spray of blood. He was killing him and the bastard still wouldn't let go! Instead of chopping in with blows, Adam tried to wriggle free – a stupid move that left him vulnerable. He caught just a glint of the blade an instant before it struck.

It sliced into his left shoulder, parting skin and muscle, ploughing in deep enough to chip the bone. All Adam experienced was a fierce burning as if he had been hit by a white-hot iron. He felt the blade suck free, slashing in again, into his rib cage this time. But the second time he felt nothing. A mad hysteria for life sustained him. He rained in more blows, seeing the man's cheekbone split. The brass ashtray went spinning from his hand and he punched him, the two of them caught in a horrifying embrace of blood and terror.

Then, just when he thought he would never break free, when he saw Cheng Tak-shing rising up and knew he would be crushed by numbers, one final blow did it. The man fell back and, sobbing with the effort, Adam threw himself through the door on to the roof garden.

On the far side, through the laundry and potted shrubs, he saw Chaiwisan standing at the top of a rusted fire escape. The Laotian was staring back at him. 'Come,' he shouted to Adam in English, pointing the snub nose of his pistol. 'Come, come!' And down the rusty steps they went, both streaming blood from their wounds, both fleeing for their lives.

As they reached street level, Chaiwisan swung round, shoving the pistol hard into Adam's chest. 'You stay with me,' he gasped. 'Try and get away and I'll kill you. God help me, I will.'

Adam was too weak, too shocked to argue. 'You said you had a car waiting.'

Chaiwisan nodded. 'This way.'

They ran no more than twenty yards, a terrified scramble, before turning into a side street. And there, its engine running, was the same red Honda that had collected Adam from his office. The two of them clambered into the back.

'Drive!' Chaiwisan shouted to the driver. 'The apartment in Happy Valley, you know where it is. Go, I said, go!'

In a screech of tyres, the Honda pulled away.

Cheng Tak-shing still couldn't believe it, the old bastard had had a gun hidden in his shirt. To get hold of a gun in Hong Kong took influence. Fuck him, the Chicken thought of everything. And now he was free, he and Blake together. Two men on the run, two sworn enemies, two men capable of destroying not only Cheng himself but Ah Leung too.

Cheng lay on the carpet watching the blood dribble from his knee. Everything was fucked up. What would Leung say? A total mess. His leg was numb from the shock; no pain yet but he knew it would come. The bullet – just a .22, thank God – had entered an inch above his right knee, exiting out the other side.

Ah Kit had managed to chop Blake, but he had paid the price. He was sitting on the sofa spitting mucus and blood. His nose was broken, his eyes were swelling. In a couple of minutes he would be half blind. They both needed medical attention, but there was only one priority now, that was to get down to the car where So Sang-on – So the Snake – was waiting and get out of the area as fast as they could. The sound of those gunshots, Cheng knew, would have the cops crawling all over Wanchai like flies on a raw wound.

At Narcotics Bureau the news was received with consternation. 'What's happening?' asked Drexel, lost amid the babble of Cantonese radio messages.

'Shots have been reported from a building in Wanchai,' said Xavier Tong.

'Any indication that Blake is involved?'

'Nothing at the moment. Our people are still checking the building. It's too early to tell.'

'No casualties?'

'None in our hands, no, but it does look like there have been casualties, serious too.'

'What makes you say that?' asked Sue Martin in a hollow voice.

'Because they've found blood,' said Xavier Tong, 'Heavy blood trails on the street.'

Adam was sure that for a time he had lost consciousness. He only vaguely remembered the Honda threading its way through the back streets of Happy Valley, twisting and turning, stopping at the countless lights and then driving on again until eventually it came to a halt outside a small apartment block.

Immediately it stopped, he heard Chaiwisan speak to the driver in a dazed voice. 'We're going upstairs, Ah Lap, apartment 2B. You know the one.'

The driver, the anaemic individual with moles on his face, thin as a stray dog, the one who had collected

Adam from Central, stared back at the two of them, mesmerised by the seeping gore. 'What do you want me to do?' he muttered.

'Park the car but don't leave it here on the street, people might see the blood on the seats. Find somewhere safe. Then come up.'

The driver pointed down the road. 'There's a parking garage at the end.'

'That's good, Ah Lap. Yes, park it there.'

'But you need a doctor.'

'No, no doctors!'

'I know one who is good,' said the driver. 'For just a small fee—'

'No doctors, I said! Just do as I say. Park the car then come up to the apartment.'

Slowly, like a man who was very tired, Chaiwisan opened the car door and stepped out. In the street light, the blood that soaked his shirt was a glistening black in colour. He pointed the square, squat pistol at Adam. 'We're going upstairs.'

Adam climbed from the car, his left arm hanging limp, and led the way through the small foyer to the elevator. There was no concierge present, nobody waiting in the foyer. They took the elevator up to the second floor. Leaning against the wall for support, Chaiwisan opened his briefcase, removing a set of keys which he used to open the outer iron grille and then the inner door of apartment 2B.

The apartment was bigger than the one in Stone Nullah Lane, more plushly furnished. Near the door leading through to the kitchen, an ivory-white telephone was mounted on the wall. Chaiwisan limped over to it, blood dribbling in his wake on to a blue and gold Chinese carpet.

As he dialled with shivering fingers, he kept glancing at Adam who had slumped down into a chair, and his beaked features were clouded with bitterness. He waited a few moments, the receiver held tight against his ear, then he spoke.

'Hullo, Ah Sing? Yes, I'll need your services. Yes, things have gone wrong. When? Tonight. It must be tonight. How long will it take you? Two hours! Why so long? You promised me—' He coughed with agitation, wiping his mouth and leaving a smear of blood across his cheek. Then he spoke again, trying to contain his panic. 'It's now nine forty-five. When can you pick me up? Eleven thirty? Is that the soonest? Okay, okay, I understand. Just be sure you're there.' And, coughing again, he replaced the receiver.

There was a chair opposite the one in which Adam sat and he made his way to it. Slowly, painfully, he lowered himself into it, unable to stifle the small whimpers of pain. The effort had caused his chest to start bleeding again. He stared down at the fresh blood, his eyes filled with dread. Then he looked across at Adam. 'You betrayed me,' he said, raising his pistol in his trembling fingers. 'I trusted you and you betrayed me. I should kill you now.'

Adam stared back at him, his face an exhausted mask. 'Go ahead,' he murmured. 'I couldn't give a damn . . .'

Down on the street, the driver of the Honda, Ah Lap, did as he was ordered and parked the car in the underground garage. But when it was done, instead of going straight up to the apartment, he went first to a nearby grocery store and asked to use the phone.

Ah Lap was a frightened man. The stench of blood was still in his nostrils. He had become involved in something big, too big. While he had been waiting in the car behind Stone Nullah Lane he had heard gunshots: two, maybe three. For all he knew, he could be involved in murder. At times like this, he thought, a man had to use his wits. Fools ended up in jail but a man who moved quickly enough might just do well.

Ah Lap had been a pickpocket and a petty drug trafficker all his adult life, a scavenger in Hong Kong's underworld. He had been employed as a driver tonight because he was Wo Shing Wo. He had nothing against the Laotian but the man was finished, that was obvious, probably dying on his feet. And where was the percentage in loyalty to a dying man?

Earlier, when he had been waiting behind Stone Nullah Lane, Ah Lap had seen four men enter Chaiwisan's building, and one of those men he had seen before.

The call he hurriedly made from the grocery store was to a friend, a man he knew to be a Sun Yee On office bearer, a White Paper Fan. The purpose of the call was to say that he had information to sell, information that might be valuable to a certain man nicknamed Dai Ngan.

It took all of Chaiwisan's strength just to hold the pistol; it quivered in his hand like a leaf in the wind. He was breathing in shallows sobs, ashen-faced, like a man who has run a great distance and is near to collapse. 'Look what you've done to me,' he muttered. 'To hell with you, you deserve to die.'

Adam looked back, unblinking, as still as a statue. 'I did what I had to do. I wanted some kind of life again.'

'I trusted you.'

Adam gave an exhausted smile. 'Tigers of deceit, that's what you called us . . .'

Chaiwisan's eyes narrowed. He gritted his teeth as if trying to find some strength from deep inside. His hand holding the pistol began to tremble more violently. Then, with a sudden sigh, he lowered the pistol to his lap. 'What's the point in killing you? What purpose will it serve? Just make things worse if I'm caught, that's all.'

Adam didn't move. Apart from a hiss of breath through his teeth, his face remained expressionless.

Slumping back in his chair, Chaiwisan put his left hand to his chest where the blood was still sleeping.

Adam could see it dribbling between the Laotian's fingers. 'We've got to have medical help,' he said.

But Chaiwisan shook his head. 'It's out of the question. The minute we're at the mercy of a doctor, the police will have us.'

'Look at you, you're still bleeding,' said Adam. 'For God's sake, you could die.'

But Chaiwisan merely shrugged. 'Then let me. I would rather die here than spend the rest of my life in jail.'

'Who said it has to be the rest of your life? You can work a deal. Surrender yourself, offer to co-operate.'

'I'm sixty-five years old, Adam, nearly sixty-six. What will be left for me, even if I do come out alive? No, it's unthinkable.'

'And what about me, what about my wounds? I'm bleeding too.'

'You initiated all of this.' Chaiwisan gave a bleak smile. 'Now you must live with the consequences. There's no way I can let you go, you must know that, not until I'm out of Hong Kong. You saw my Indonesian passport lying in the briefcase, you're aware of my petty disguise. No, Adam, for good or bad, you and I are in this together – blood brothers, mmm?' And he laughed softly.

'All right,' said Adam, 'if you won't agree to the two of us seeing a doctor, then let me bring somebody here, somebody we can both trust.'

'One of your DEA agents, that blonde woman, Martin, is that who?' Chaiwisan gave a dry chuckle. 'Trust? For you the word is meaningless.'

'There's one person,' said Adam, ignoring the cynicism, 'one person who'll come, I'm sure of it. There'll be no betrayal, no report to the police.'

Chaiwisan pondered the matter, his breath punctuated by shallow moans.

'For God's sake,' groaned Adam, 'do you think I want to sit here bleeding to death? Do you think I want to see either of us die?'

Reluctantly, Chaiwisan asked, 'Who is this person you say I can trust?'

And Adam answered, 'Her name is Nicky du Bois.'

The telephone was on the wall by the kitchen. As Adam limped over to it, he was silently praying: Please God, let her be home, let her not reject me as I rejected her, let her just say yes. He dialled the number and waited, interminably, while it rang. She's not there, he thought, his heart sinking. Oh God, what do I do now?

Then suddenly the receiver was lifted. He heard her voice and he could have sobbed for joy. 'Please, Nicky,' he said, 'please, my darling, you've got to help us . . .'

The desperation in his voice rang as clear as a bell and Nicky didn't hesitate. 'What is it?' she asked. 'What do you want me to do?'

Stumbling over his words, half incoherent, Adam tried to explain. 'We've been wounded,' he said, 'both of us . . . we're bleeding badly. We need bandages, needle and thread, antiseptic to clean the wounds. Get whatever you can . . .'

'But you need a hospital, Adam, you need proper attention—'

'No, not at the moment! Please, Nicky, just do as I say. I'll try and explain when you get here. Please, darling, hurry.'

Nicky tried to gather her wits. 'Where are you?' she asked.

Adam looked across at Chaiwisan. 'She needs the address. Where the hell are we?'

'Apartment 2B, Dragon Villas, 32 Tsoi Tak Street.'

Adam repeated the address to Nicky.

'And no police,' snapped Chaiwisan, lifting his pistol. 'Tell her that, no police.'

Adam spoke into the phone again. 'Trust me, Nicky,' he said. 'As crazy as this sounds, please, just do as I say. Get the stuff from a pharmacy and come straight here.

Don't tell anybody, you understand? No doctors, no police. Nobody.'

Cheng Tak-shing got out of Wanchai by the skin of his teeth, huddled in the back of So Sang-on's car with Ah Kit bleeding all over him.

As he had anticipated, within minutes the Wanchai area was crawling with cops. But Cheng's destination was Chai Wan, way out at the eastern end of the island. There was a doctor in Chai Wan whom Cheng had used before, an inveterate gambler in heavy to the loan sharks, a man who would attend to wounds with no questions asked.

The doctor complained that both Cheng and Ah Kit needed hospitalisation. He was a general practitioner, he said, not a surgeon. 'You should get proper treatment,' he grumbled, clearly terrified. 'I can't be held responsible.'

'Tomorrow,' said Cheng, 'when all the fuss has died down . . . tomorrow. Now just get on with it.' And he lay back on the surgery table, his head spinning.

Trying to cope with the quickening tides of pain was bad enough, but trying to sort out the confusion in his head was worse. What did he do now? Everything was a mess. He knew what Ah Leung would tell him – find Chaiwisan, find Blake, and kill them both. Get the job done properly the second time. But that was easier said than done. He had no idea where either of them were and had only limited means of tracking them down. Blake was probably back under police protection by now.

As the doctor was probing at his wound, the pager on

Cheng's belt began to bleep. So Sang-on was in the room and Cheng asked him to deal with it. So was one man he could trust.

Cheng had failed. It hurt him to admit it, the humiliation as painful as the bullet wound. But he had to accept it. Maybe it was time to start thinking of himself. But what should he do? Lie low? Find a place in the New Territories? Or get out of Hong Kong entirely? Should he try and cross the border into China – the doctors there would butcher his leg – or fly to Taiwan? Everything was a fuck-up. He had lost face and put his future at risk. He'd never failed this badly before.

The doctor was bandaging Cheng's wound when So returned to the surgery. There was a smile on his face. 'Luck is with you, big brother.'

Cheng sat up. 'Who was it?'

'One of Chaiwisan's people.'

'What does he want, settlement talks?'

'He has information to sell.'

Cheng couldn't believe it. 'The Chicken and Blake?'

So nodded. 'He says they're holed up together in an apartment near the racecourse.'

Now it was Cheng's turn to smile. 'How much does he want?'

'We agreed fifteen thousand.'

'Have you got the cash?'

'I can get it.'

'And?'

'I'm meeting him in forty-five minutes.'

As soon as Ah Lap entered the apartment, Chaiwisan

swung on him. 'Where have you been? I told you to come straight up. It's been nearly half an hour.'

The driver replied with a look of sullen insolence, scratching at the moles on his cheek. 'The garage was full. I had to wait. Everything in Hong Kong is full.'

Chaiwisan glared at him, trying to root out the truth behind those anaemic grey eyes. Then, with a short, frustrated sigh, he collapsed back into his chair. Adam could see it written on Chaiwisan's face: the terrifying uncertainty of having to place his trust in strangers.

'We're going to need the car again,' said Chaiwisan.

Ah Lap lit a cigarette, a toasted American brand. Blue smoke curled around his face. 'What time?' he asked.

'How long will it take to get to Aberdeen?'

'The harbour?'

'Yes, near the Ap Lei Chau power station.'

'About twenty minutes, half an hour.'

'Then we must leave in an hour and a half.'

'I can't park right at the water's edge.'

Chaiwisan looked directly at him. 'So?'

Ah Lap sniffed, picking at shreds of tobacco on his lip. 'You're going to have to walk a distance. I mean no disrespect, Uncle Chicken, but Aberdeen is a crowded place.'

'Get to the point.'

'With all that blood on your clothes, with everything ripped and torn like that – within two minutes somebody will have phoned the police.'

Chaiwisan sat for a time staring pensively at the floor. 'Are there any clothes in the apartment here?'

Ah Lap coughed as he exhaled smoke. 'I doubt it.'

'Check, will you.'

'If you wish.' And, with the cigarette dangling from his lip, he went through to the bedroom.

There was something about the man's attitude that worried Adam, a flippant kind of arrogance that hadn't been there before. If he had been a little less in shock, suffering a little less pain, he would have taken it further. As it was, the kernel of his concern was quickly crushed under the weight of his other emotions. They were all under stress, Ah Lap too.

Adam could see that Chaiwisan was on the verge of collapse. His eyes were hooded and he breathed with short, shallow gasps, clinging desperately to consciousness.

'So that's it,' said Adam, 'that's how you intend to get out of Hong Kong. You have a boat picking you up at Aberdeen. Always an alternative.'

'That's the way I survive.'

'What kind is it?' Adam asked with weary sarcasm. 'Some sleek cruiser?'

'No, a simple fishing junk.'

'Yes, of course, suitably anonymous. Where do you intend to sail to? China, Macau?'

Chaiwisan considered whether to answer. Then he murmured, 'Macau . . . I have refuge there, friends on the island of Coloane . . . a doctor who owes me favours . . .'

'Provided you live that long.'

Chaiwisan gave a dazed shrug. 'If I don't, I don't . . .'

'What if your boat is intercepted by the police?'

'That's a chance I take.'

'Leung and Cheng Tak-shing will still be looking for you. And Ah Leung, they say, has resources, even in Macau.'

Chaiwisan gave a heavy-lidded smile. 'What are you trying to suggest?'

'There's still a way out of this. Let me try and make a deal with the police.'

The Laotian laughed mirthlessly. 'Yes, why not? By now they must know I'm wounded, on my last legs. They must know I'm in hiding in a strange city. Tell me, Adam, what do you think you can secure for me from a position of such strength?'

'Give me a chance at least. You never know until you try.'

But Chaiwisan just shook his head. 'No, I've told you already, I'd rather die than spend even a day in jail.'

Ah Lap came out of the bedroom. 'There are no clothes in there,' he said. 'Just some pillows and a couple of sheets.'

Chaiwisan spoke without looking at him, 'Can you find some for us elsewhere?'

'There are shops still open in Causeway Bay but it could take half an hour or more. I have to get there, get back.'

Chaiwisan nodded. 'Leave the car keys here.'

Ah Lap took the keys out of his pocket, placing them on a sideboard. 'The car's on the second level close to the exit ramp,' he said.

And for the first time, Chaiwisan turned to him, a timbre of menace in his voice. 'Be careful, my friend. Just get the clothes and return, do you understand?

Don't get any ideas of profiting out of tonight, finding yourself perhaps some financial reward.'

Ah Lap blinked, his mouth falling slack. 'I swear, Uncle Chicken—'

'Yes, I know, it never entered your mind.' Chaiwisan seemed to look right through him. 'But just remember, you have loyalties, and revenge has a long arm.'

Ah Lap gave a frightened jerk of the head. 'I'll be back as soon as I can, half an hour, no more, I swear. What kind of clothes do you want?'

'Dark, unobtrusive. Use your common sense.'

'Of course, Uncle Chicken, of course. I have the necessary money. Let me do this for you. It is my privilege.' And the driver headed for the door.

Outside in the elevator lobby, a sweat broke out on his pallid brow. His fingers began to tremble. He hammered at the elevator button, prodding it again and again, terrified that the apartment door might open and Chaiwisan would be standing there. For a time, inside the apartment, he had been certain Chaiwisan knew. The Laotian had been suspicious, there was no doubt about it, profoundly so.

Considering himself fortunate to be alive, Ah Lap took the elevator down to the ground floor. When he got out on to Tsoi Tak Street, he was so desperate to be gone that he broke into a run, fleeing down the rutted pavement. That was the reason he never saw the BMW 735 draw up and never saw Nicky du Bois climb out.

It was Adam who opened the door for her, standing there like a blood-soaked apparition, his left arm dangling almost useless by his side. On the way there Nicky had tried to prepare herself but she had not imagined anything like this. 'Oh God,' she said with a gasp of horror. 'What's happened to you?'

Adam gave a foolish, shattered kind of smile. His face was grey, his cheeks speckled with blood. 'Thank you for coming,' he said. 'I had no right to ask.'

'No, no, Adam my darling—' And she reached out to touch his cheek.

There were tears suddenly sparkling in his eyes. 'I'm just so sorry . . .'

'Sssh,' she whispered, putting a finger to his lips. 'We can talk later. But first we've got to do something about those wounds. Oh God, I had no idea it was so bad.'

Adam closed the outer iron grille then the main door into the apartment. He took her arm but she was the one who had to help him back into the lounge.

Chaiwisan remained in his chair. The pistol was still in his hand. He looked up at her and the briefest zephyr of a smile passed across his lips. 'Excuse me for not getting up,' he said in the tones of an old world gentleman. 'As you can see, we are both in some distress. My name is Chaiwisan.'

All Nicky could do was nod. She stared at his torn, blood-drenched shirt and saw the palsied tremble of his fingers.

'The two of you should be in hospital,' she said. 'I'm not a nurse. I've never even done a first aid course.'

Chaiwisan smiled at her. 'Do what you can. That will be more than enough. I suggest you treat Adam first. I can wait.'

Ashen-faced, Nicky set to work. She had antiseptics

with her, gauze dressings and bandages that she had purchased at a late-night pharmacy in Causeway Bay. She went through to the kitchen, filling a plastic bowl with warm water. She added antiseptic to it so that it turned a cloudy white. Then she carried the bowl back into the lounge.

'My shoulder is the worst,' said Adam.

Nicky studied the mashed gore of cloth, cotton, skin and blood and her stomach churned. 'I'm going to have to get your jacket and shirt off first,' she said.

Adam climbed to his feet and, gingerly, Nicky helped him to remove the bloodied clothes. Once he was bare-chested, the harness for the tape recorder could be seen round his waist, that and the wires running up his spine and over his shoulders into the crook of each collarbone. But for Nicky the recording device was peripheral, part of some nightmare labyrinth of events that was beyond her comprehension. Her only concern was Adam's wounds.

Adam's left shoulder had been cleaved open, the skin lying back in rubbery flaps. 'Did you bring the needle and thread?' he asked.

'Oh no,' murmured Nicky, appalled. 'Oh no, Adam, I'm sorry, I can't do it, I just can't . . .'

'Please, Nicky, just a couple to hold it together. That's the worst part, the way the skin flaps back.' He gave her a gritty smile. 'Don't worry, it's still numb. There's no real pain, not yet.'

Taking a wad of cotton wool, Nicky dipped it into the bowl of warm antiseptic liquid and began to dab gently at his shoulder wound. 'This is all part of it, isn't it?' she said. 'Something that began when Harry was arrested . . . hiding here like this, your wounds . . . it's all part of what tore us apart.'

Adam put his head back, closing his eyes. 'Yes,' he said, 'you're right. It did begin with Harry.' And, haltingly, with Chaiwisan as a silent witness, he began to tell her how it had really been.

They met at a backstreet *dai pai dong*, a cooked food stall which consisted of a dirty clutter of fold-up tables and stools under a greasy awning. So Sang-on, the Snake, had two teenage boys with him, two young thugs who followed him in the Triad way and called him 'older brother'. Ah Lap came alone. Bowls of noodles were served with cabbage and pork and greasy glasses of tea.

So handed over a brown paper bag containing the cash, fifteen thousand Hong Kong dollars as agreed. Then he asked, 'So where are they?'

'Tsoi Tak Street, Dragon Villas,' said Ah Lap, clutching his bag of money. 'Apartment 2B.'

Using Chinese characters, So scribbled down the details on a piece of paper. 'Does Chaiwisan still have the gun?'

'He carries it all the time.'

'Mmm . . .' So didn't like it.

'But he's weak. He has lost much blood,' Ah Lap assured him. 'Blake too. Both have been hurt bad. They can barely walk.'

'Is there some way we can get into the apartment?'

'There's an iron grille, then the main door.'

'And the back?'

'Locked and bolted.'

So slurped at his noodles.

Ah Lap sipped his tea. 'You'll never get in without them knowing. Your best way is to get them when they leave.'

'And when is that?'

'In about an hour.'

'Where to?'

'Aberdeen Harbour, below Ap Lei Chau.'

'To get a boat?'

'A fishing junk to Macau, that's what he said.'

So spat a piece of pork gristle on to the pavement. 'And how are they getting from the apartment to Aberdeen?'

'I left the keys of a hired car in the apartment,' said Ah Lap. 'It's parked in an underground car park across the road from the block. It's a red Honda, second level down, close to the exit ramp.' He smiled nervously. 'That would be a good place. It's dark, mostly deserted.'

So finished his noodles, using chopsticks to shovel them from the bowl into his mouth. Then he looked up at Ah Lap and gave a venomous grin. 'Spend your money well, little brother.'

Cheng received the news at the Chai Wan surgery with more relief than exultation. Time, he knew, was running out. Desperation was beginning to creep in.

He had no delusions about his position. If either Blake or Chaiwisan were picked up by the cops, they could put him away for twenty years. And they wouldn't hesitate, he knew it. Twenty years could be a death sentence in itself; in 1997, when the mainland communists took over Hong Kong, he would still be in jail. The communists had their own way of dealing with convicted criminals: a quick march outside and a single bullet into the back of the head, paid for by the next of kin.

So there could be no compromises now. It was his life or theirs. Chaiwisan, if he managed to get away, might just scuttle back to his jungle. But Blake was a different story, a police agent; he would be back, facing him across a courtroom. Blake especially had to die.

Cheng looked at his watch. It was 10.35 p.m. He should have reported back to Ah Leung at least two hours ago. But he had delayed, knowing what Leung's reaction would be. Now, however, with better news, he gathered the courage to make the call.

As expected, Leung was in a withering fury. 'For two hours I have been waiting. Did you do it or not?'

'There have been a few problems, big brother.'

'Problems? What kind?'

'We got to them okay and we hurt them bad. But Chaiwisan had a gun.'

'Are you telling me he's free, Blake too – both of them? Chaiwisan knows me, do you realise that? He knows all about me.'

'He knows me, too, big brother.'

'I pay you to protect me. Look at the mess!'

'But I know where they are now. I'm going to finish it, I swear to you—'

'I should have listened to my instincts in the beginning,' said Leung. 'Why did I listen to people? Now look where I am!'

* * *

It had taken Nicky nearly an hour. She was squeamish at the best of times. Just to glimpse an operation on television turned her stomach. The sight and smell of blood brought her close to fainting. How she had managed to push the needle into Adam's flesh and then draw the cotton through she would never know, but somehow she had persevered.

Both of Adam's wounds – the one to the shoulder and the shallower one that had laid open the side of his chest – had stopped bleeding. She had cleaned them, applied gauze and bandaged them.

Chaiwisan's wound, if anything, had been easier although trying to tend to him while he held that gun in his hand had only added to Nicky's traumas. His wound at least had been clean, one continuous knife cut that ran diagonally from the right shoulder almost to the groin.

When finally Nicky was done, Chaiwisan smiled across at her. 'It may seem strange to say it with a gun in my hand,' he said, 'but thank you. I'm in your debt.'

'What do you intend to do now?' Adam asked him. 'It's getting close to your deadline to leave. What about Nicky and me?'

Chaiwisan looked genuinely saddened. 'I'm, sorry, I have no choice. You both have to come with me.'

'Why don't you just leave us here? We won't go to the police.'

Chaiwisan smiled. 'You'll give me a sporting chance, is that it, like an English gentleman?'

'I just want to ensure that Nicky doesn't get hurt,' said Adam wearily. 'I've had enough of it. We'll do nothing until dawn, I promise you.'

But Chaiwisan just shook his head. 'You can see for yourself, Adam, Ah Lap, the driver, hasn't returned. So now you are even more essential to me. I need you to get me to Aberdeen. I don't know Hong Kong, I don't know the way.'

'But will you at least leave us on the shore?'

'I wish I could.'

'Why not? You'll be on board a vessel,' said Adam angrily. 'You'll be gone.'

'But still in Hong Kong waters, and I know what'll happen when my vessel draws away from the shore – Miss du Bois will take you to the nearest hospital.'

'Not before dawn, I said.'

There was a low chuckle in reply. 'I may have lived in the mountains but I am not a fool. Your wounds must be close to unbearable now. How much more so in an hour or two? Of course you will go to a hospital. That is human nature. And that means the police will be involved. It is so very easy for a radio message to be sent, so easy for a patrol boat to set itself on an interception course. No, Adam, I'm sorry, until I can set foot in Macau, until I know I've got refuge, there's no way I can let either of you go.'

Very slowly, wincing with pain, Chaiwisan climbed to his feet. Then, almost impishly, he smiled at Adam. 'I know what's been going through your mind. Several times I've been able to read it in your eyes, just how easy it would be to get this pistol off me, make me your prisoner and end it. I can understand you thinking that way, I must look like an old man ready to die. But you're hurt as bad as I am, Adam, maybe worse. Remember, too, that I haven't spent my life in a carpeted office watching a computer and drinking tea. I've lived hard. In a strange way that you won't understand, right at the moment I see ourselves as allies almost, not enemies. So please, Adam, don't do anything foolish. The risks we face are already great enough.'

It was true of course. Adam had considered trying to wrestle the pistol from him. But he had also rationalised it the same way. The risks weren't worth it.

Chaiwisan glanced at his watch and then picked up his briefcase. 'Very well,' he said, 'let's be on our way.'

So Sang-on wanted a reputation. More than anything, he wanted face. The events of tonight, he knew, would give it to him. Ten seconds, he had calculated that's all it would take. Ten seconds and he would be a man to be remembered. He felt the excitement brimming inside. He had never killed a man before. From where he stood at the exit of the car park, he could see down Tsoi Tak Street to the apartment block. They should be coming out any minute, two wounded men – easy meat.

At first the gun that Chaiwisan carried had worried him. But he knew now that it would be no problem. He had been down to the second level of the car park and seen where the Honda was parked. It was just as Ah Lap had said. There was a door to the internal stairs only a few feet away and large square pillars right next to it. He and his two men had only to step out of the shadows.

As a boy of thirteen, raised on the fishing junks of Aberdeen, So had tried to impress his Sun Yee On peers by eating snakes live, biting off their heads as they wriggled in his mouth. That was how he had acquired his nickname in the back streets and gambling dens around the harbour.

He worked now as a crew member, the lowest of the boat boys, on Leung Chi-ming's motor cruiser, the *China Jewel*. It was a job he had secured through Cheng Tak-shing's influence, a small Triad perk. Cheng had looked after him well and he wanted to repay him. But there was more to it than that. In comparison to killing a man, biting the head off a snake was a childish thing. He was twenty-three now, a full-grown man, and he needed to prove it.

His two followers, both just sixteen, were waiting down on the first level for his signal. Each of them was armed with a melon knife. So himself carried a square meat chopper concealed under his denim jacket. He lit a cigarette to calm his nerves. Any minute now . . .

He saw the foyer door of the apartment block swing open and froze, waiting. A figure appeared, tall, lean, hair greying – that had to be Blake. He was walking slowly, almost hobbling, looking nervously around.

But there was somebody with him, a woman. Ah Lap hadn't said anything about a woman. She looked European. He flicked away his cigarette, every muscle tense. The woman complicated matters.

Chaiwisan emerged from the apartment block, walking three or four steps behind. Even at that distance So could see the small black blur of the gun in his fist.

He gave one shrill whistle to alert his two followers. He stepped back into the shadows, watching the three as they came along the pavement, as slow as a funeral procession, step by step towards the car park.

Then suddenly, to his amazement, they stopped. The breath caught in So's throat. The woman stepped over to a car. What was she doing? She had keys in her hand. It was *her* car!

Nicky was behind the wheel of the BMW 735, one of her few indulgences, an elegant thoroughbred of a vehicle with black leather upholstery and its own car phone. Adam sat beside her in the front seat while Chaiwisan sat slumped in the rear.

'Which is the quickest way?' she asked as she pulled out onto the road. 'I can't think straight.'

Adam shook his head. 'I'm not sure myself . . .' He was mentally exhausted, too, his mind numb. 'Up Blue Pool Road probably and then along Wong Nei Chung Gap—' Movement caught his eye. Swinging his head to his left, he shouted: 'Watch out!'

Nicky saw the darting figure, too. But she couldn't believe that he was coming straight for them, couldn't comprehend that the instrument in his hand was a butcher's cleaver. Her instinctive reaction – bred out of innocence – was to slam on the brakes to avoid an accident. The BMW came to a jarring halt, throwing Chaiwisan forward. And in the next second Nicky appreciated the fatal error she had made.

Vaulting on to the bonnet, So Sang-on smashed at the windscreen with his heavy butcher's blade. The glass only inches in front of Nicky's face shattered inwards and she screamed as shards of it peppered her face.

'Don't stop!' Adam shouted to her. 'Go, go!'

So Sang-on was still hacking away, puncturing further holes into the windscreen, trying to smash open the barrier between them and hack at her arms.

'Go!' yelled Adam. But Nicky seemed paralysed, her eyes wide, screaming with every blow.

Another figure appeared at the side of the car, tugging at Adam's door and slashing in a frenzy at the window. '*For God's sake, go!*' Adam bellowed above Nicky's terrified sobs. 'They're going to kill us!'

In a wild kind of trance, Nicky grabbed the wheel. Mercifully, her foot found the pedal. The BMW lurched forward, throwing So Sang-on to the road. Nicky accelerated away, swerving wildly, half blinded by the opaque maze of what was left of the windscreen.

Swivelling round, his lap and legs covered in crystals of glass, Adam looked back and saw the three attackers standing in the middle of Tsoi Tak Street, their weapons dangling in their hands. They made no attempt to run. They just stood there watching the BMW as it swung into Blue Pool Road and up the hill.

In the back seat of the car, Chaiwisan appeared to be in a state of near catatonic shock. 'It was your driver,' Adam shouted at him. 'It was Ah Lap. It had to be. He sold you out!'

Chaiwisan could only manage the barest shadow of an acknowledgement. There were fresh bubbles of blood on his lips, fresh blood seeping through the buttons of his shirt.

'You're going to get us all killed,' said Adam in white-hot anger. 'If Ah Lap told Cheng's people we were in the apartment, he must have told them we were heading for Aberdeen too. They'll be waiting for us. Listen to some sense, won't you? Let me try and do a deal with the police. If you don't trust them, at least trust me!'

Chaiwisan stared at him, a vacant look in his eyes. He was barely conscious. 'I'm not going to prison. I'd rather die. Give me your word, Adam, go on, do it – give me your word that you won't do a deal that puts me into jail. I'll kill you if I have to.'

'For Chrissake, do I try or not? Will you testify?'

Chaiwisan hesitated.

'Damn you!' shouted Adam. 'What loyalty do you owe them? Look at you!'

Chaiwisan's head fell back, the pistol lay limp in his blood-streaked hand. Then, as if it took a great effort of will, he nodded his head. 'Do what you can . . .' he mumbled.

'Thank God,' said Adam. 'At last . . .' And, as the BMW sped up the long curving hill of Blue Pool Road, he reached for the car telephone.

It was Xavier Tong who called to Drexel across the Control Room. 'It's Blake! He's on the telephone. He says he'll only speak to you.'

Drexel barged his way across the room, grabbing the phone. 'Where in hell are you?' he asked. 'Are you okay? We've been worried sick—'

'Just listen to me,' said Adam. 'I've got Chaiwisan with me. Between us we can deliver Leung to you. We'll testify, both of us, we'll do whatever is necessary.

Between us we'll put him away – him and Cheng Tak-shing. But there's a condition.'

'Okay, spell it out.'

'We both want full immunities.'

'Chaiwisan, too? No, you're crazy!'

'It must be both of us. Do you understand that? Both of us! Otherwise there's no deal.'

'Just tell me where you are, Adam,' said Drexel, his voice low and calm. 'Once we know you're safe, we can work something out. We can't do it over the phone, not like this. We're going to get Chaiwisan anyway. It's only a matter of hours.'

'We do a deal now or never,' said Adam, the anger and the desperation giving a fierce energy to his voice. 'We're both wounded. Chaiwisan is still bleeding, bleeding badly. Cheng's killers are closing in on us.'

'Look, Adam, I know what you must have been through tonight.' Drexel was trying to play it by the book. 'If you will testify against Leung and Cheng, I can organise an immunity. I'm authorised to do that.'

'That means a *full* one,' Adam retaliated. 'It's got to cover everything from the minute I first got involved in this nightmare. The New York conviction has to be set aside. I want a clean slate, do you understand?'

'Yes, yes, I understand. I can swing that for you. But Chaiwisan is another matter. He's too big a fish. And I just don't have the authority, not here in Hong Kong.'

'Then you'd better get hold of the man who does,' said Adam, the firmness in his voice allowing for no opposition. 'And you've only got a few minutes to do it. Chaiwisan is sinking fast.'

'Why are you protecting him?' asked Drexel, barely able to contain his temper. 'What do you care about Chaiwisan? Don't be stupid, Adam. I've already guaranteed you full and absolute immunity. Just give me your present location. I can help you—'

'Sure,' interjected Adam, his voice dripping cynicism, 'just as you did when you set me up for tonight's meeting. When Cheng came to kill us, he knew everything.'

Drexel, normally so controlled, gave a gasp of astonishment. 'What are you talking about? That just couldn't happen.'

'How do you know what could or couldn't happen?' Adam screamed at him over the line. 'I'm the one with half my arm cut away and my ribs hacked in. He knew I was working for you, he knew about Sue Martin, he knew I was carrying a recording device – everything! And that had to come from somebody in the DEA or somebody you've been shouting your mouth off to! So don't you tell me what could or couldn't happen!'

Drexel's mouth fell slack. There was no way he could reply, no words would come. The shock, like a poison in his veins, had paralysed his ability to respond. Instinctively, he looked across the crowded control room to where Danny Abbott sat in the corner. And he knew . . .

He could hear Adam's voice over the line. 'I want those two immunities.'

'I'll see what I can do,' he answered in a dazed voice. 'But how do I contact you?'

'I'll contact you,' said Adam. 'Fifteen minutes, that's about as long as we've got.'

'For Pete's sake, Adam, just tell me where—'

But he had rung off.

Drexel replaced the receiver. He felt numb, ice-cold inside. He turned to Xavier Tong, not wanting even to look at Danny Abbott, and asked him in a voice so low that it was almost a mutter, 'Okay, who the hell do we contact to get Chaiwisan an immunity?'

Immunity from prosecution, said Xavier Tong, was a legal decision, not one for the police. In a case like this, of this importance, the only person who could grant it was the DPP himself, Hong Kong's Director of Public Prosecutions.

'Okay,' said Drexel, 'let's get him on the line.'

But nothing was ever that simple. First, it had to be cleared through the commanding officer of Narcotics Bureau. Only then could the DPP be approached. And, at this time of night, both he and the DPP could be just about anywhere.

Cheng Tak-shing was just a block away when he received So's call and knew immediately from the flat tone of his voice that it had gone wrong again.

'We were waiting just as you said. I saw them come out of the apartment block,' said So despondently. 'But they had a woman with them – we were never told about a woman – and she had her own car. It was parked right there in front of the block, a big BMW. I'm sorry, big brother . . .'

'So they got clear?'

'We tried. But what could we do?'

'Which way did they go?'

'Up Blue Pool Road.'

'How long ago?'

'A minute or two, no more.'

'So they'll get to Aberdeen harbour ahead of us,' said Cheng. 'But there's still a way. I won't lose to those bastards, not a third time. Are you still with me?'

'Yes, big brother, always.'

'The *China Jewel*, can you operate it?'

'I don't have a master's certificate—'

'But can you operate it?'

'Yes, yes.'

'Then wait for me on the street, you and the others.'

Cheng knew what he had to do. It was a desperate move but what else was open to him? At night, out in the sea lanes, with no other vessels nearby, he was sure he could get away with it. But first he needed Ah Leung's clearance to take out the *China Jewel*.

This time, Cheng had no reticence in telephoning. Matters had reached a critical stage. Caution had to be thrown to the wind. It was time for Leung to come down off his rich man's mountain. If Chaiwisan and Blake survived until morning, if they got to Macau or the police got to them first, then Leung and he were finished. Their lives were forfeit.

He dialled Leung's number, the number that he always used to contact him. He knew Leung would answer. He went nowhere without the portable phone. It was like an extra limb. But this time it rang and rang with no reply.

Cursing the delay, every second wasted, Cheng tried again. But still it remained unanswered. Only then did he realise . . . yes, it was always with Leung, always, with only one exception – when he left Hong Kong.

Carl Drexel couldn't leave it. One way or the other it had to be resolved and it had to be resolved that night. For all these months he had placed his trust in Danny Abbott, confided in him as a brother. The thought that Danny could have been responsible tore at Drexel's innards. It was incomprehensible. How could it be him? But that's where the evidence pointed, to one person and one only – Danny Abbott.

He saw Xavier Tong, a telephone cupped in his shoulder, waving to him across the Control Room. He went to join him. 'That was the Chief Superintendent,' said Tong. 'It took a bit of persuasion but he's agreed to support Chaiwisan's immunity. Now let's try the DPP.'

Back through the window, in the smaller room, Drexel could see Danny Abbott drinking coffee and all the emotions that had hit him when he first realised that it had to be Danny – the anger and despair, outrage and bewilderment – welled up inside him again.

Xavier Tong was speaking to the DPP's house. 'Is Mr Calder there? He's out you say. Whereabouts? Yes, I know it, the Red Pepper. No, don't worry, I'll try and get him there.'

'Just our luck,' said Drexel. 'It's always a merry-go-round.'

Xavier Tong checked the time. 'Eleven twenty. It's late. Let's hope he's still there.' At that time of night it was quicker to dial Enquiries than scramble through a telephone directory. Xavier Tong obtained the number and got straight through. He spoke in rapid Cantonese to whoever was at the other end, then, with a small grunt of frustration, put down the phone.

'They're closing up,' he explained to Drexel. 'Yes, they remember him leaving about fifteen minutes ago. A tall *gweilo*, smoking a pipe, a stiff leg from some old injury. That's the DPP. It will take him at least another ten to fifteen to get home.'

'So we wait?'

'I'm afraid we have no choice.'

Drexel glanced back into the smaller room. Sue Martin had joined Danny Abbott. Now was the time, he thought. 'What about some coffee?' he suggested and he and Xavier Tong went through.

When they entered, Danny Abbott looked up. 'Any developments?' he asked.

Drexel did his best to remain outwardly calm although inside he was churning. 'We're just waiting on the DPP now. Apparently he's driving home after a night of bean curd and chilli prawns.'

Drexel poured two coffees, black for himself, and took a seat at the table. 'There's something I should tell you all,' he said. 'It's to do with Blake. When I spoke to him on the phone, he had more than one bombshell to drop. He told me that when Cheng Tak-shing arrived at tonight's meeting he knew all about his undercover role. Every last detail, even the fact that he was wired for sound.'

When Drexel said the words, Danny Abbott was just three feet away from him, divided by the span of the table. There was a look of shock on his face, but that was only to be expected. It was on the faces of Sue Martin and Xavier Tong, too. But Carl Drexel saw more. He saw Danny's surgically-shaped features shift through half a dozen almost imperceptible changes of expression in a matter of seconds: surprise then fear, puzzlement, a flicker of panic. Those expressions put it beyond doubt.

Xavier Tong was mortified by the revelation. 'I told nobody,' he said. 'My officers knew there was an operation on but they knew none of the details. The matter will be investigated, Carl, I can promise you. If what you say is true, it's terrible, just terrible.'

Drexel nodded. 'Thank you, that's all I ask, Xavier.' But his eyes were on Danny all the time, boring into him.

Danny Abbott shifted in his seat, beginning to look uncomfortable. 'Excuse me,' he said.

'Where are you off to?' asked Drexel amiably.

'Just to the John.'

'I'll go with you.'

They walked through together. It was a small room: white tiles and basins, a mop and pail in the corner. Danny walked up to the urinal but Drexel hung back. Danny turned. Their eyes met.

There was a moment's tense silence.

Then Drexel said in a low voice, 'Why, Danny, that's all I want to know. How could you bring yourself to do it?'

'What are you talking about? For Chrissake, Carl, you don't seriously think—'

'It has to be you, Danny. There's nobody else. It's not Tong, it's not Sue Martin. Now it all makes sense, your reaction this evening when you learnt so late what was happening. Where did you phone from, right here in the Bureau?'

'This is crazy. You've got water on the brain, Carl. I hate Leung Chi-ming as much as you!'

Drexel nodded. 'I don't deny it.'

'Don't you think I want revenge on the bastard?'

'But there are all sorts of revenge, aren't there?'

'I don't know what you mean . . .'

'Money for example.'

It was as if Danny Abbott had been hit by an invisible fist. And Carl Drexel knew he was right. It was money. He spoke softly then, rationally, because there were matters he had to know. 'Whatever you say in here, Danny, is between the two of us, one man's word against another's. I'm not interested in hauling you before the courts. What's the good of another scandal? It does us all harm.' He smiled with a cold, deadly cynicism. 'Check for yourself – Blake might be, but I'm not wired for sound.'

Danny Abbott gave a contemptuous grunt. But the blood had drained from his face. There were beads of sweat on his forehead.

'You're lower than shit to me now,' said Drexel. 'It turns my stomach to look at you. But all I'm concerned about is damage control. How many other men like Blake are riding on a knife edge out there? Tell me that and you can go. It's other men's lives that concern me.'

'You're mad. I don't have to listen to this.' Danny tried to move past to get out of the toilet but Drexel blocked his way.

'You're going to tell me, one way or the other. How do

you want it? It's up to you. A full enquiry with a jail term at the end of it or here and now, just between the two of us? Either way, I'll find out in the end.'

Danny was so pale he looked as if he might faint. He swallowed hard. Then he said in a whisper, 'There are none, Carl. Blake was the first.'

Drexel nodded. 'How long have you been supplying Leung with information?'

'Just a few weeks.'

'How did you get to him?'

'Through Cheng Tak-shing.'

'Why, Danny, why?'

'Just as you said, Carl, revenge. Look at me, look what he did to me. Don't I deserve some compensation? Why should I waste my life away in this crappy job?'

'Is that how you really see it?'

'I'm making him bleed the only way I know how.' After the initial shock, his ego was slowly coming back to him and Drexel knew that he would justify everything, no matter how unjustifiable. 'Money, Carl, yes, money. Why should I be in debt all my life? That car outside, the yacht, my family debts back home, at least now they're all covered. At least I have *something*. What about you? A scrapbook full of half-arsed memories, a few good busts, is that going to be enough?'

Drexel stared back at him and felt as if he was looking at a dead man. Danny Abbott had thrown his life away a year and a half ago, he had lost it in that restaurant in Tsim Sha Tsui the night they were attacked. Carl Drexel felt nothing but contempt for him. 'You had better get out of the police force as soon as you can,' he said. 'And you had better pray, too, that Adam Blake survives. If he dies, Danny, you'll be his murderer. And then I promise you, you'll pay with much more than money.'

The BMW with its shattered windscreen drove slowly down the winding roads under the residential towers of the Ap Lei Chau estate. Nicky had never been in this area before, nor had Adam. They had no map and had to sense their way, constantly turning up dead-end lanes while Chaiwisan fretted in the back. Finally Nicky came to a halt behind a row of tin-roofed boat builders' sheds. 'That's it,' she said. 'I can't get any closer.'

Chaiwisan staggered out of the car, his pistol in one hand, his briefcase in the other. He was so weak that he had to lean against the car to regain his strength. But he still clung tenaciously to consciousness.

Nicky and Adam led the way, with Chaiwisan a couple of paces behind. Slowly, one step dragging after another, they approached the water's edge along dark alleys that ran with water and stank of gutted fish. It took them five minutes to reach the quay, constantly peered at by old amahs and young urchin boys.

When they stepped out on to the quay, into the air again, Chaiwisan said, 'Yes, yes, this is it. This is where Lau said he would be waiting. I came here with him.' He peered at his watch in the darkness. It was 11.35 – five minutes past due time. But the quay was deserted. The only sound was the lap of the water and the soft groaning of the junks moored hull to hull.

'He'll be here,' muttered Chaiwisan, 'he'll be here.' But they all knew his options were running out.

'Let me contact Drexel again,' said Adam. 'He must have news by now.'

Chaiwisan shook his head. 'It's a waste.'

Adam ignored him. It was the last hope they had of avoiding a sea trip to Macau with wounds that would bleed again, the last chance they had of safety. 'The portable telephone in your briefcase,' said Adam. 'Give it to me.'

Immediately the number rang, Drexel answered. 'We're trying, Adam, believe me, we're trying. We've got police clearance but we've still got to get the top law man's consent. Give me a few more minutes, that's all I ask. But you've got to give us your location.'

Drexel's words carried clearly and Chaiwisan answered. 'Tell Drexel, tell the American that he gets nothing until I get an immunity. Go on, tell him that!'

Adam began to repeat the message when, further along the quay, there was a sudden whistle. A squat figure in tattered shorts and a vest was gesturing to them. 'This way, this way!' he called in Cantonese.

Chaiwisan's fishing junk had arrived.

The *China Jewel* was the kind of vessel Cheng Tak-shing dreamt of possessing one day. Sixty foot long, burnished brilliant white, it had its own state room and, with two turbo-charged high-speed engines, was capable on a good flat sea of hitting thirty knots. And tonight, thought Cheng, was perfect for it.

The moon was high and the Lamma Channel, he knew, would be as flat as a plate. If they could just locate the fishing junk, they could get the job done. But, as So had warned, finding it might prove impossible. Hundreds of fishing vessels went out every night. How did you find one small junk with no name, no flag, just a scruffy wooden boat no different from a thousand others?

Cheng was determined it would be done. The alternative didn't bear contemplation. If necessary, they would zigzag the shipping lanes all the way to Macau and lie off Coloane where Chaiwisan intended to land. If it took them a week, they would do it. Ah Leung might have fled but Cheng still had himself to think of, and Blake, like a black shadow, kept looming before him – Blake, the accuser.

Cheng sat on the bridge next to So. His leg was now as stiff as a board, throbbing with pain. But in the tension of the moment it was almost forgotten. Slowly, the *China Jewel* pulled away from the marina. With its huge engines purring, it wound its way through the harbour past the endless rows of green-hulled fishing junks. The water was black but it danced like fire with the reflection of a million lights. A piebald dog started to bark from a darkened deck. Ahead and to his left, Cheng could see the chimneys of the Ap Lei Chau power station silhouetted against the night sky.

So Sang-on may only have been a deckhand but he handled the vessel with consummate ease. 'We're getting close to the place where Chaiwisan said the fishing junk would collect him,' he said. 'It's a little further ahead, on the lefthand shore.'

'Slower then, slower,' said Cheng. He looked at his watch as the big cruiser wallowed back in the water. It was 11.40. Ten minutes too late.

'There!' said So, pointing excitedly. 'There, can you see it? A fishing junk coming out from the quay.'

'Yes,' said Cheng, 'Yes, I do!' And a triumphant smile settled on his face. As the fishing junk swung ahead of them into the main channel, in the luminous green sheen of its navigation light, Cheng had glimpsed the tall, spare frame of a man. He had seen it only for the briefest moment but there was no doubt in his mind. It was Adam Blake.

'I've got him!' shouted Xavier Tong, his hand covering the telephone. 'He's just walked in.'

'At long bloody last,' said Drexel and he came over as Tong began to explain the position to Hong Kong's Director of Public Prosecutions. Questions were asked, answers given. But it was all achingly slow. Drexel paced up and down like a worried animal in a cage. More questions, more answers. God, he thought, bloody lawyers! Precious seconds were ticking away. Lives were in the balance. Make a decision, damn you!

As the fishing junk hit the open waters of the Lamma Channel, proceeding at a steady six knots, it began to yaw and roll more noticeably. It was a small grubby vessel stinking of brine and grease, a working man's craft, not designed for comfort. There was a crew of three; Lau the captain, the squat man in the ragged khaki shorts, and his two sons.

Lau wanted to take Chaiwisan into the wheelhouse and lay him on a bunk. He was terrified Chaiwisan was going to expire on him right there and then. But the old

Laotian refused, laying himself on the deck near the stern with his back to the wheelhouse instead. They were still too close to shore, still in too much danger. 'Later,' he kept murmuring, 'later . . .'

Adam, too, could see how critical Chaiwisan's medical condition was becoming and, despite everything, God knows why, he didn't want the man to die. 'Let me try Drexel again,' he said.

'Try,' said Chaiwisan with the weakest glimmer of a smile. 'But I keep telling you, Adam, you're wasting your time. What court wants to deal with an old opium dealer like me? The Director of Prosecutions, whatever he is, will never agree.'

'I think you're wrong,' said Adam, clinging to hope, and, taking Chaiwisan's portable phone, he dialled the hotline number for the third time. As it was, he didn't even have to ask.

'I've got it!' shouted Drexel. 'You can tell the old bastard that I've got him his immunity!'

With a deep sigh of relief, Adam turned to Chaiwisan. 'Did you hear? You've got it! It's authorised. What did I tell you. Now, for God's sake, let's turn round. Let's get back to shore!'

Then Drexel's voice interjected. 'But it's subject to conditions, tell him that, too.'

Oh God, no, thought Adam, and his heart sank. 'What kind of conditions?'

'The man I want is Leung Chi-ming. If Chaiwisan can give us credible evidence to put him away, then he gets his immunity. If not, he can rot in hell. Do you understand me, Adam? I'm not interested in Cheng or any other financiers he's dealt with in the past – it's Leung Chi-ming.'

Adam turned to where Chaiwisan lay. 'Did you hear that? The immunity is conditional upon you testifying against Leung Chi-ming.'

He expected Chaiwisan simply to nod in reply. But instead there was a look of bewilderment on his face. 'No,' said Chaiwisan. 'I never dealt with Leung Chi-ming, I don't know what they're talking about.'

Adam was flabbergasted. 'But who was going to finance our deal? Surely that was Leung?'

Chaiwisan nodded. 'Leung, yes, but not Leung Chi-ming. It was his son, that's who I've always dealt with – Leung Choi-lam.'

'Teddy Leung?'

'Yes, it was never the father, always the son.'

Carl Drexel couldn't believe it. For all these months he had been pursuing the wrong man. Every piece of evidence that had convinced him it was the father was equally evidence against the son. Father and son – they shared the same surname, the same mansion, the same wealth, even the same cars. That was the way of it with the Chinese. How could he have been so blind? Leung Chi-ming, the pillar of the Hong Kong community, the man of charity, was exactly that. Drexel felt sick inside. But there was no time for regrets.

'It's the son, not the father,' he said to Xavier Tong. 'The man you have to arrest is Leung Choi-lam.'

A wind had arisen in the west, curling across the water from Lamma, and Adam had to concentrate with the telephone pressed against his ear to catch snatches of

Drexel's words. 'Okay now . . . your position . . .'

'We're in the Lamma Channel heading towards Chung Chau. But we're turning now, heading back towards harbour. Can you hear me?'

Yes, loud and—'

A searchlight hit them. It lit up the junk, drenching it in a fierce white neon. Adam spun round, his eyes dazzled by the bright star bearing down. The other vessel was directly astern but catching up fast, its bows high in the water, a silvery wake left behind. It had to be doing twenty knots or more.

'What the hell is it?' asked Adam, his nerves jangling. 'Who could it be?'

Lau, the captain, was peering back, trying to define something behind the starburst of the light. 'It must be Marine Police,' he said, 'one of their patrol boats.'

Adam began to relax again. 'Are you sure?'

Drexel's voice came over the phone again. 'Are you okay there? What's going on?'

Adam had to smile. 'No problems,' he replied. 'There's a police patrol boat bearing down on us. Coming fast as hell. They'll be disappointed when they realise it's all over.'

'No, I'm wrong!' shouted Lau, a look of apprehension verging on fear on his face. 'Look, look, can you see the hull? It's white, not grey. It's not the cops.'

In the light of the moon reflecting off the water, Adam could just make out the tall, sleek superstructure. It was a cruiser of some kind, fifty foot, even longer. But why was it coming so fast, bearing down on them like that? Oh God, he thought, no . . . And he screamed into the portable telephone, 'It's Cheng Tak-shing, it's got to be him! Oh Christ, what in hell do we do?'

There was silence at the other end, Drexel equally stunned. Adam was shouting into the phone, 'You've got to send help!' But all he could hear in reply were snatches of words, the rest blown away in the wind. 'Take evasive action . . . there's an air force chopper lifting off from Tamar . . .'

Adam tried to control his panic. He took Nicky's hand. Her face was drenched by the white light of the pursuing vessel. The fear was stark in her eyes.

Adam turned to Lau. 'Can't we go any faster?'

'Faster?' There was now a look of abject terror on the captain's face. 'Seven knots, that's the best we can do. Chug, chug, chug. That thing is doing thirty! We don't have a hope.'

'But if we take evasive action, keep turning away from it?'

Lau's eyes were popping from his head. 'Seven knots, I said. We're like an old man walking in the park! What evasive action? In a minute it will be alongside. There's no way we can stop it. Then they jump on board, don't you understand? They have choppers, we have nothing. Chop, chop – and we're dead. All of us dead!'

'There has to be something we can do,' said Adam, 'some way of avoiding it, slowing the bloody thing down. There has to be something!' He couldn't bring himself to believe that after everything he had been through, after the endless weeks of worry and torment, now that it was all over, now that suddenly there was a new life ahead, it could all end here. An anger was building inside him, not fear – a rage, a compulsion to hit back, to say: 'No more, you bastards!'

Then, from the deck, he heard the barest murmur. 'The nets . . .' It was Chaiwisan, his eyes rolling back in his head. 'Use the nets . . .'

'Yes,' said Lau, 'the fishing nets. If we throw them overboard at the right time, yes, maybe . . .'

'Maybe what, for God's sake?'

'We can foul their propellers, get the nets caught in their engines. Yes, yes, that will slow them!' And with a sudden, desperate energy bred of terror, Lau and one of his sons began frantically to haul the nets towards the side.

Adam helped as best he could but only one arm was functioning. His left arm hung useless. And every time he bent, the pain shot through him. 'Let me do it,' said Nicky and she hauled at the nets, too. The cruiser was less than fifty yards behind them now, a white whale in the water; impregnable, invincible. It edged to starboard, intending to draw alongside.

'Now!' shouted Lau. 'Now!'

Nicky didn't understand Cantonese but the sharp yell was all she needed and she strained to hurl the nets out into the water across the bows of the cruiser.

The searchlight swung wildly, sweeping across the blackness. The nets had been seen, their orange floats like beacons. But the cruiser was close, too close. It swerved out in a wide arc, turning back in towards the small junk.

But then, clearly, above the whip of the wind, Adam heard its engines whine and one of them suddenly cut.

They had slowed the damn thing, half crippled it. Adam could see that it was trailing orange floats. But, half crippled or not, it could still do double the speed of the junk. They might be able to evade it for a minute or two longer but the end result was certain.

Adam looked towards Nicky. He had brought her to this, placed her life in jeopardy. It was waste enough for him and Chaiwisan to die, but her . . . And suddenly nothing mattered but giving Nicky a chance for life and hitting back at Cheng, repaying him for every injustice, every cruelty.

He looked down at Chaiwisan, expecting some response. But he lay still, his eyes closed. At last, there on the rolling junk, the wounds had defeated him. He knelt by him, hearing his shallow breathing. So he was still alive. But for how long? He took the pistol, having to prise it from the unconscious fingers.

Standing at his shoulder, Lau was wailing, 'It's coming alongside again. We've got no chance, no chance!'

Adam stood up, grabbing him by the shoulders. 'Do you want to live? Do you want to survive?'

Lau gawked at him. 'But there's no way of stopping them, none.'

'There's one,' said Adam, 'just one. Can you and your sons swim?'

Lau nodded, too terrified to question him.

'Then take Chaiwisan, the three of you. Hurry now!' He looked across at the white cruiser which was less than thirty yards to port, so close that he could see the figures on the foredeck, see the eighteen-inch blades in their hands. 'Get over the side, go on, do it now!' He took the wheel of the junk. 'Go, go!'

In a mad, panicky scramble, lifting Chaiwisan's inert figure, the father and two sons did as he had commanded. Adam heard the dim splashes, caught a glimpse of heads surfacing in the silvered sea. Then they were lost to view.

He looked again to port. The cruiser was less than ten feet distant now, two of Cheng's men waiting to spring across the gap. Adam waited. It came closer, closer. And he swung the wheel hard to starboard.

The little junk rolled wildly but it took the turn, cutting away sharply, while the cruiser, its manoeuvrability impaired, made a bigger, broader, clumsy sweep. Within seconds the distance between them was twenty yards or more.

Adam shouted to Nicky. 'Swim, darling, it's your only chance!'

She looked back at him. 'What about you?'

'I'll be okay, I promise. Now go!'

Nicky hesitated a moment. She was a strong swimmer, the water didn't worry her. But she didn't want to leave him.

Adam yelled above the wind and the screech of the junk's engine. 'Don't endanger us both! Dive over. Please, I beg you, go!'

With a last, lingering glance, Nicky threw herself over the starboard side, down into the green-black waters. She's safe, thought Adam, thank God.

He looked at the cruiser and a grim smile was set on his face. 'If we go down, we all go down together,' he said.

And he swung the wheel hard back to port – on a direct collision course with the cruiser's midships.

The distance between them was small, no more than thirty yards. There was no way the collision could be avoided. Adam saw the figures on the deck staring back, stupefied. He stood firm by the wheel, holding the course steady. Chaiwisan's pistol was in his hand.

The hull of the cruiser loomed up, a huge white wall engulfing him. Adam fired, just two shots high into the bridge, then he turned, scrambling towards the stern. And, in the second the two vessels struck, he hurled himself overboard.

Even under the water he sensed the concussion of impact. The water was cold, dark, disorientating. He spluttered for breath, so feeble that he could barely strike for the surface, swallowing water, choking on it. I'm going to drown, he thought, after everything I've been through, I'm going to drown.

But, even crippled, the buoyancy of his body brought him up and he broke the surface gasping for air. He could see the two vessels locked together, the wooden junk being dragged under first but dragging the motor cruiser with it.

A fierce fire had broken out on the junk. Old kerosene-fuelled navigation lights had fallen, shattering on the deck. Carried by the wind, flames were devouring the dry fan-shaped sails and were already scorching the hull of the great white whale. Both vessels were doomed.

Adam began to tread water, so weak he could barely keep his head above water. He was in agony from the salt sea that cauterised his wounds. If he could just stay afloat for a few more minutes. In the distance, from the sparkling lights of Hong Kong Island, he could hear a helicopter approaching. Just a few more minutes, that's all . . .

Then closer, he heard a shout. 'Adam! Adam!' He swivelled in the water and there she was. He could see her waving, one slim arm silhouetted against the orange aurora of the two burning vessels. She struck out towards him, swimming strongly. Nothing else mattered. Nicky was alive, he was alive. A life that was lost to him had been reclaimed.

AFTERMATH

'No man in our society, no matter how rich or influential, stands above the law. The accused, members of the jury, believed that his wealth made him invincible, a law unto himself. He believed that he could traffic in drugs and order men's deaths with impunity because somehow that wealth was a shield and his influence a sword of Excalibur. But now you see him today, head bowed, with no shield, no sword, just a man like any other.'

Those words, spoken by the Crown Prosecutor, opened the trial of Teddy Leung in the High Court of Hong Kong before a jury of his peers.

Cheng Tak-shing had been fished from the Lamma Channel with three ribs broken and the skin burnt off his back, lucky to be alive. But Teddy Leung had almost made it to safety, unscathed. The China Airlines flight bound for Taiwan had in fact been poised for take-off on Kai Tak's single runway when police had taken him, protesting his innocence, from the plane. The first press photographs had shown him being dragged across the tarmac. The second, taken forty-eight hours later, had depicted him being driven in a prison van from the Central Magistracy after his offer of bail in the sum of five million dollars cash plus a surety in the same amount – a total of ten million – had been unceremoniously rejected.

Knowing that he faced a life sentence, Cheng Tak-shing appeared to forget his Triad bonds and loyalties of the past. A deal was struck with the prosecution. For a substantial reduction in sentence, which would at least give him some chance of seeing the outside world again, he agreed to plead guilty to charges of conspiracy to murder and conspiracy to traffic in dangerous drugs. He further agreed to testify against Teddy Leung.

While awaiting trial, he was placed in special protective custody undergoing methadone treatment to try and rid him of his heroin addiction. But Cheng never did testify. One evening, after a day of brooding contemplation, when his guards weren't watching, he managed to hang himself from the bars of his window. He left two written messages, one absolving his prison guards of any blame, the other to his father saying that he was a dishonoured man and asking only that his body be cremated.

But even without Dai Ngan, the evidence against Teddy Leung remained formidable. Five months after his arrest he stepped into the prisoner's dock in the High Court thirty pounds lighter than he had been at the time of his arrest, pale and emaciated, a pathetic shadow of the privileged playboy he had once purported to be.

Tinko Chaiwisan, fully recovered from his wounds,

was the first Crown witness to testify. His evidence in chief took two full days, his cross-examination double that. Teddy Leung's counsel, an English QC, vilified him as a man steeped in the cult of drugs, an unrepentant opium trafficker who would sell his soul to escape incarceration; a man, he said, whose testimony was a 'vindictive tissue of lies'. But Chaiwisan – Uncle Chicken, as the Chinese press delighted in calling him – was too wily a bird to be provoked. The more stinging the questions, the more disarming his answers. When eventually he stepped down from the witness stand, bowed solemnly to the judge and walked from the court, Carl Drexel, who had been there every day, felt like applauding.

Adam testified in the second week. The Crown Prosecutor described him to the jury as a 'co-operating civilian witness who had worked undercover for the DEA', a neat little euphemism which disguised the true nature of his original role. Adam had had no direct dealings with Teddy Leung and, after the fiasco with Chaiwisan, the defence thought it safest not to challenge him directly. As a result he had an easy time of it and he, too, stepped down from the witness stand unshaken.

At the close of the prosecution case, Teddy Leung elected not to give evidence on his own behalf nor were any witnesses called. As his QC later commented: 'Under cross-examination he would have been slaughtered. He was damned if he testified and damned if he didn't.'

The Hong Kong jury of seven persons – four Chinese businessmen, one American engineer and two Australian housewives – deliberated for less than a morning before returning unanimous verdicts of guilty to the charges of conspiracy to murder and to traffic in dangerous drugs. When the verdicts were announced to a packed courtroom, Teddy Leung wept openly in the dock. The following day he was sentenced to life imprisonment.

In Hong Kong, life imprisonment means exactly that; there is no commutation, no possibility of parole. Teddy Leung will spend the rest of his natural days in confinement until at last he is committed to an unmarked grave behind the looming, white-washed walls. As the Crown Prosecutor had said, no man stands above the law.

Devastated by the revelations of his son's crimes, Teddy Leung's father, the legendary Leung Chi-ming, suffered a stroke two weeks before the trial began and was unable to attend court.

For a man who prized his position of eminence in Chinese society, the loss of face brought upon him by his son's criminal activities was beyond redemption. Partially paralysed and confined to a wheelchair, Leung Chi-ming abandoned his commercial interests, retiring to his Peak mansion where he still lives today. He has never once visited his son in jail.

Teddy Leung wrote just one letter begging his father's forgiveness. He never explained directly why he had involved himself in the business of drugs, the nearest he came to it were the semi-poetic, formalised Chinese characters: *I wanted so much to stand as tall as you, I wanted so much to reach across the ocean*. The letter, however, remains unanswered.

With his testimony completed, Tinko Chaiwisan spent a month in Singapore cloistered with DEA agents. He told them a great deal, much of it being used in ongoing narcotics operations. But he did not tell them everything. His friends and those who had placed their trust in him, he protected to the bitter end and none have since been arrested. Yu Wen-huan, for instance, still manages his modest tribal crafts shop in Chiang Mai and still brokers opium as his father did before him.

Chaiwisan is retired now, living on the Indonesian island of Bali in a well-guarded estate. There have been several attempts on his life. Most of his children live with him and it is one of life's small ironies that he has a son in the United States studying to be an attorney at the University of Pennsylvania Law School.

As for Danny Abbott, terrified that Carl Drexel would renege on his undertaking or that somehow his 'paid informer's' role would come out when Teddy Leung and Cheng Tak-shing were questioned by the police, he resigned his commission overnight, cashed in his pension and flew down to the Philippines, a country chosen because it has no extradition arrangements with Hong Kong. He stayed there for a year, living the life of a beach bum on the island of Cebu, drinking cheap beer and buying even cheaper whores. It was only when Teddy Leung's trial was a matter of history and his money had run out that he thought it safe to return home to New Zealand. That is where he now lives, working for an Auckland security company, an embittered loner, chronically in debt.

Carl Drexel and Sue Martin remain in the DEA, still

operating out of New York. 'Snow White' was a resounding success for both of them. But Drexel has been in the business too long to think of it as anything more than a well-executed skirmish. The war goes on, he says. But maybe, just maybe, he can sense a turn in the tide . . .

Adam and Nicky were married at long last a month after Teddy Leung's trial had finished. The wedding took place in Canada in the same small Burnaby chapel where Nicky had been christened as a child. They managed a three-day honeymoon up in the Rockies – the longest either of them could spare from their business commitments – and then flew back to Hong Kong where the foundations of the Swiss Federal Bank building were emerging from the reclaimed soil of the city's waterfront.

The design that Adam had agonised over and once despairingly labelled a 'post-modernist chop suey emporium' has won a quiverful of international design awards and has led to commissions throughout the Far East, everything from hotels to shopping complexes. Adam has two new partners, his staff has doubled – and Nicky still complains that he spends his life on aeroplanes.

Adam's future may now be well set, his reputation as an architect assured. But those few desperate weeks he endured as a drug trafficker will always be with him. Every month, without fail, he visits his brother in Stanley Prison, talking to him through a wall of glass just as he had done in the beginning. Harry hasn't changed. He suffers occasional bouts of depression but most of the time he remains as incorrigible as ever, hustling deals behind the bars or scheming how to make a quick million when he is released.

For Adam, no matter how close he and his brother might be, every visit is a short season spent in purgatory. Every time the prison doors shut behind him and he steps out into the sunshine again, with that first breath of freedom, it hits him. Every time, knowing how perilously close he once came to sharing Harry's fate, his heart begins to thud in his chest; and every time, the echoes of those distant, dark terrors return.

A selection of bestsellers from Headline

FICTION		
THE EIGHT	Katherine Neville	£4.50 □
THE POTTER'S FIELD	Ellis Peters	£5.99 □
MIDNIGHT	Dean R Koontz	£4.50 □
LAMPLIGHT ON THE THAMES	Pamela Evans	£3.99 □
THE HOUSE OF SECRETS	Unity Hall	£4.50 □
NON-FICTION		
TOSCANINI'S FUMBLE	Harold L Klawans	£3.50 □
GOOD HOUSEKEEPING EATING FOR A HEALTHY SKIN	Alix Kirsta	£4.99 □
SCIENCE FICTION AND FANTASY		
THE RAINBOW SWORD	Adrienne Martine-Barnes	£2.99 □
THE DRACULA CAPER Time Wars VIII	Simon Hawke	£2.99 □
MORNING OF CREATION The Destiny Makers 2	Mike Shupp	£3.99 □
SWORD AND SORCERESS 5	Marion Zimmer Bradley	£3.99 □

All Headline books are available at your local bookshop or newsagent, or can be ordered direct from the publisher. Just tick the titles you want and fill in the form below. Prices and availability subject to change without notice.

Headline Book Publishing PLC, Cash Sales Department, PO Box 11, Falmouth, Cornwall, TR10 9EN, England.

Please enclose a cheque or postal order to the value of the cover price and allow the following for postage and packing:
UK: 60p for the first book, 25p for the second book and 15p for each additional book ordered up to a maximum charge of £1.90
BFPO: 60p for the first book, 25p for the second book and 15p per copy for the next seven books, thereafter 9p per book
OVERSEAS & EIRE: £1.25 for the first book, 75p for the second book and 28p for each subsequent book.

Name ....

Address ....

....

....